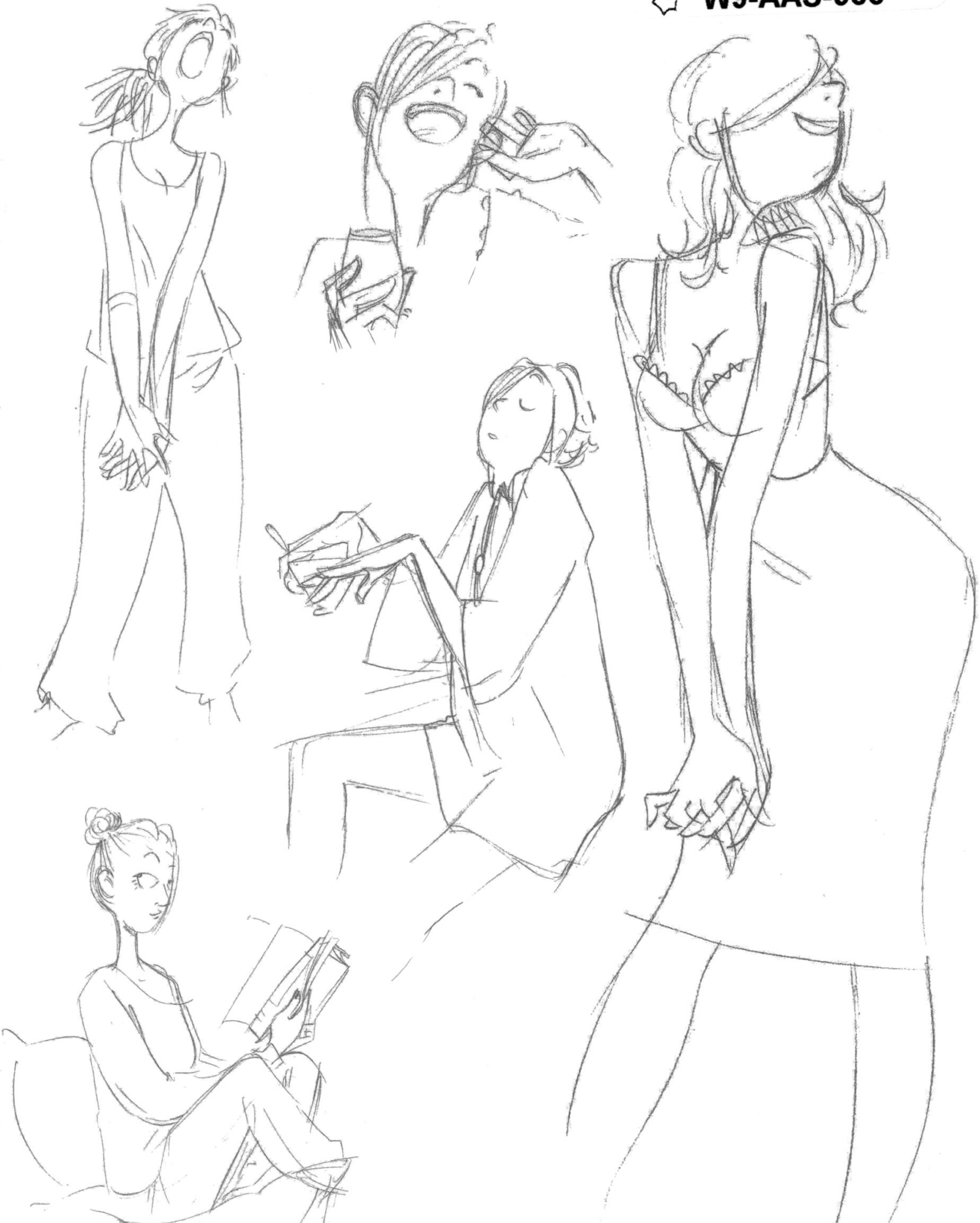

First published in English in 2012
by SelfMadeHero
5 Upper Wimpole Street
London WIG 6BP
www.selfmadehero.com

English translation © 2012 SelfMadeHero

Written and Illustrated by: Margaux Motin
Translated from the French edition by: Edward Gauvin

Editorial Assistant: Lizzie Kaye
Marketing Director: Doug Wallace
Publishing Director: Emma Hayley
With thanks to: Dan Lockwood

First published in French by Marabout in 2009
© Hachette Livre (Marabout), Paris, 2009

A CIP record for this book is available from the British Library

ISBN: 978-1-906838-46-1

10 9 8 7 6 5 4 3 2 1

Printed and bound in England

Margaux Motin

But I really wanted to be an anthropologist...

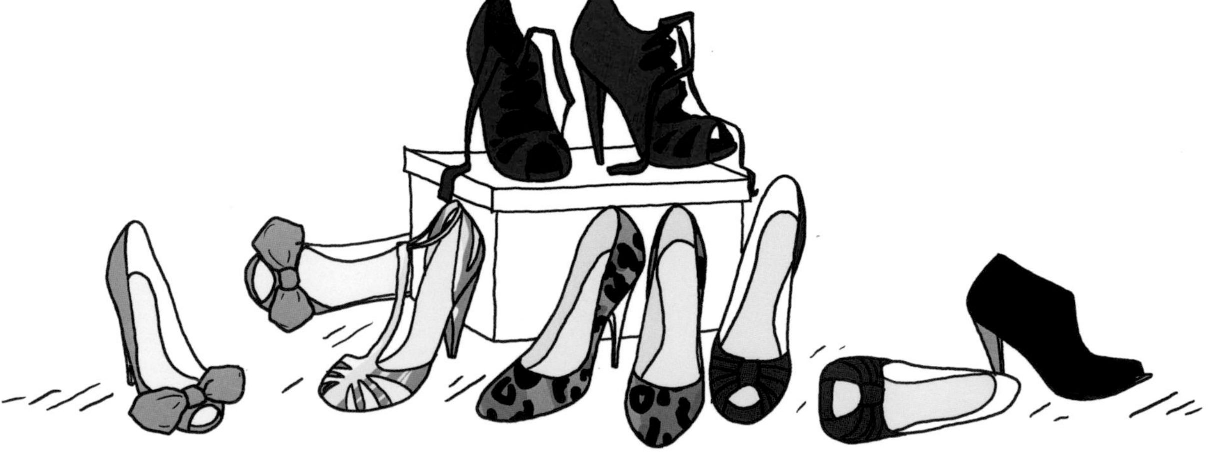

I turned out to be an illustrator, but I really wanted to be…

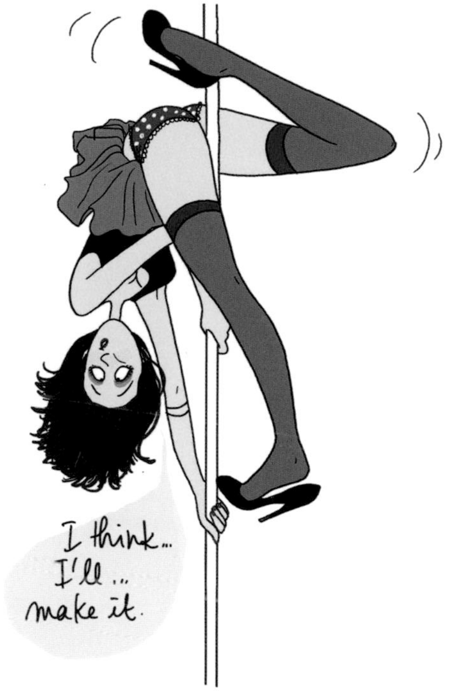
I think... I'll... make it.

A CHAMPION POLE DANCER

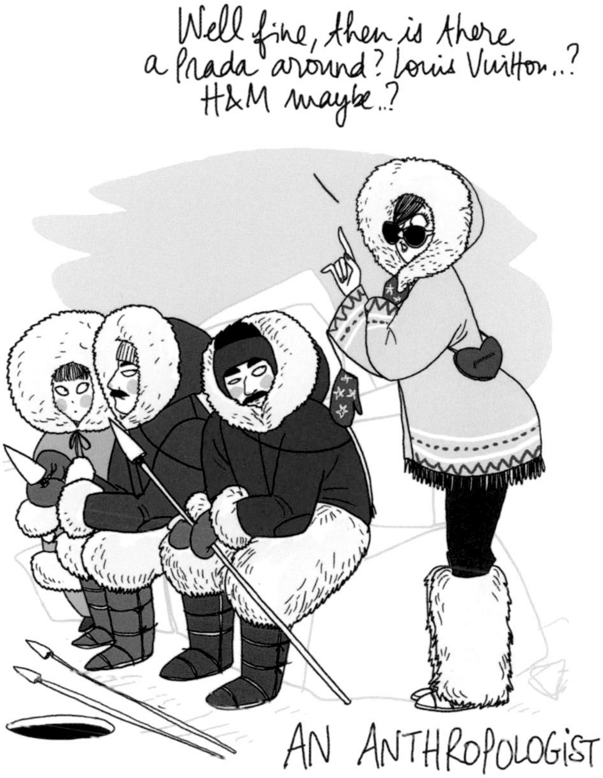
Well fine, then is there a Prada around? Louis Vuitton..? H&M maybe..?

AN ANTHROPOLOGIST

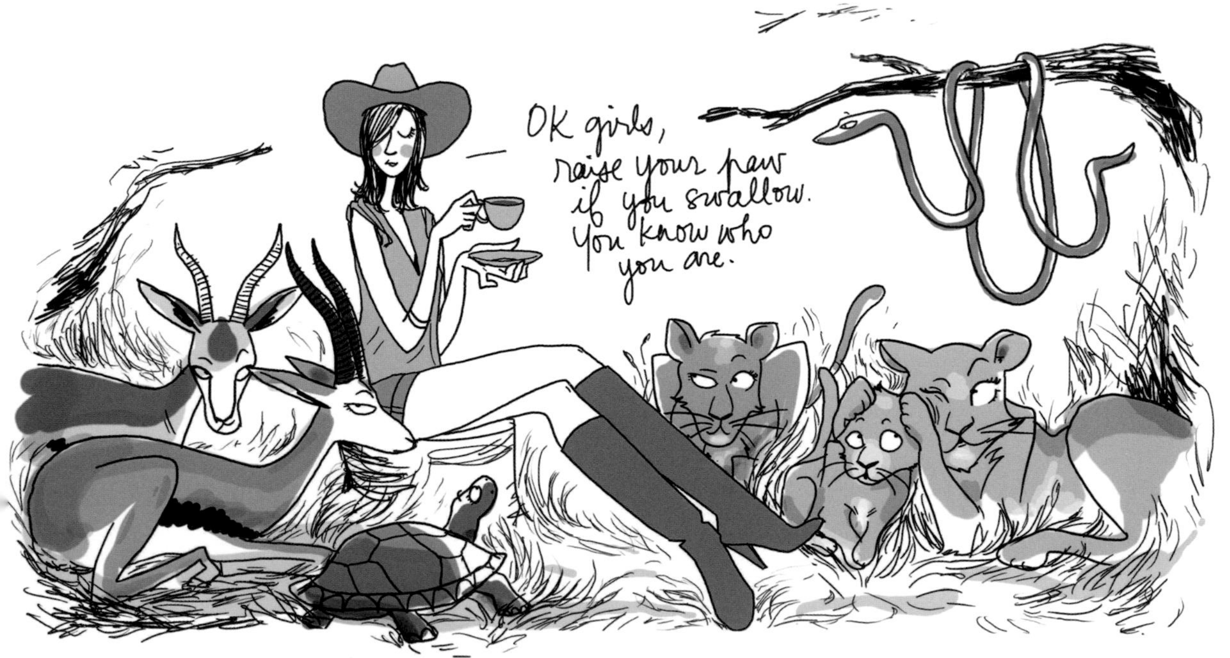
OK girls, raise your paw if you swallow. You know who you are.

OR A GIRL WITH A GIFT FOR TALKING TO ANIMALS.

... BUT ALL I REALLY KNOW IS HOW TO DRAW.

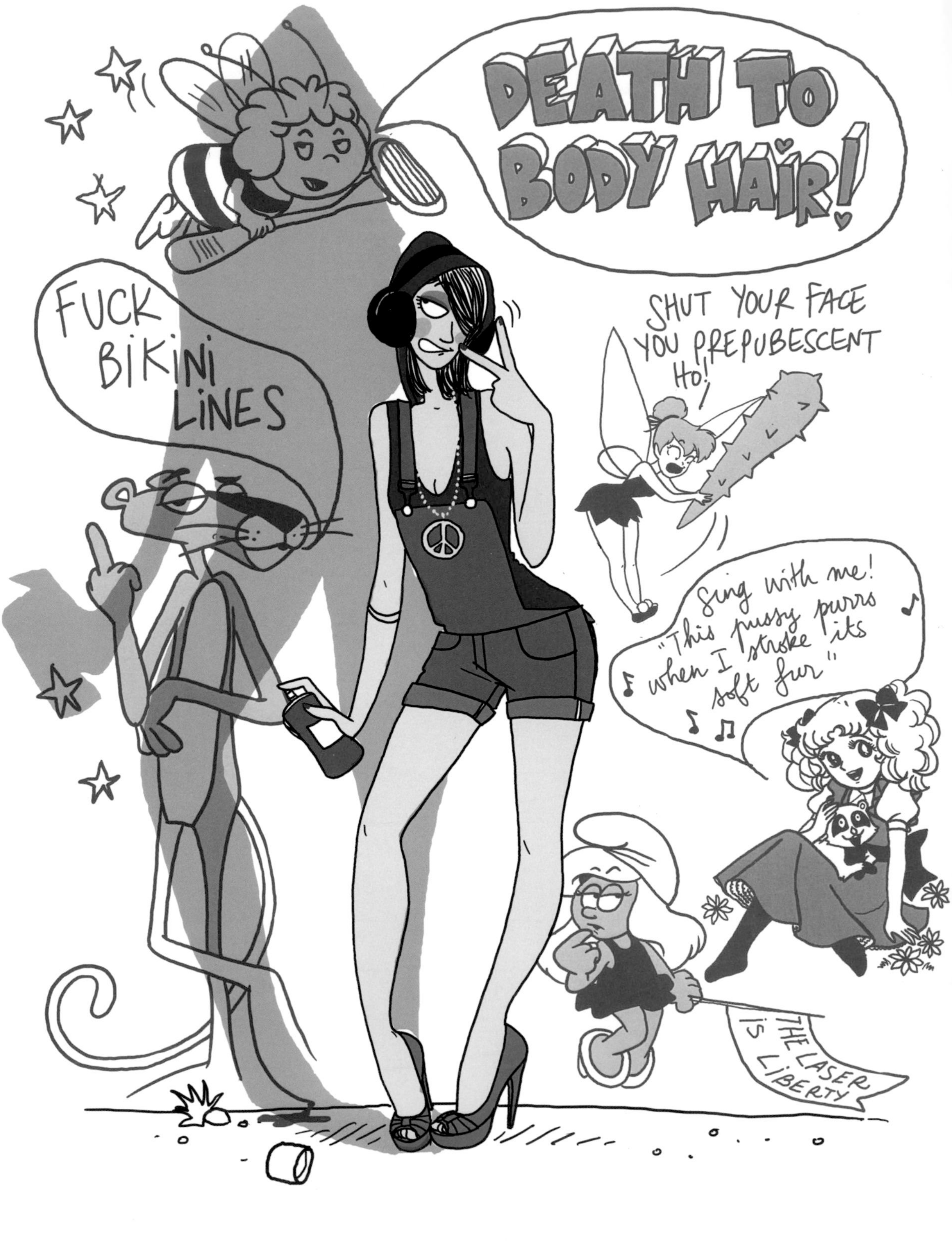
DEATH TO BODY HAIR!
FUCK BIKINI LINES
SHUT YOUR FACE YOU PREPUBESCENT HO!
Sing with me! "This pussy purrs when I stroke its soft fur"
THE LASER IS LIBERTY

A few things you should know about me:

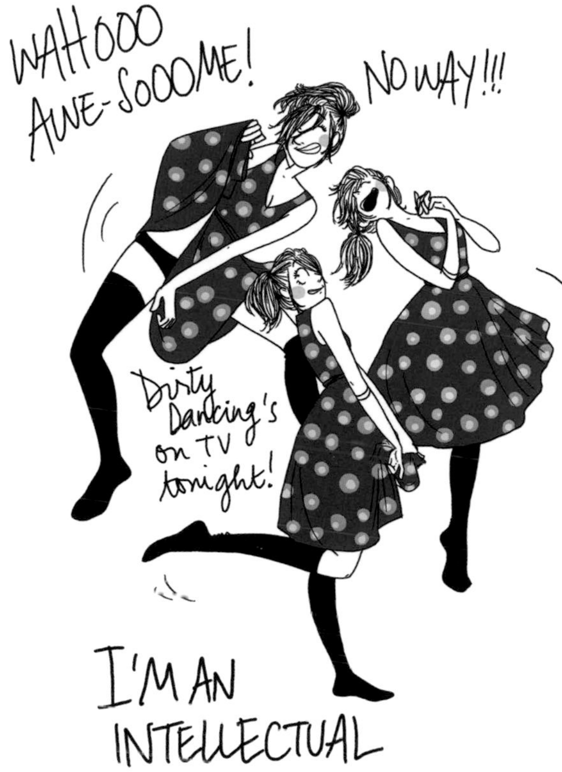
WAHOOO AWE-SOOOME!
NO WAY!!!
Dirty Dancing's on TV tonight!
I'M AN INTELLECTUAL

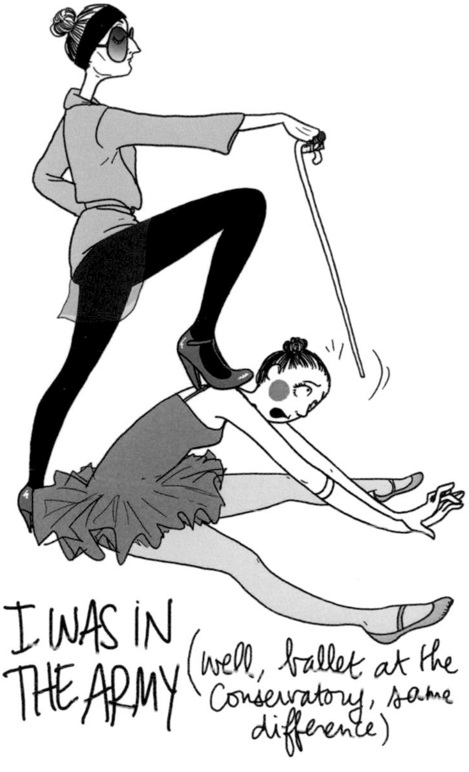
I WAS IN THE ARMY (well, ballet at the Conservatory, same difference)

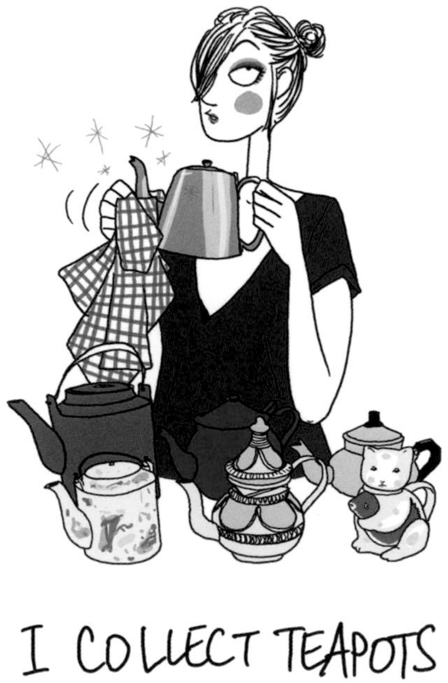
I COLLECT TEAPOTS

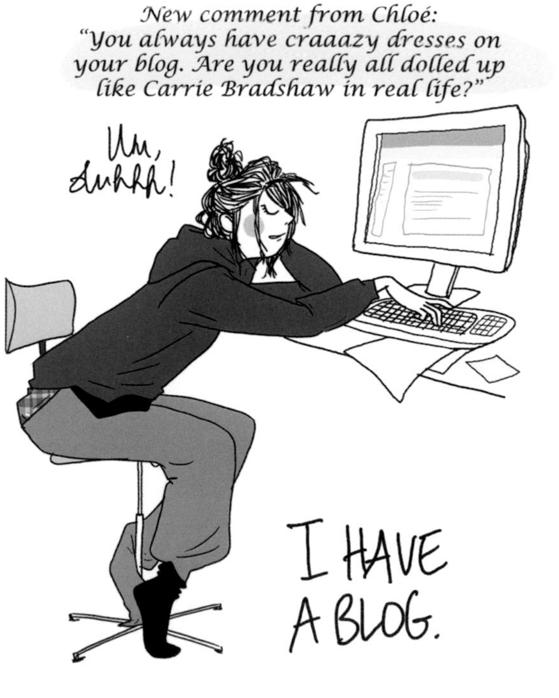
New comment from Chloé:
"You always have craaazy dresses on your blog. Are you really all dolled up like Carrie Bradshaw in real life?"
Um, duhhh!
I HAVE A BLOG.

The best thing about working from home…

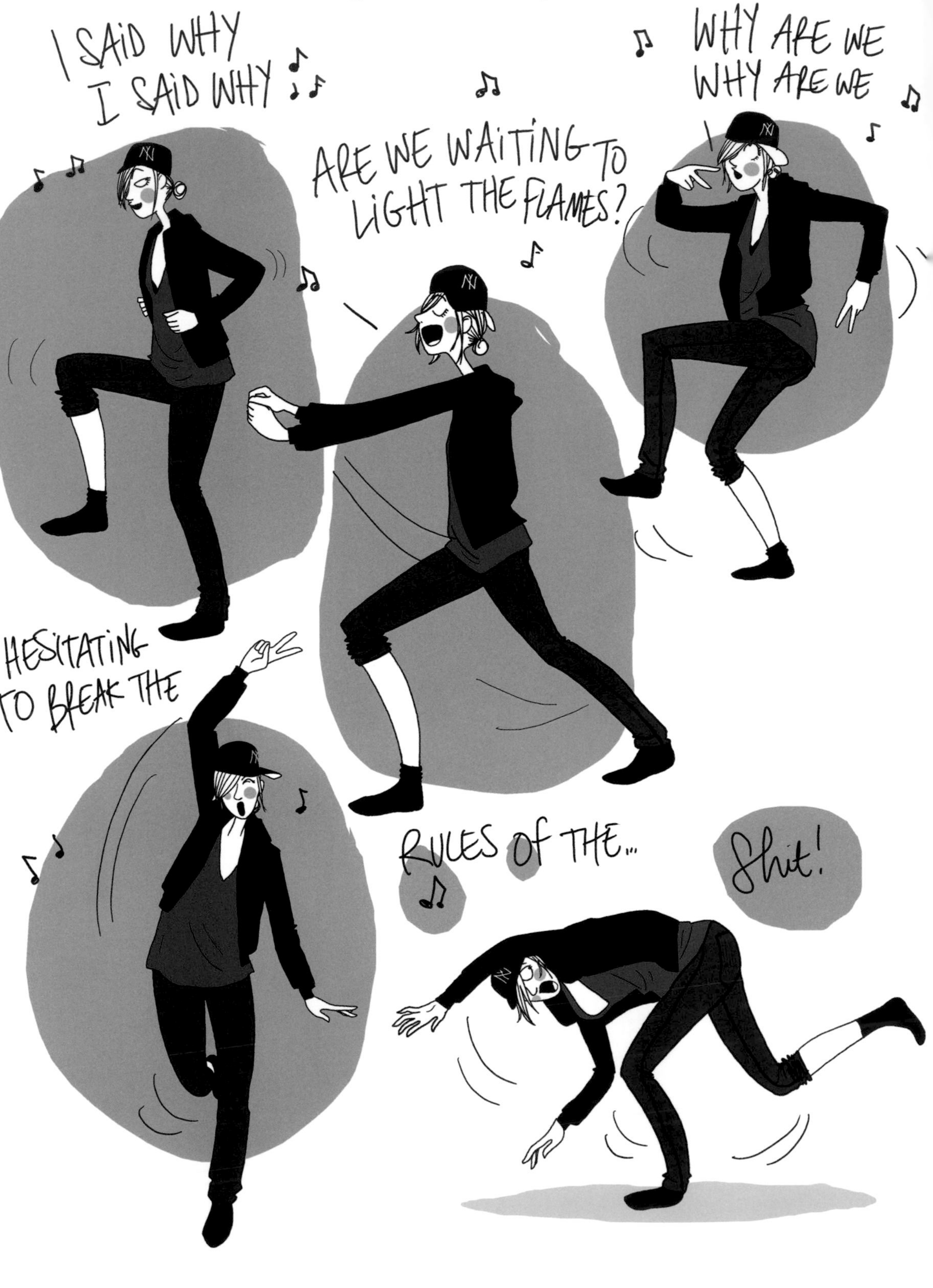
I SAID WHY I SAID WHY
ARE WE WAITING TO LIGHT THE FLAMES?
WHY ARE WE WHY ARE WE
HESITATING TO BREAK THE
RULES OF THE…
Shit!

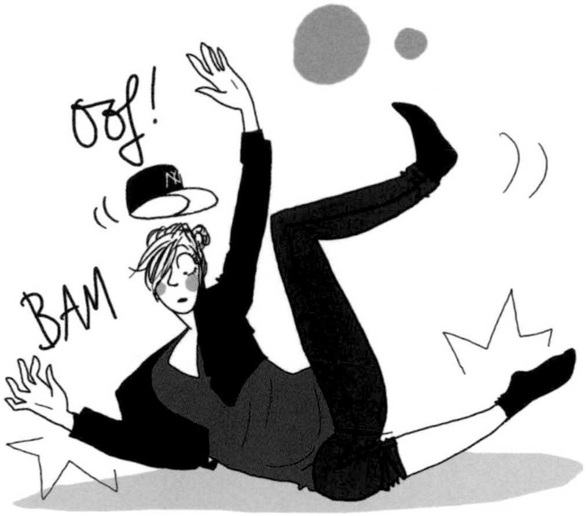
Oof!
BAM

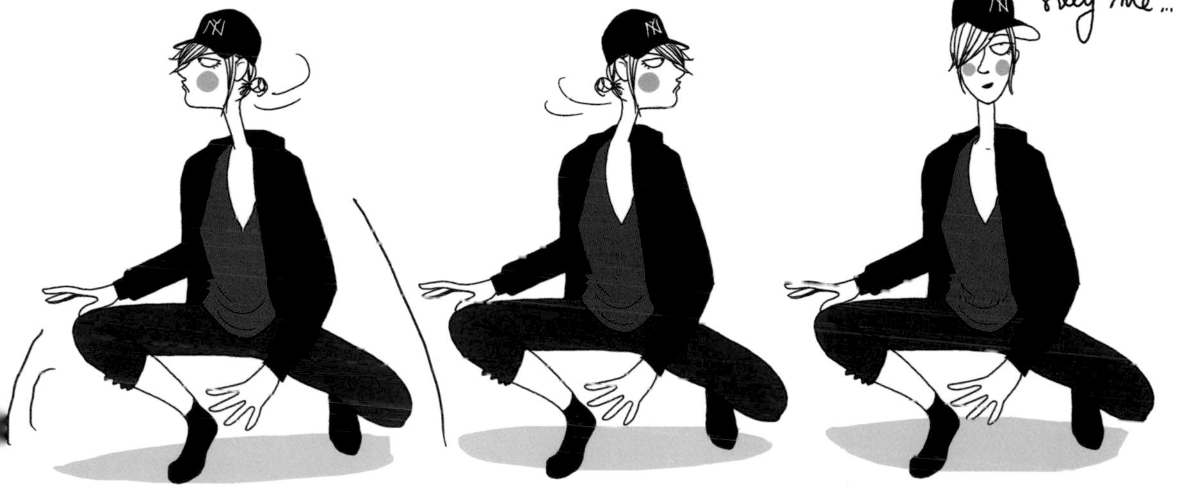
Oops, silly me…

…is not having
co-workers.

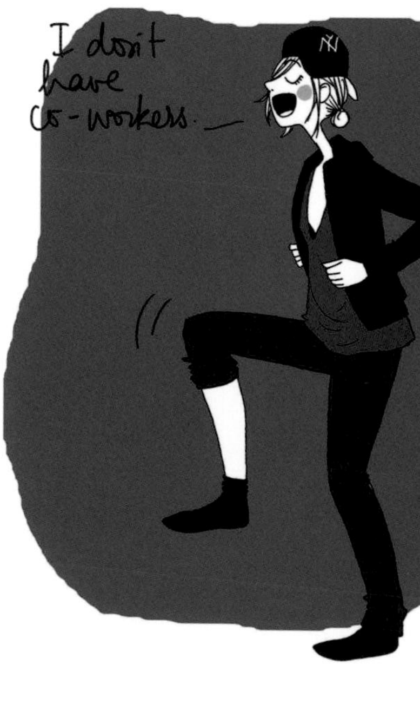
I don't have co-workers…

The worst thing about working from home...

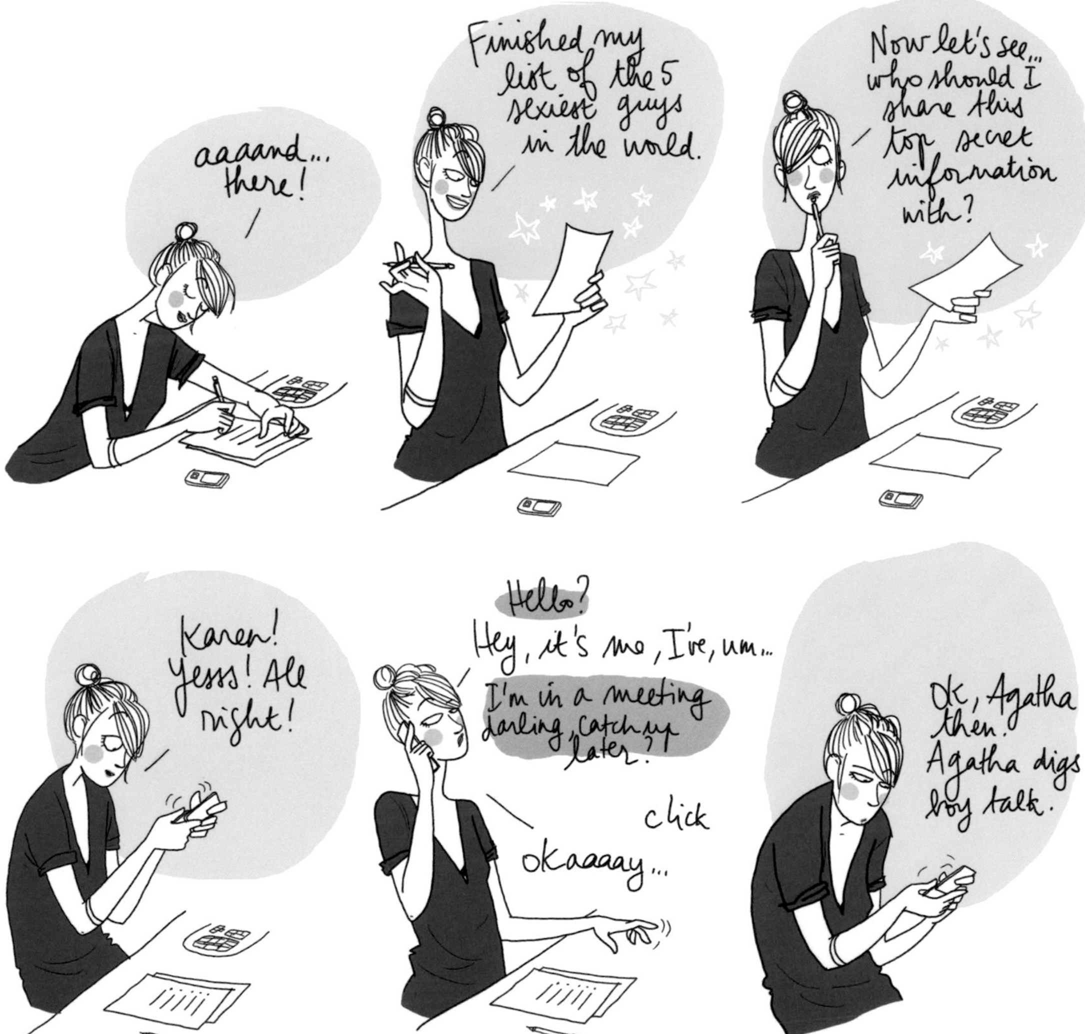
aaaand... there!
Finished my list of the 5 sexiest guys in the world.
Now let's see... who should I share this top secret information with?
Karen! Yesss! All right!
Hello?
Hey, it's me, I've, um...
I'm in a meeting darling, catch up later?
click
okaaaay...
OK, Agatha then. Agatha digs boy talk.

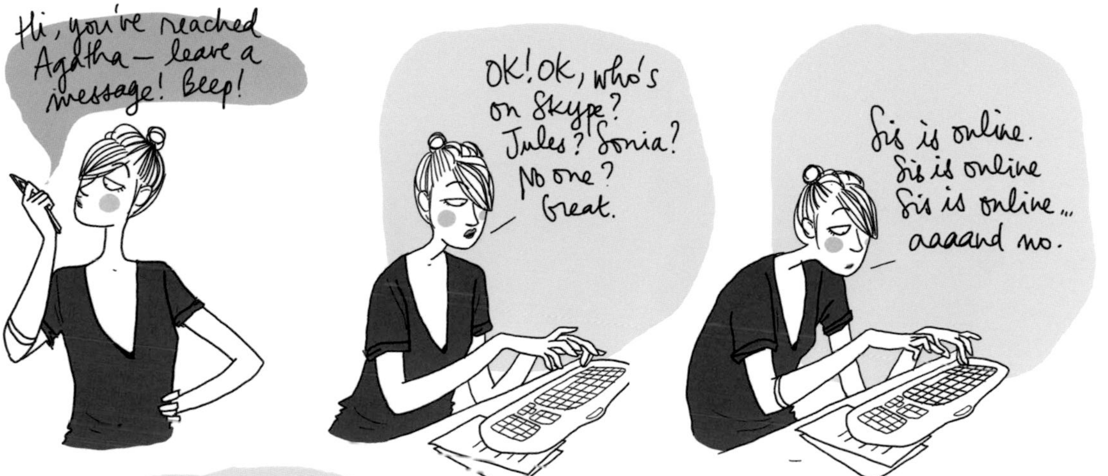
Hi, you've reached Agatha – leave a message! Beep!
OK! OK, who's on Skype? Jules? Sonia? No one? Great.
Sis is online. Sis is online Sis is online... aaaand no.

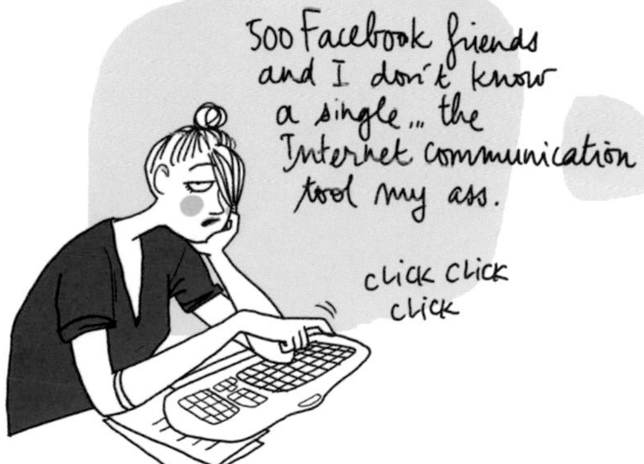
500 Facebook friends and I don't know a single... the Internet communication tool my ass.
CLICK CLICK CLICK

...is not having co-workers.

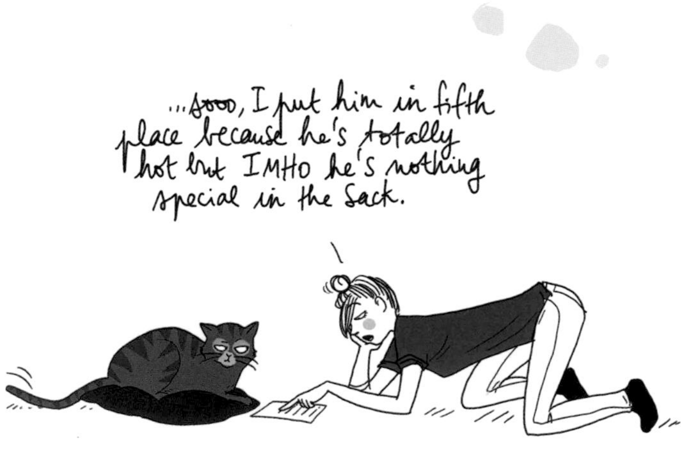
...sooo, I put him in fifth place because he's totally hot but IMHO he's nothing special in the sack.

Welcome to real life

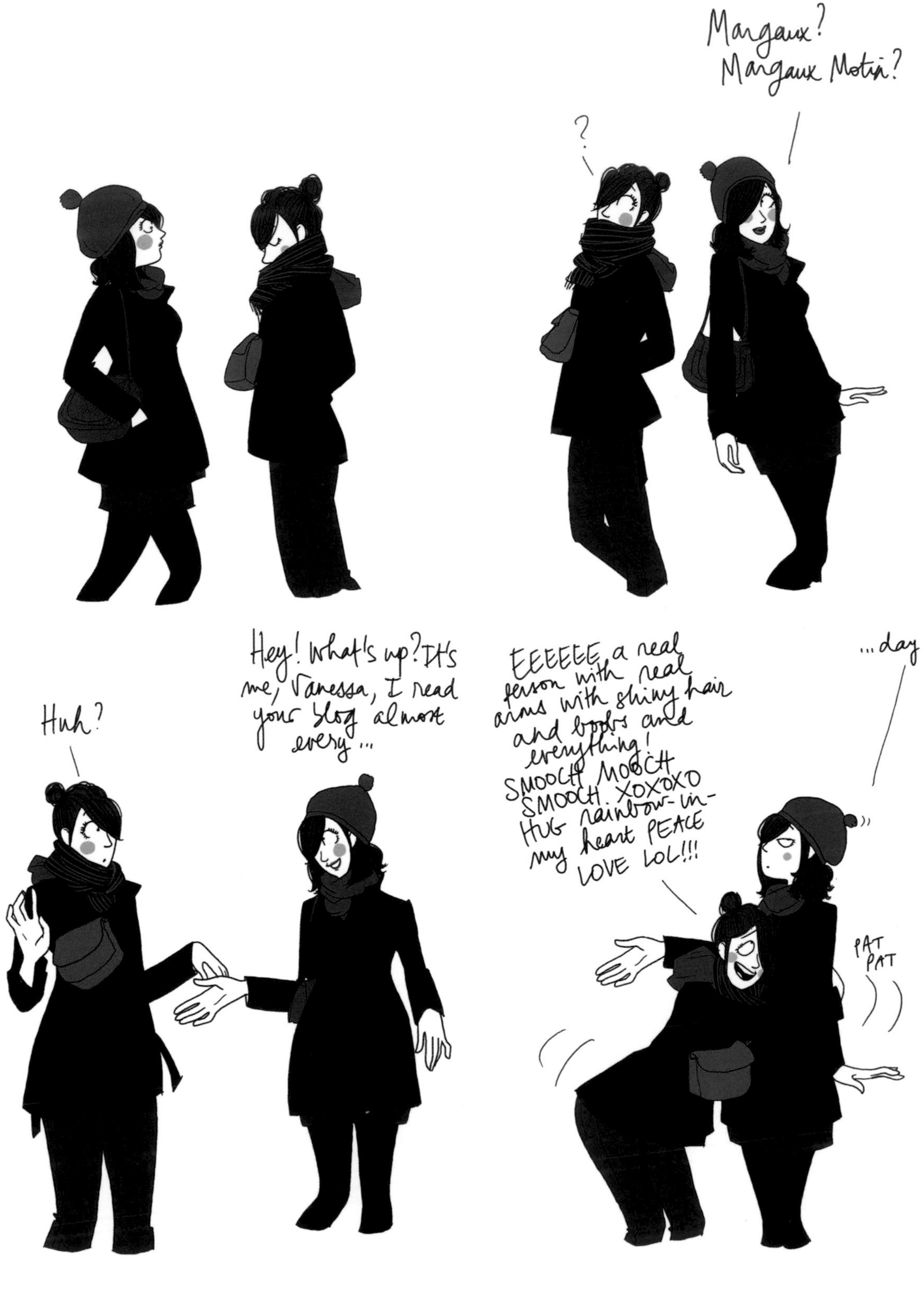
Margaux? Margaux Motin?
?
Huh?
Hey! What's up? It's me, Vanessa, I read your blog almost every...
EEEEEE a real person with real arms with shiny hair and boobs and everything! SMOOCH MOOCH SMOOCH XOXOXO HUG rainbow-in-my heart PEACE LOVE LOL!!!
...day.
PAT PAT

My new hero

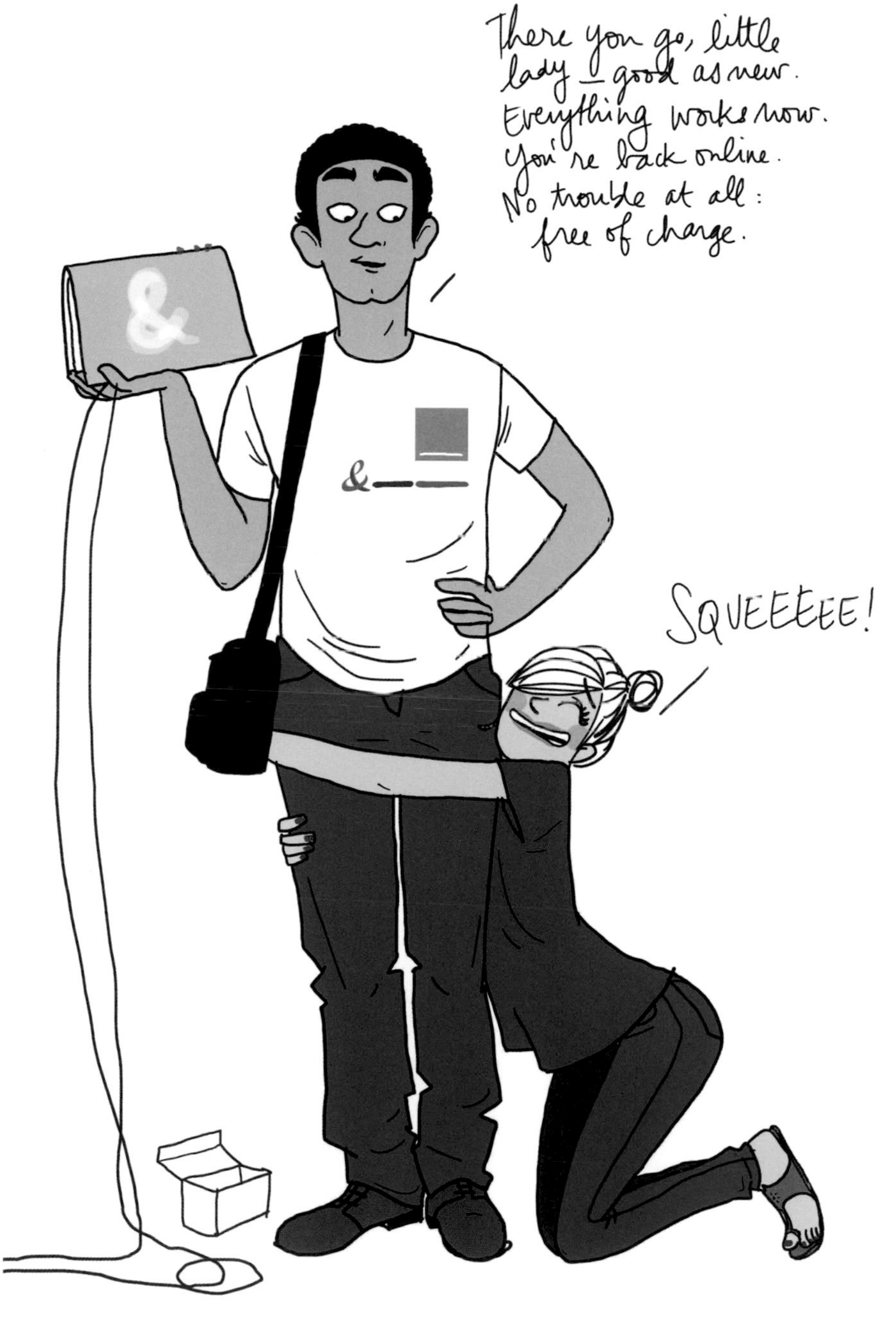
There you go, little lady – good as new. Everything works now. You're back online. No trouble at all: free of charge.
SQUEEEEE!

I like to...

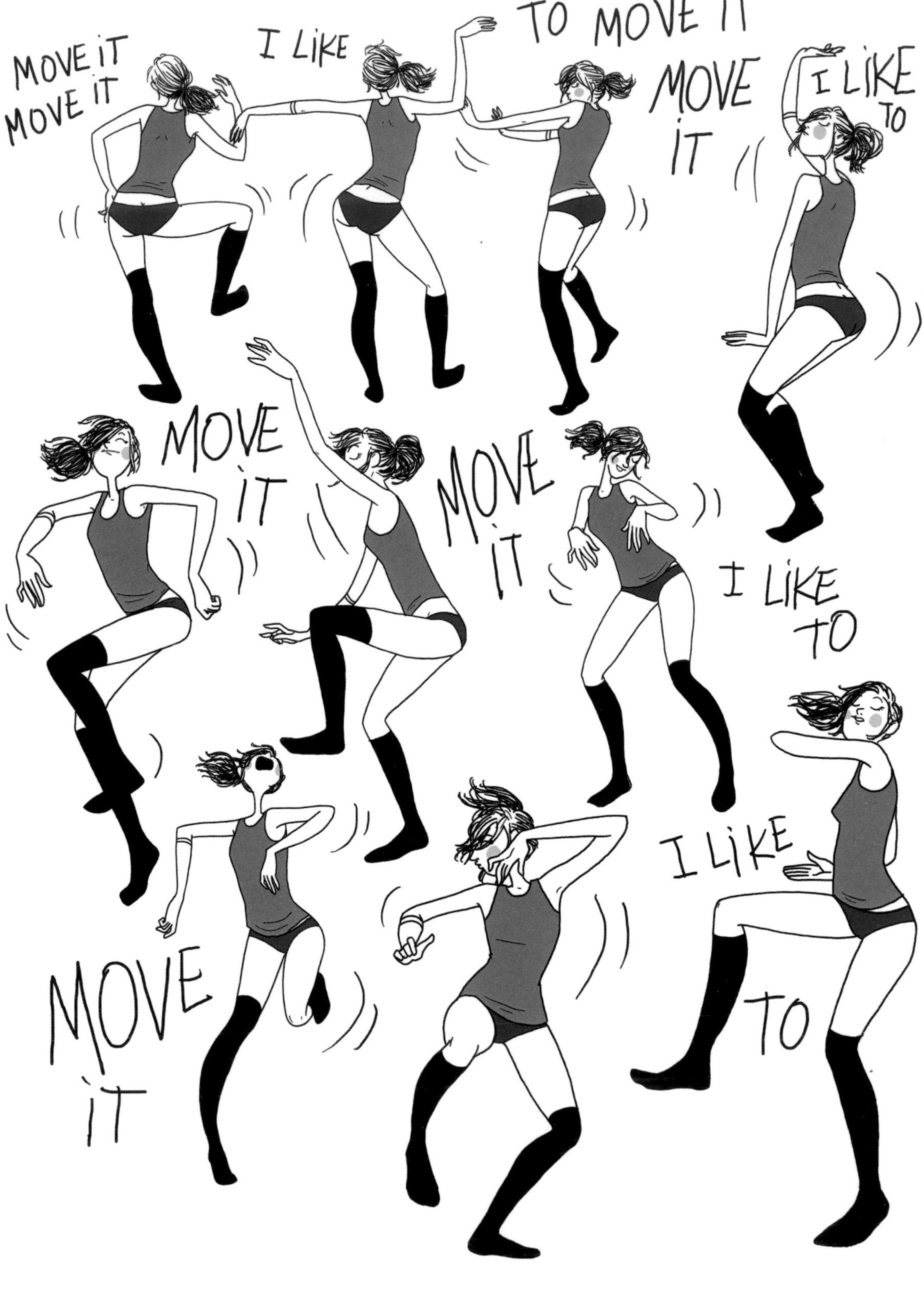
MOVE IT
MOVE IT
I LIKE
TO MOVE IT
MOVE IT
I LIKE TO
MOVE IT
MOVE IT
I LIKE TO
I LIKE
MOVE IT
TO

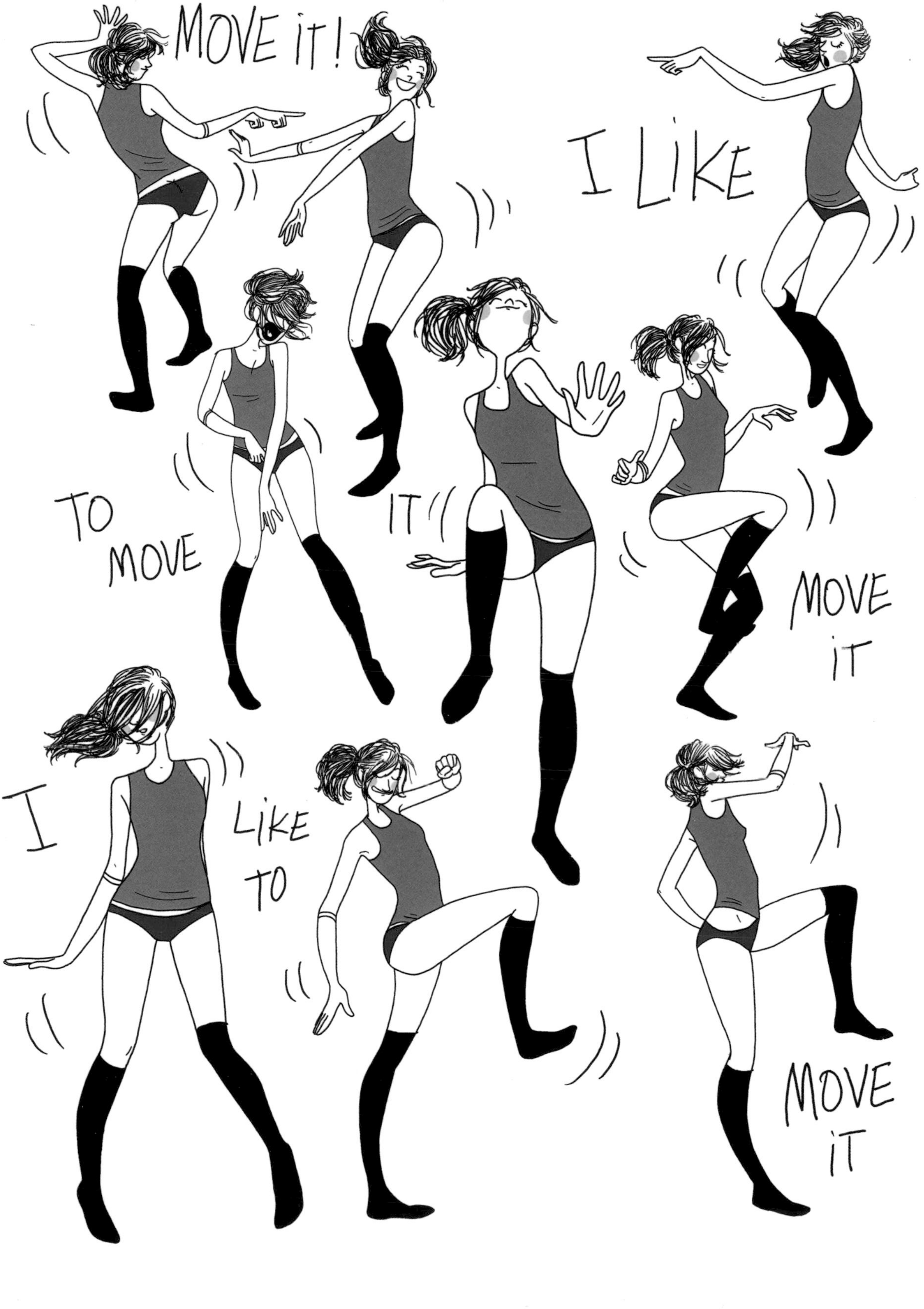

MOVE IT!
I LIKE
TO MOVE
IT
MOVE IT
I
LIKE TO
MOVE IT

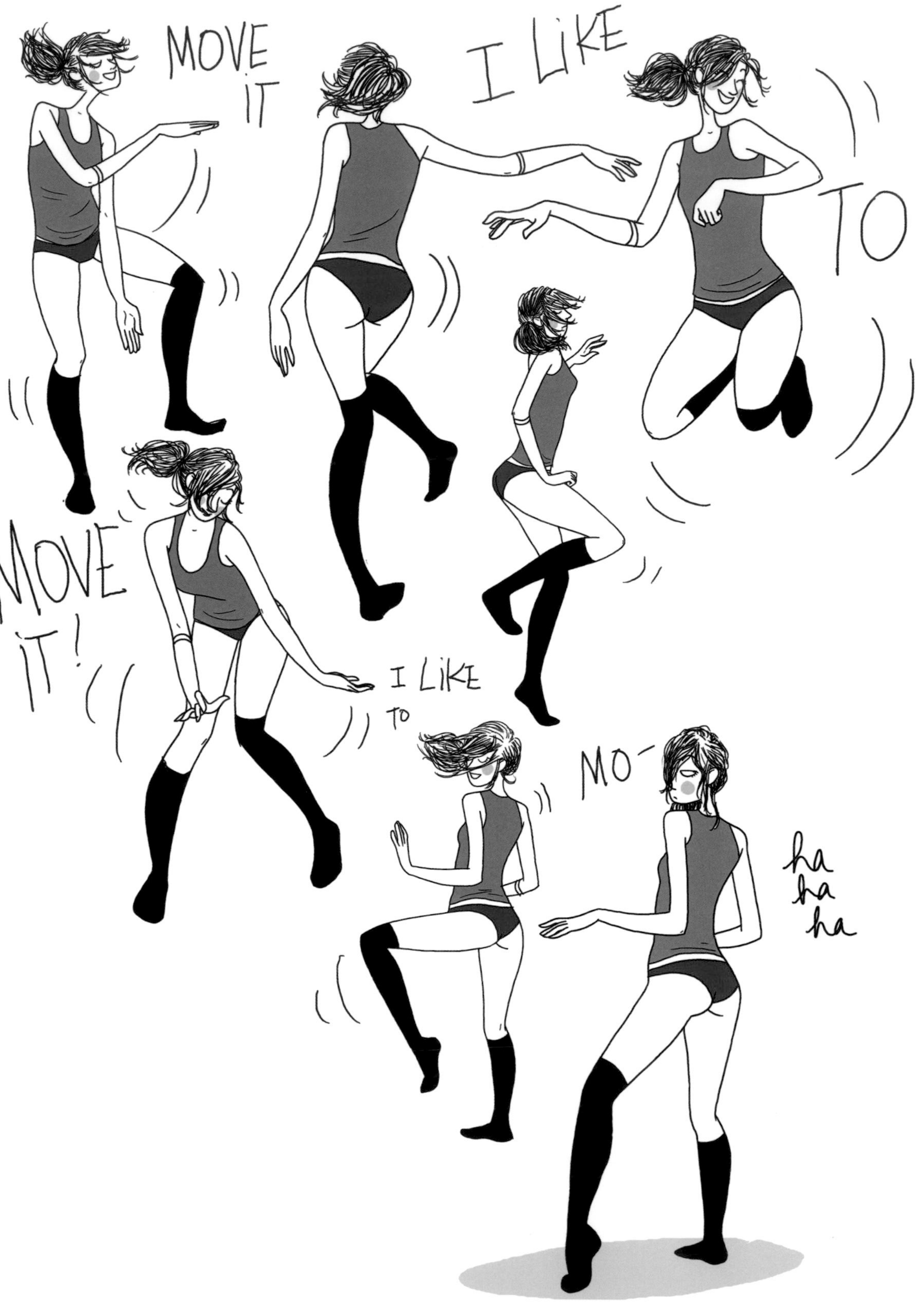
MOVE IT
I LIKE
TO
MOVE IT!
I LIKE TO
MO-
ha ha ha

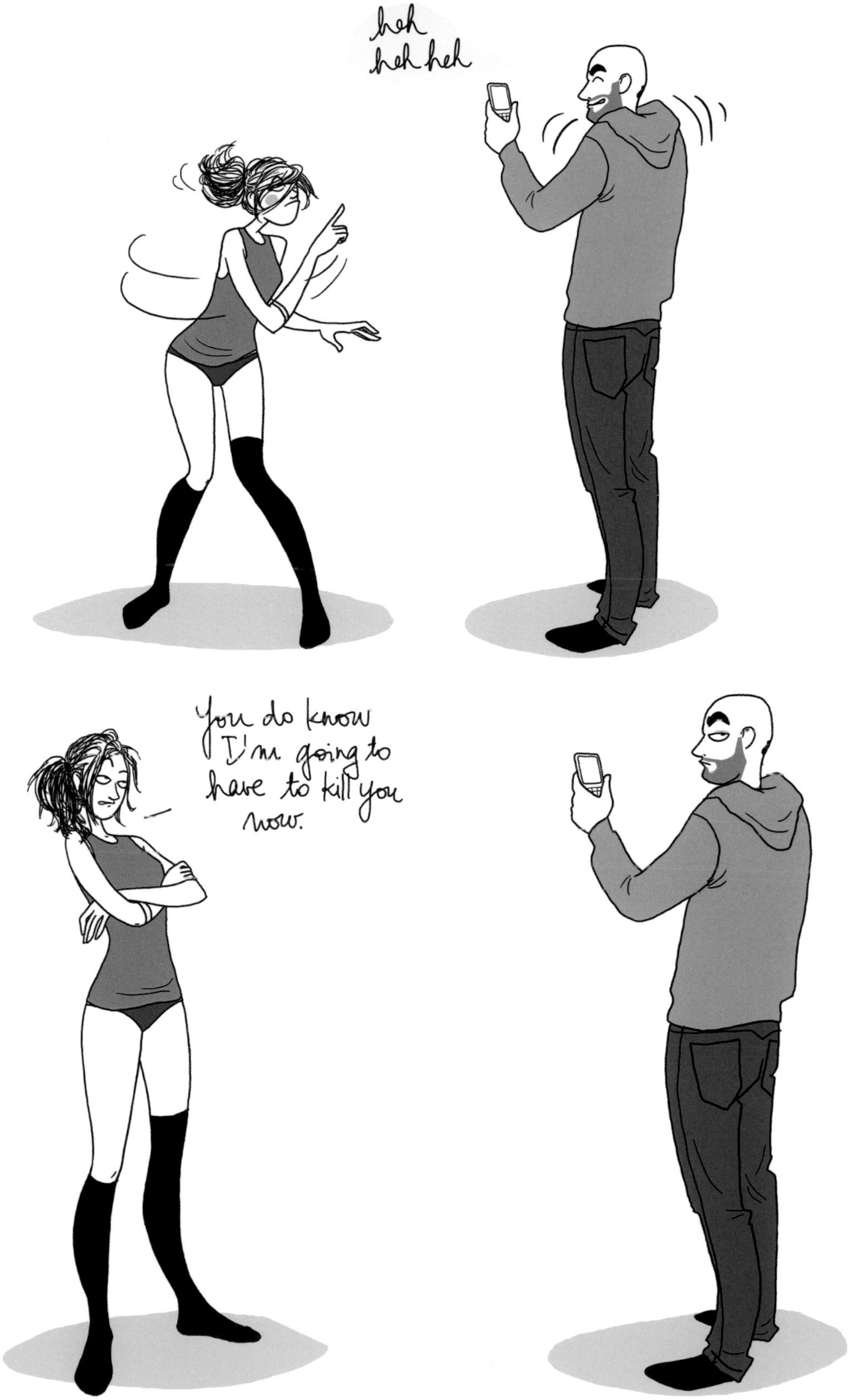
heh
heh heh
You do know I'm going to have to kill you now.

Last night, Jill Scott concert

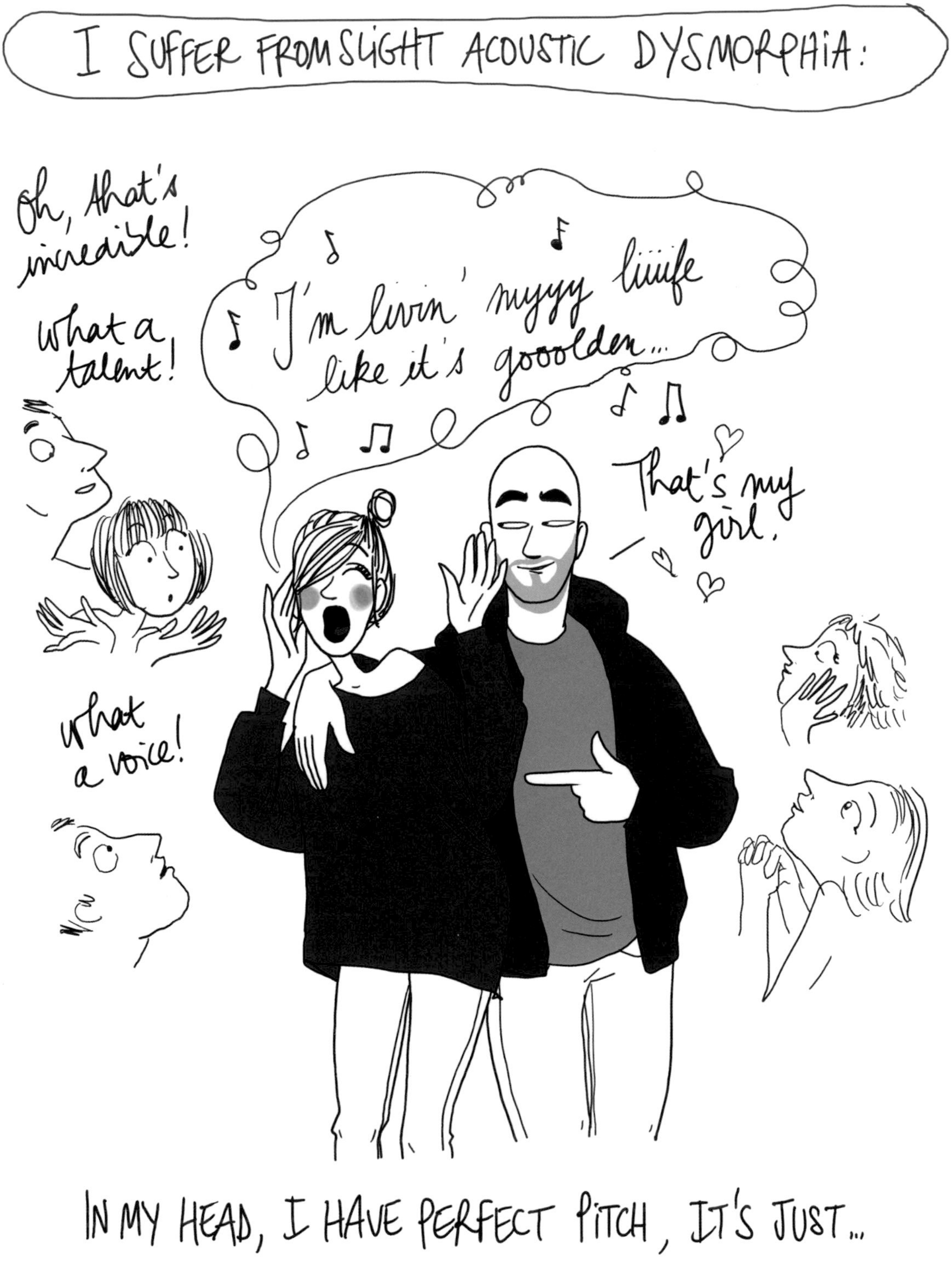
I SUFFER FROM SLIGHT ACOUSTIC DYSMORPHIA:
Oh, that's incredible!
what a talent!
what a voice!
I'm livin' myyy liiife like it's gooolden...
That's my girl.
IN MY HEAD, I HAVE PERFECT PITCH, IT'S JUST...

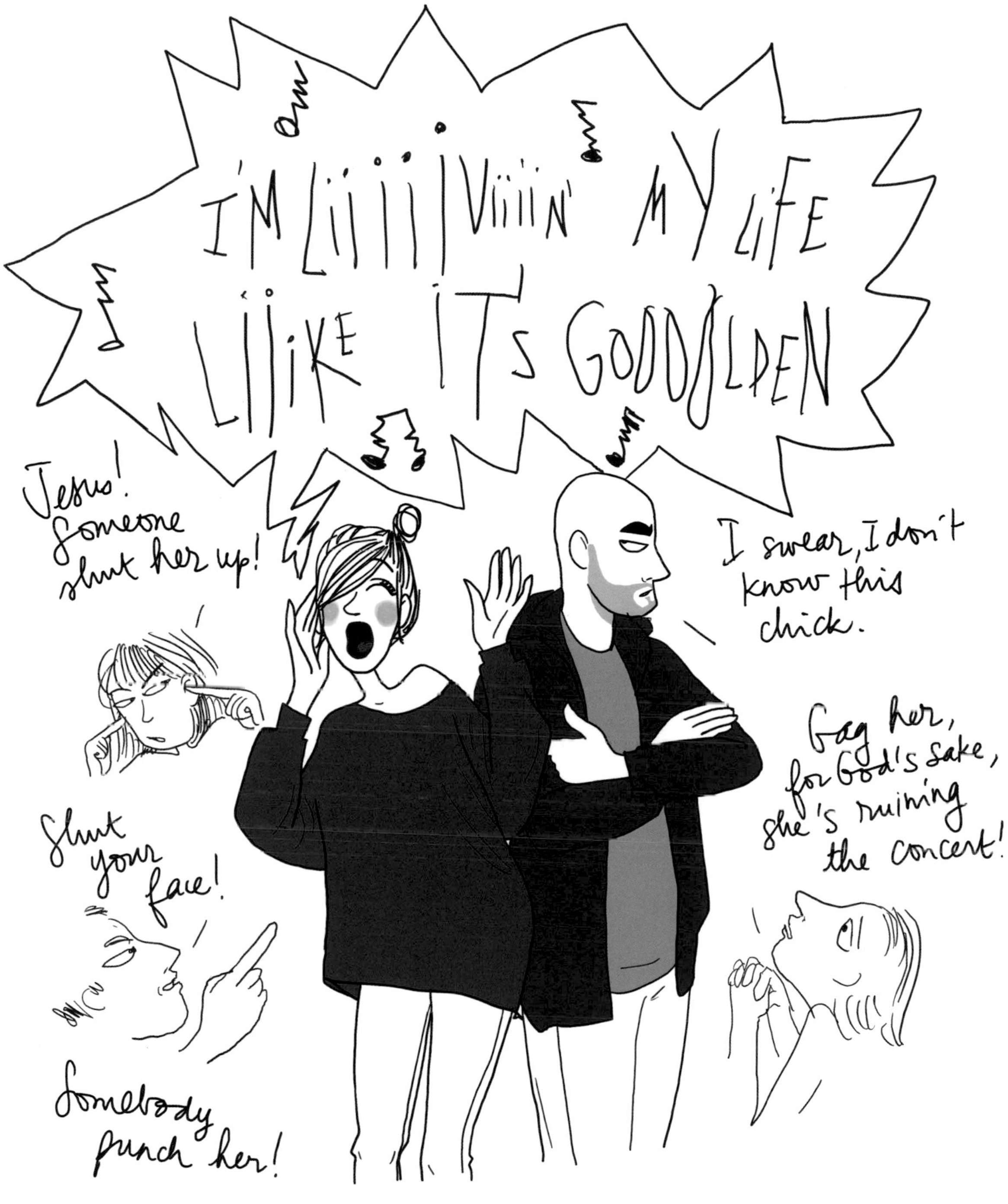
I'M LiiiiiVIIIIN' MY LiFE LiiiKE iT's GOOOOLDEN
Jesus! Someone shut her up!
I swear, I don't know this chick.
Gag her, for God's sake, she's ruining the concert!
Shut your face!
Somebody punch her!

... THE REST OF THE WORLD THINKS I'M OFF KEY

Of sound mind and body

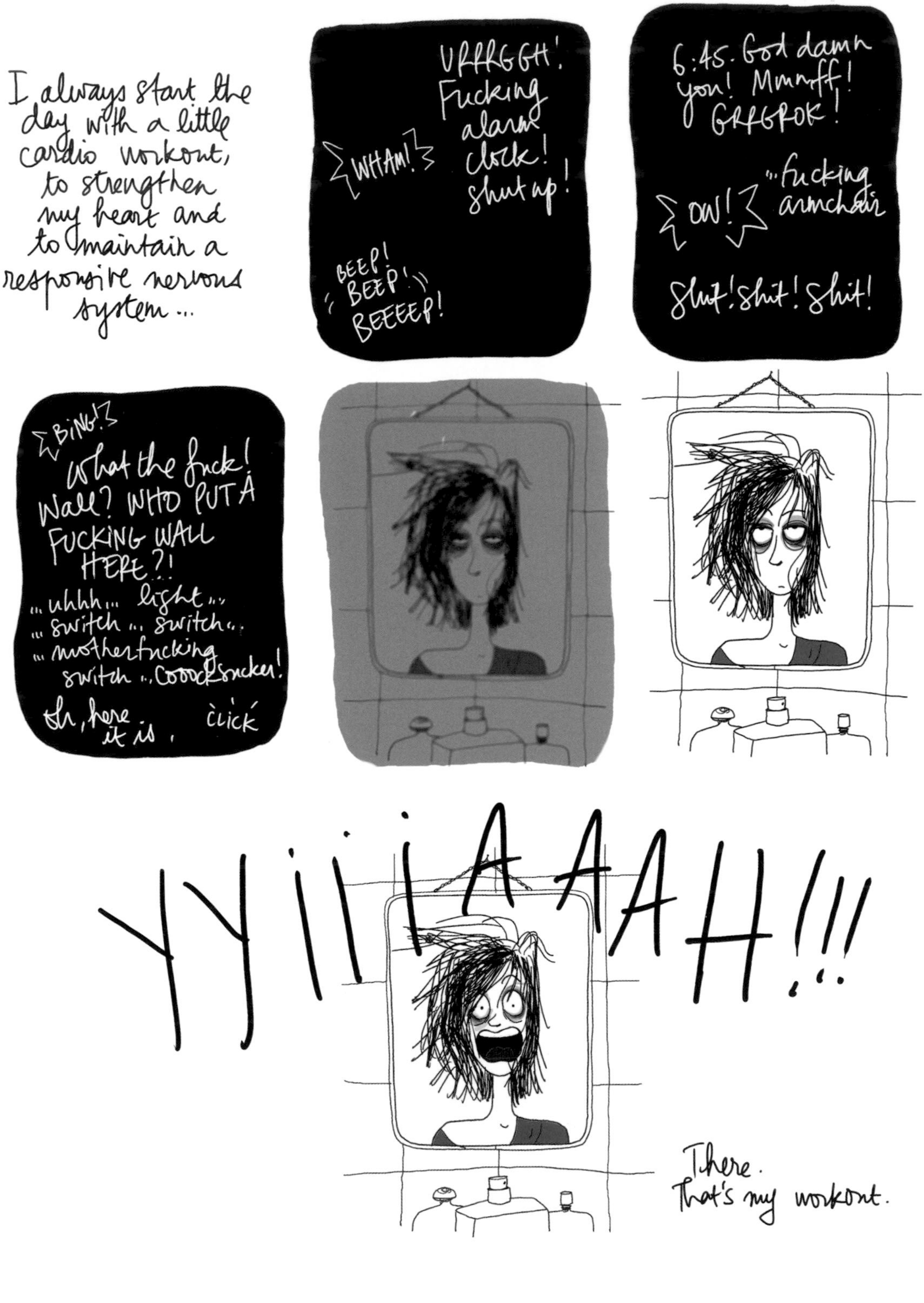
I always start the day with a little cardio workout, to strengthen my heart and to maintain a responsive nervous system...
WHAM!
URRRGGH! Fucking alarm clock! Shut up!
BEEP! BEEP! BEEEEP!
6:45. God damn you! Mmmff! GRRGROK!
OW!
...Fucking armchair
Shit! Shit! Shit!
BING!
What the fuck! Wall? WHO PUT A FUCKING WALL HERE?!
...uhhh... light... ...switch... switch... ...motherfucking switch... Cooocksucker!
Oh, here it is.
CLICK
YYIIIIAAAH!!!
There. That's my workout.

The tyrants

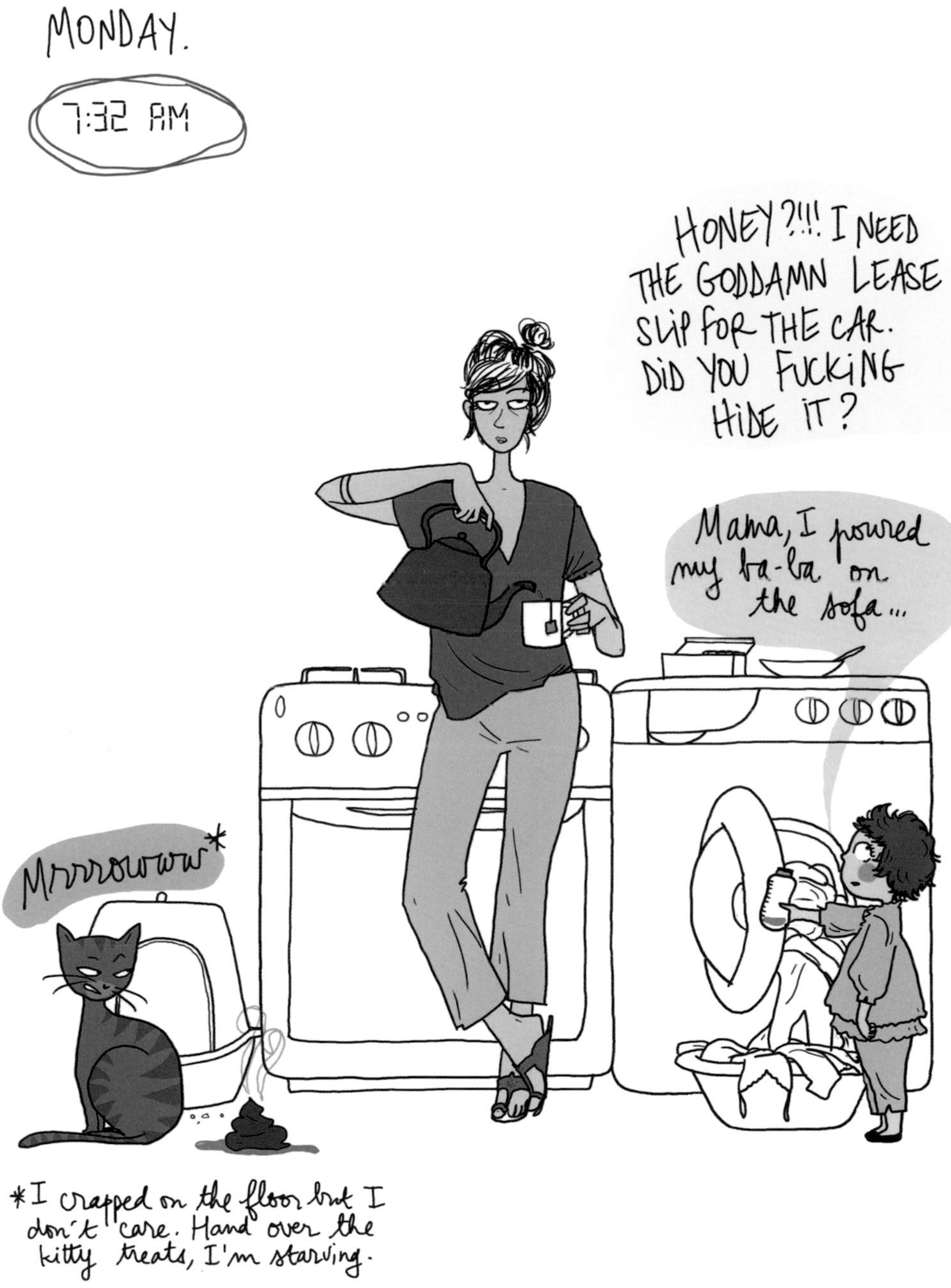
MONDAY.
7:32 AM
HONEY?!!! I NEED THE GODDAMN LEASE SLIP FOR THE CAR. DID YOU FUCKING HIDE IT?
Mama, I poured my ba-ba on the sofa...
Mrrrowww*
*I crapped on the floor but I don't care. Hand over the kitty treats, I'm starving.

Be fruitful and multiply, they said…

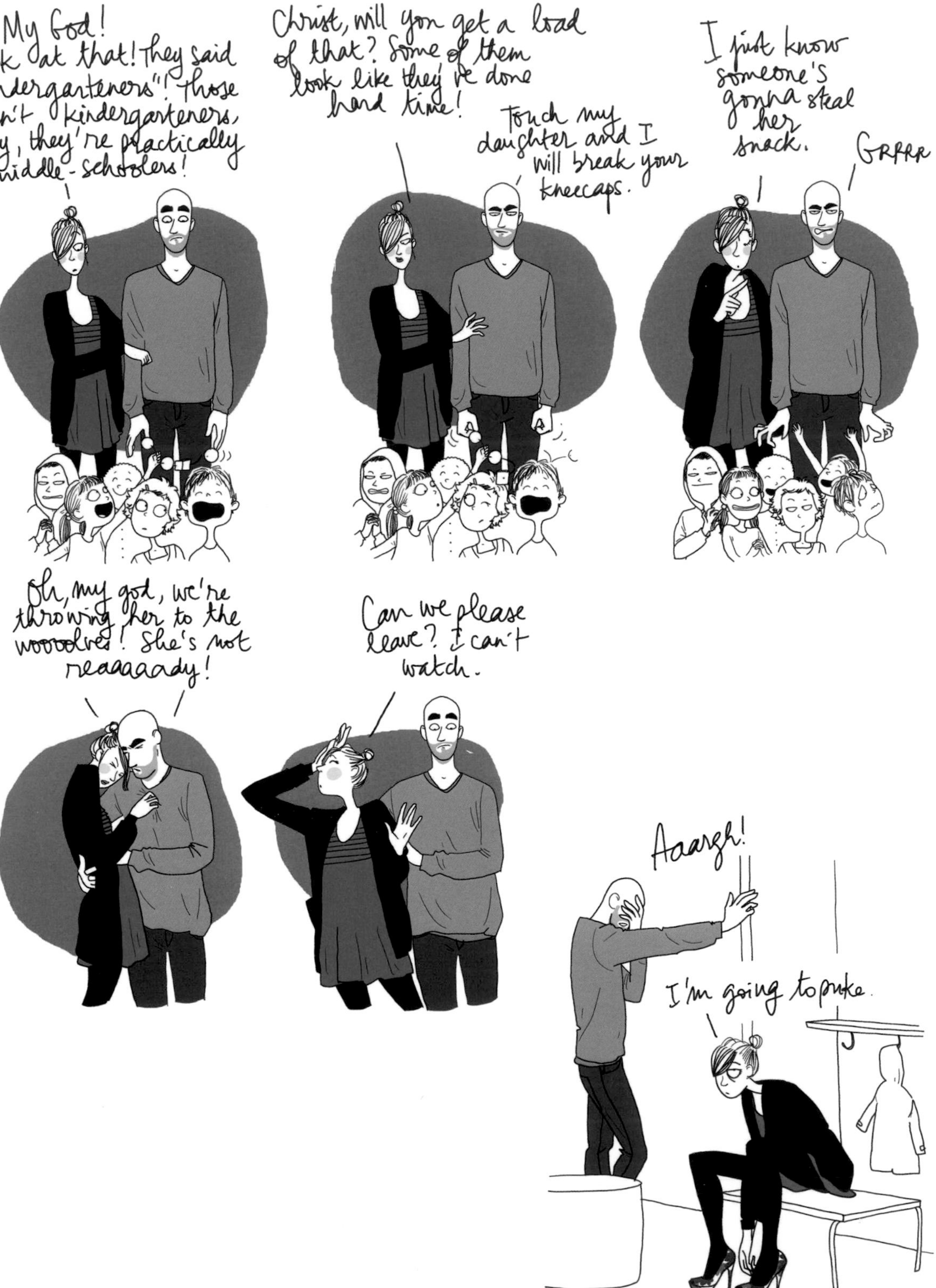
My God! Look at that! They said "kindergarteners"! Those aren't kindergarteners, honey, they're practically middle-schoolers!
Christ, will you get a load of that? Some of them look like they've done hard time!
Touch my daughter and I will break your kneecaps.
I just know someone's gonna steal her snack.
GRRRR
Oh, my god, we're throwing her to the woooolves! She's not reaaaaady!
Can we please leave? I can't watch.
Aaargh!
I'm going to puke.

Kids are like alcohol

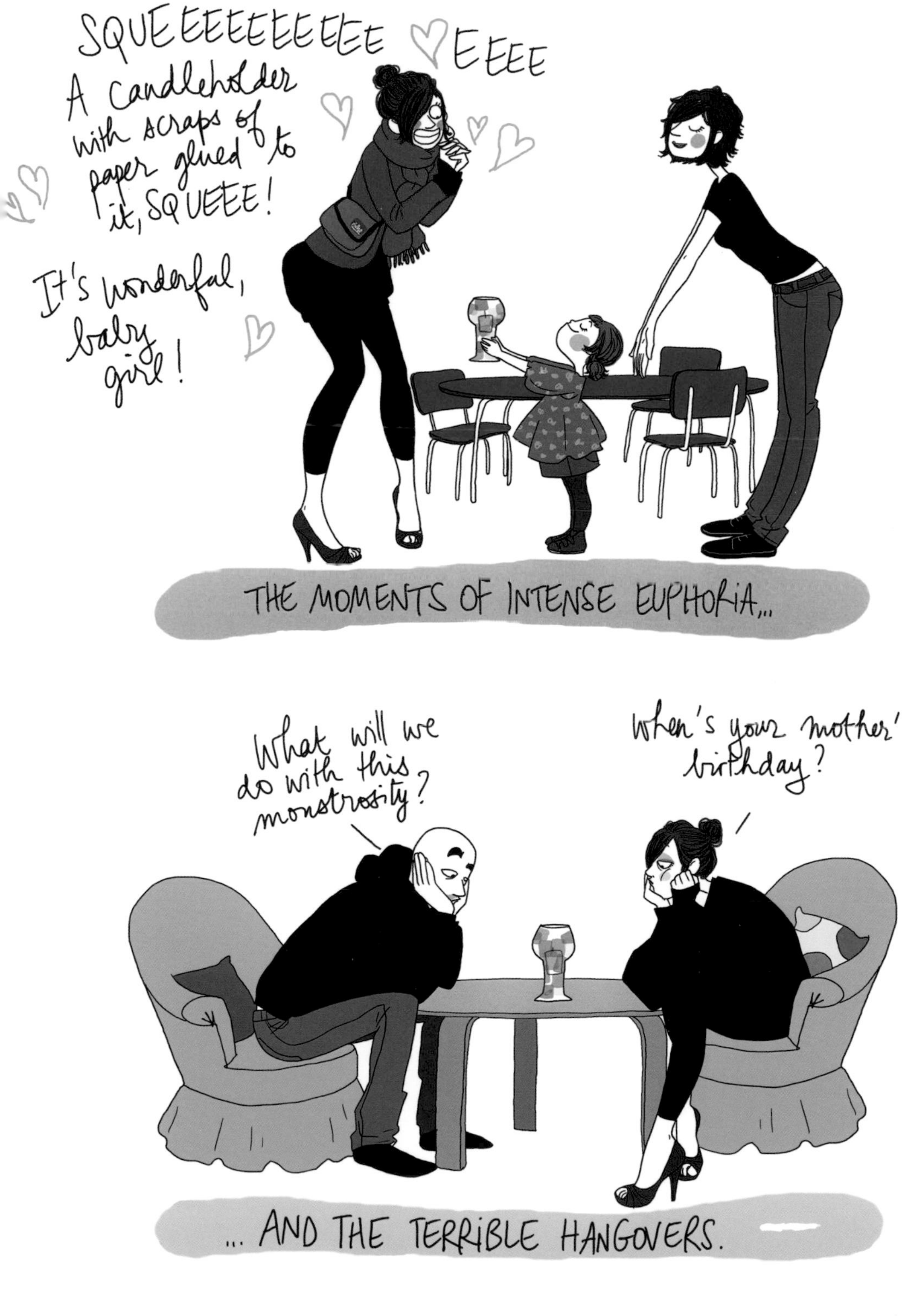
SQUEEEEEEEEEE EEEE
A candleholder with scraps of paper glued to it, SQUEEE!
It's wonderful, baby girl!
THE MOMENTS OF INTENSE EUPHORIA...
What will we do with this monstrosity?
When's your mother's birthday?
... AND THE TERRIBLE HANGOVERS.

It's fine, it's not like she has to drive home, right?

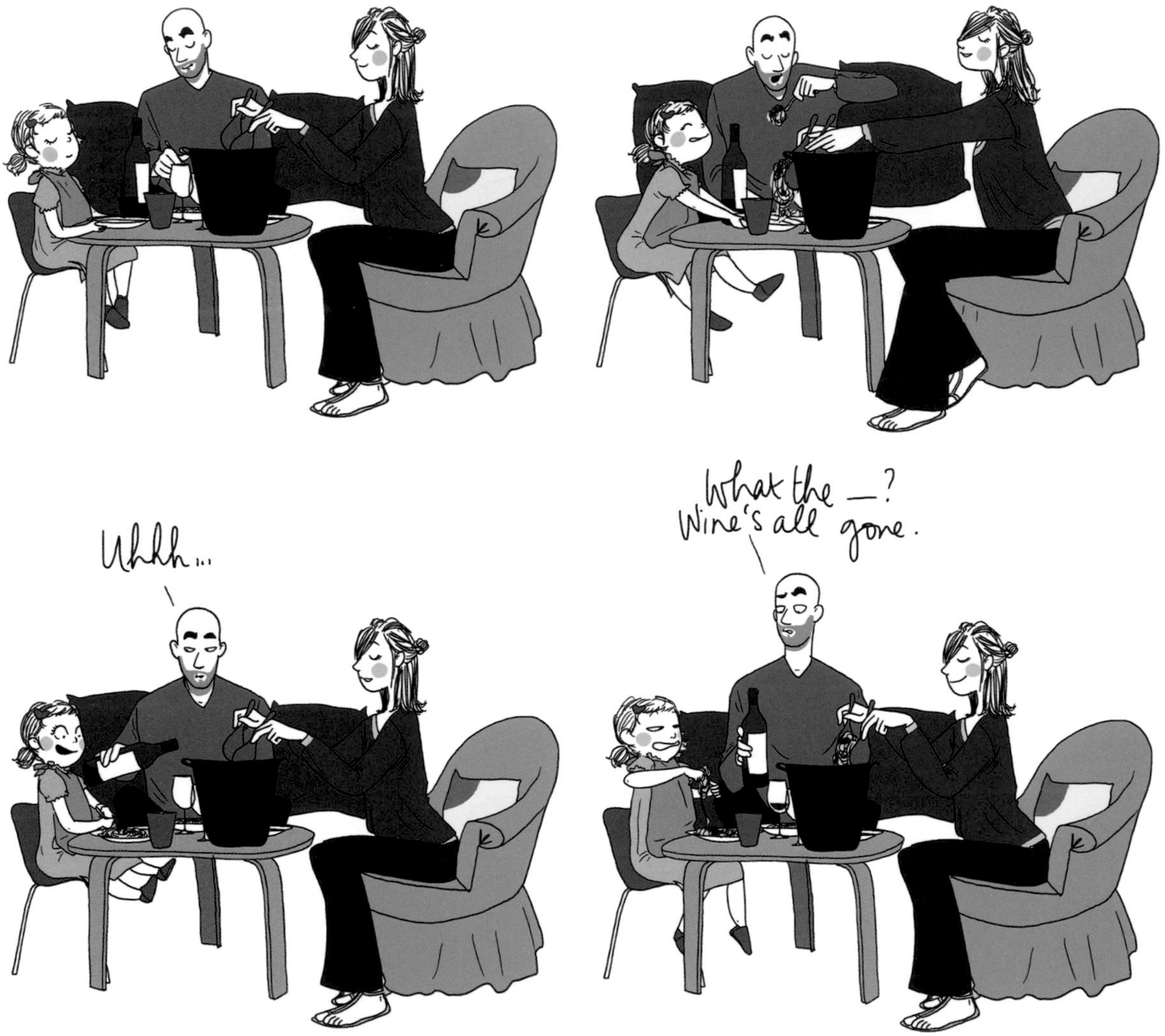
Uhhh...
What the —?
Wine's all gone.

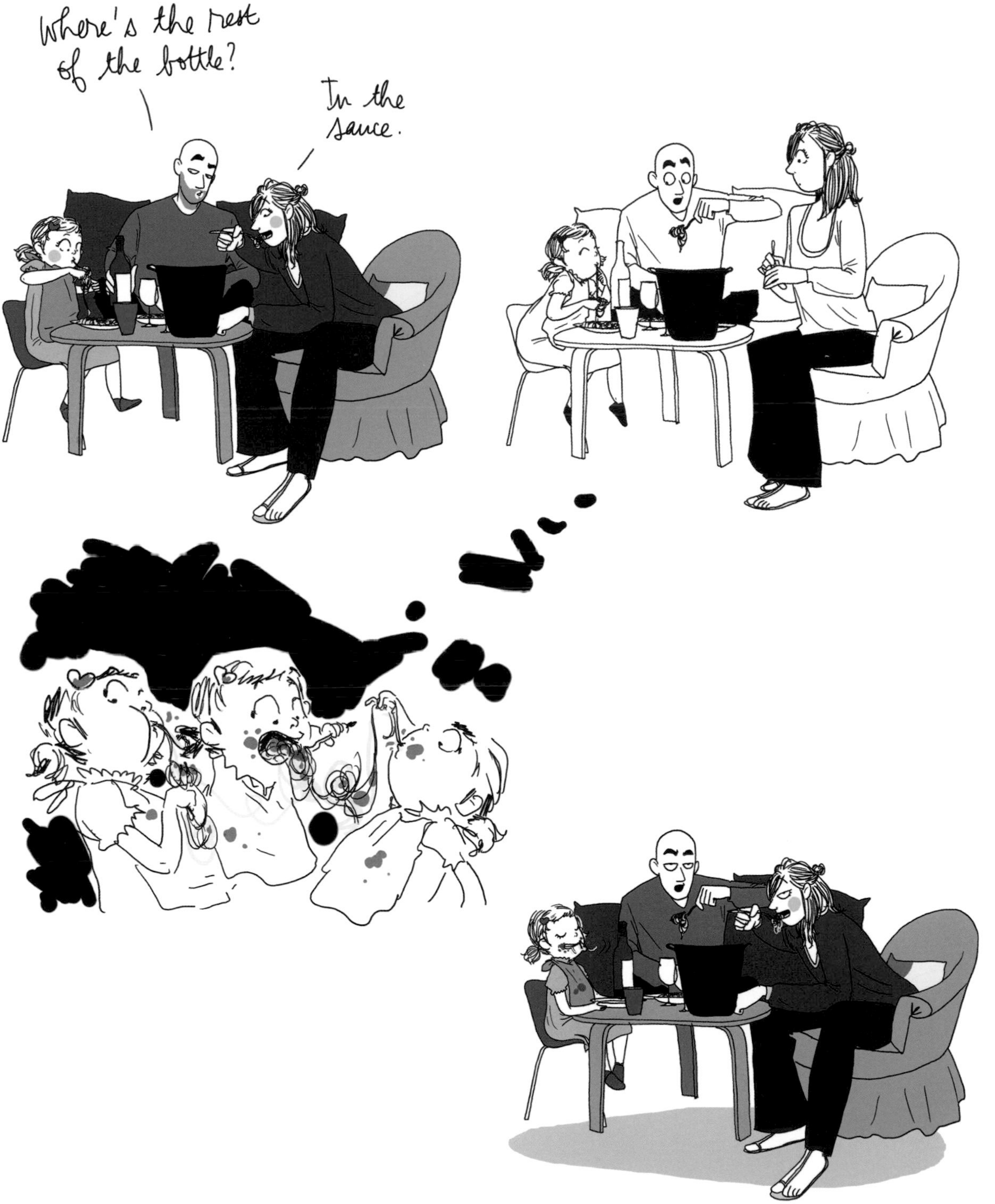
Where's the rest of the bottle?
In the sauce.

Even little victories count...

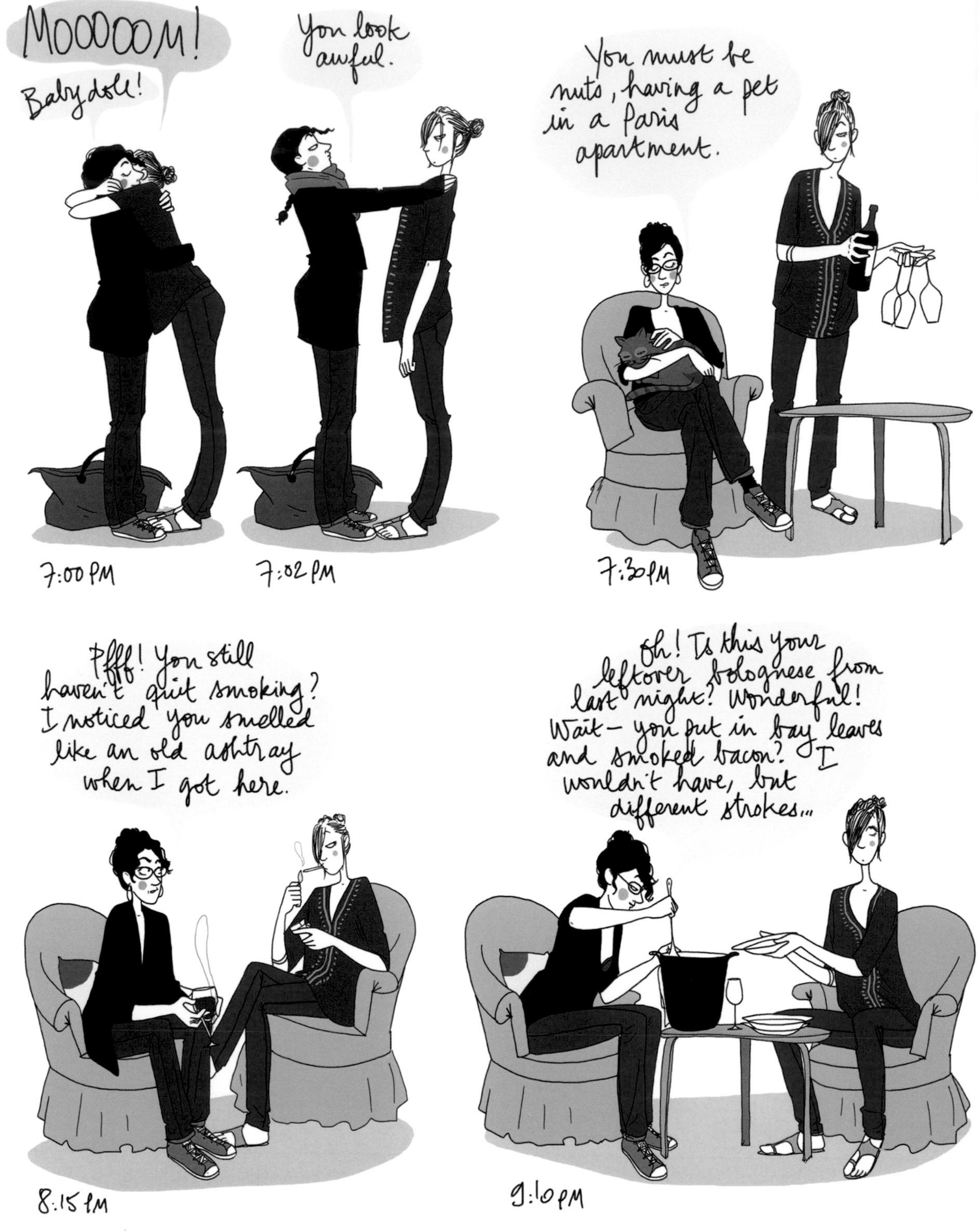

MOOOOOM!
Babydoll!
7:00 PM
You look awful.
7:02 PM
You must be nuts, having a pet in a Paris apartment.
7:30 PM
Pfff! You still haven't quit smoking? I noticed you smelled like an old ashtray when I got here.
8:15 PM
Oh! Is this your leftover bolognese from last night? Wonderful! Wait– you put in bay leaves and smoked bacon? I wouldn't have, but different strokes...
9:10 PM

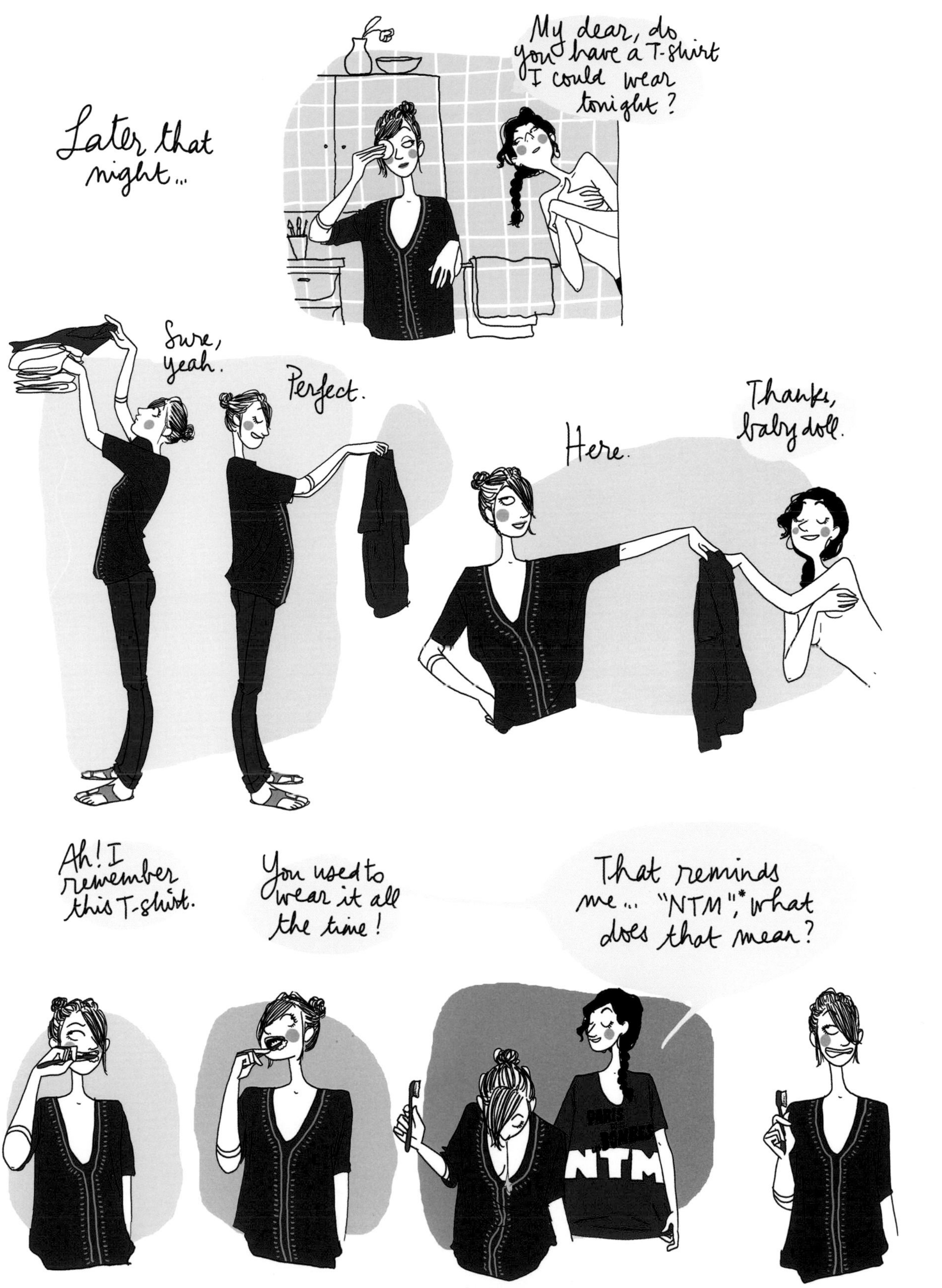
Later that night...
My dear, do you have a T-shirt I could wear tonight?
Sure, yeah.
Perfect.
Here.
Thanks, baby doll.
Ah! I remember this T-shirt.
You used to wear it all the time!
That reminds me... "NTM",* what does that mean?
NTM

*NTM was a Parisian rap duo from the 1980s and 1990s. Their name comes from the popular French insult "nique ta mere" meaning... "fuck your mother".

Total non-assumption of my responsibilities

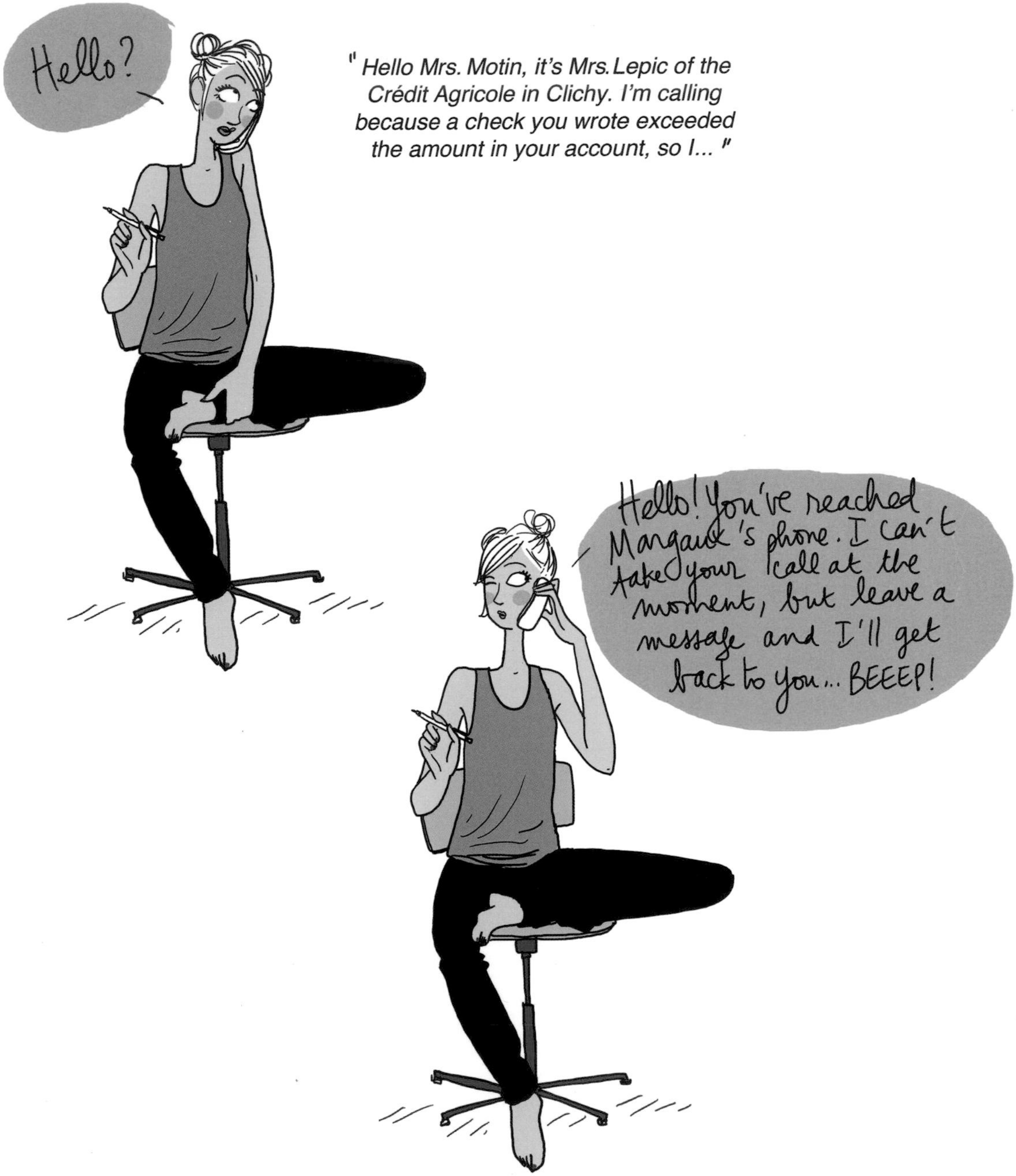
Hello?
" Hello Mrs. Motin, it's Mrs. Lepic of the Crédit Agricole in Clichy. I'm calling because a check you wrote exceeded the amount in your account, so I... "
Hello! You've reached Margaux's phone. I can't take your call at the moment, but leave a message and I'll get back to you... BEEEP!

Unfit mother

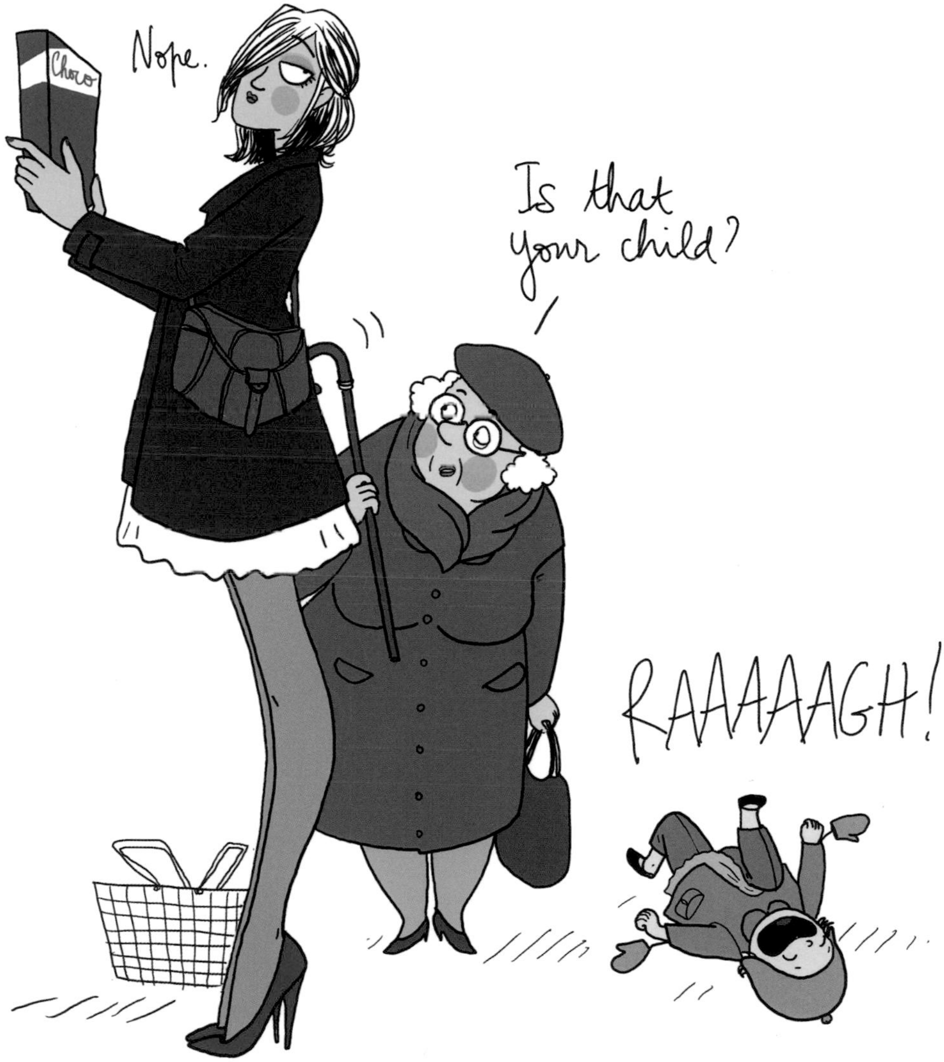
Choco
Nope.
Is that your child?
RAAAAAGH!

In good faith

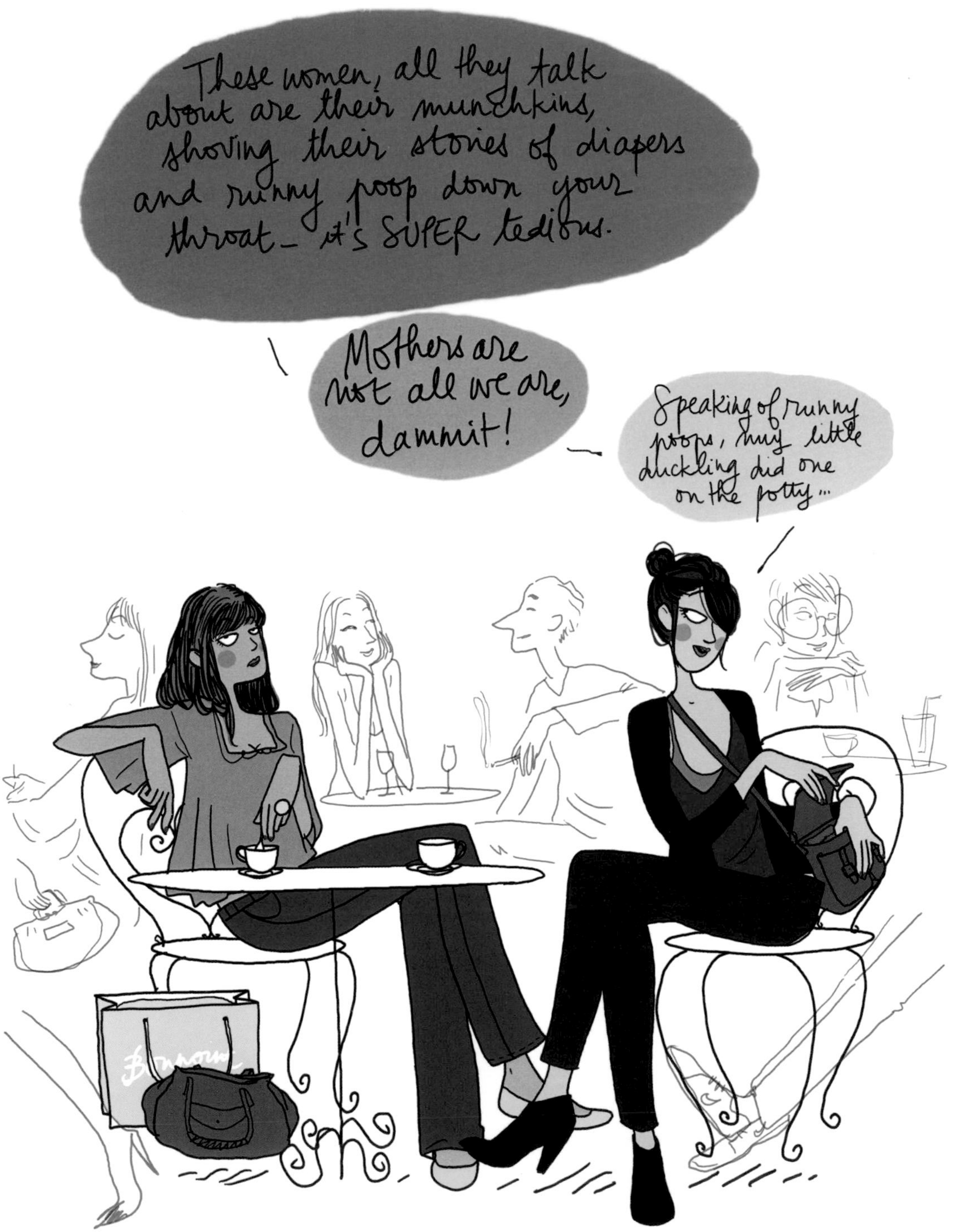
These women, all they talk about are their munchkins, shoving their stories of diapers and runny poop down your throat – it's SUPER tedious.
Mothers are not all we are, dammit!
Speaking of runny poops, my little duckling did one on the potty...
...wanna see pictures?

"Love is looking in the same direction." Yeah, right...

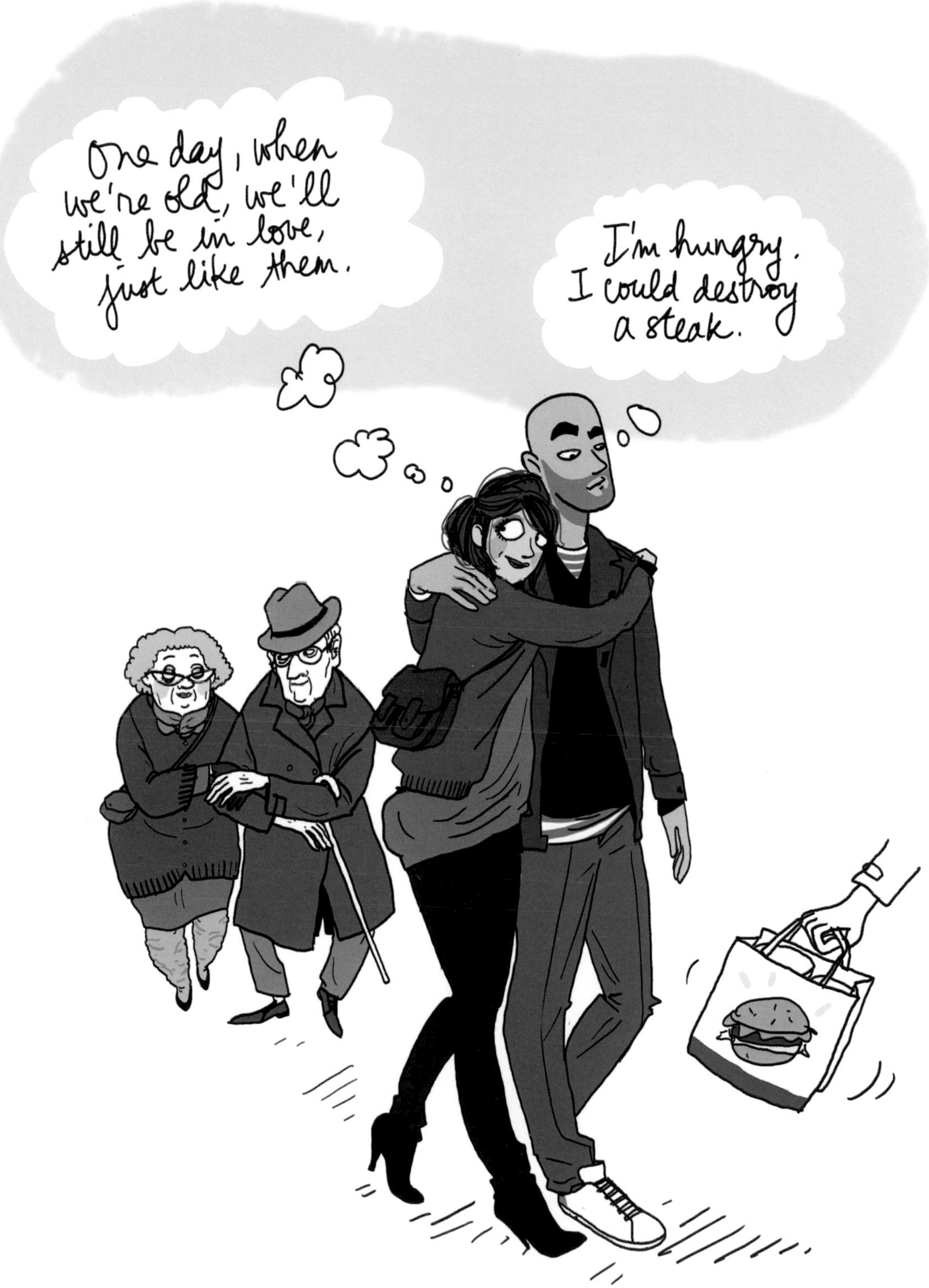

One day, when we're old, we'll still be in love, just like them.
I'm hungry. I could destroy a steak.

Oh ye of little faith

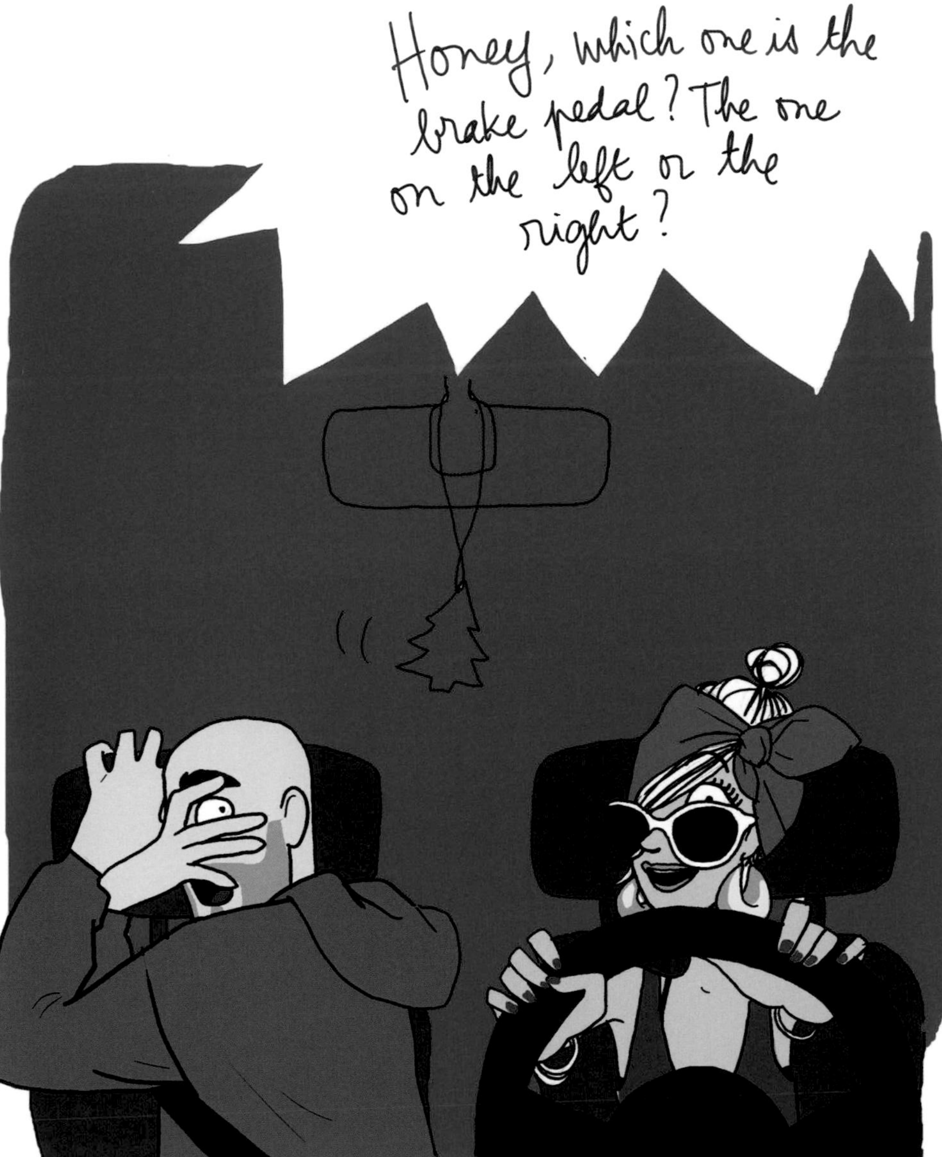
Honey, which one is the brake pedal? The one on the left or the right?

(I got my license a year ago. I haven't touched a car since.)

Sure! And then we'll make loincloths from
banana leaves and live off ants!

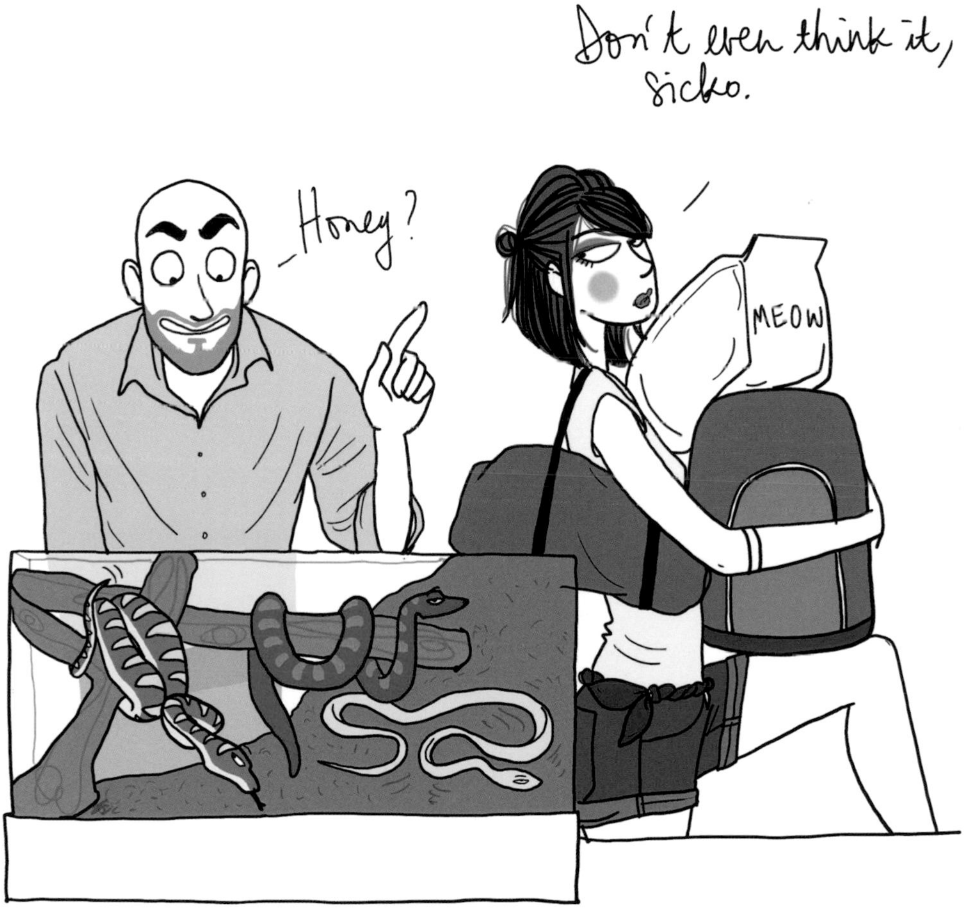

Don't even think it, sicko.
Honey?
MEOW

Crappy housekeeping

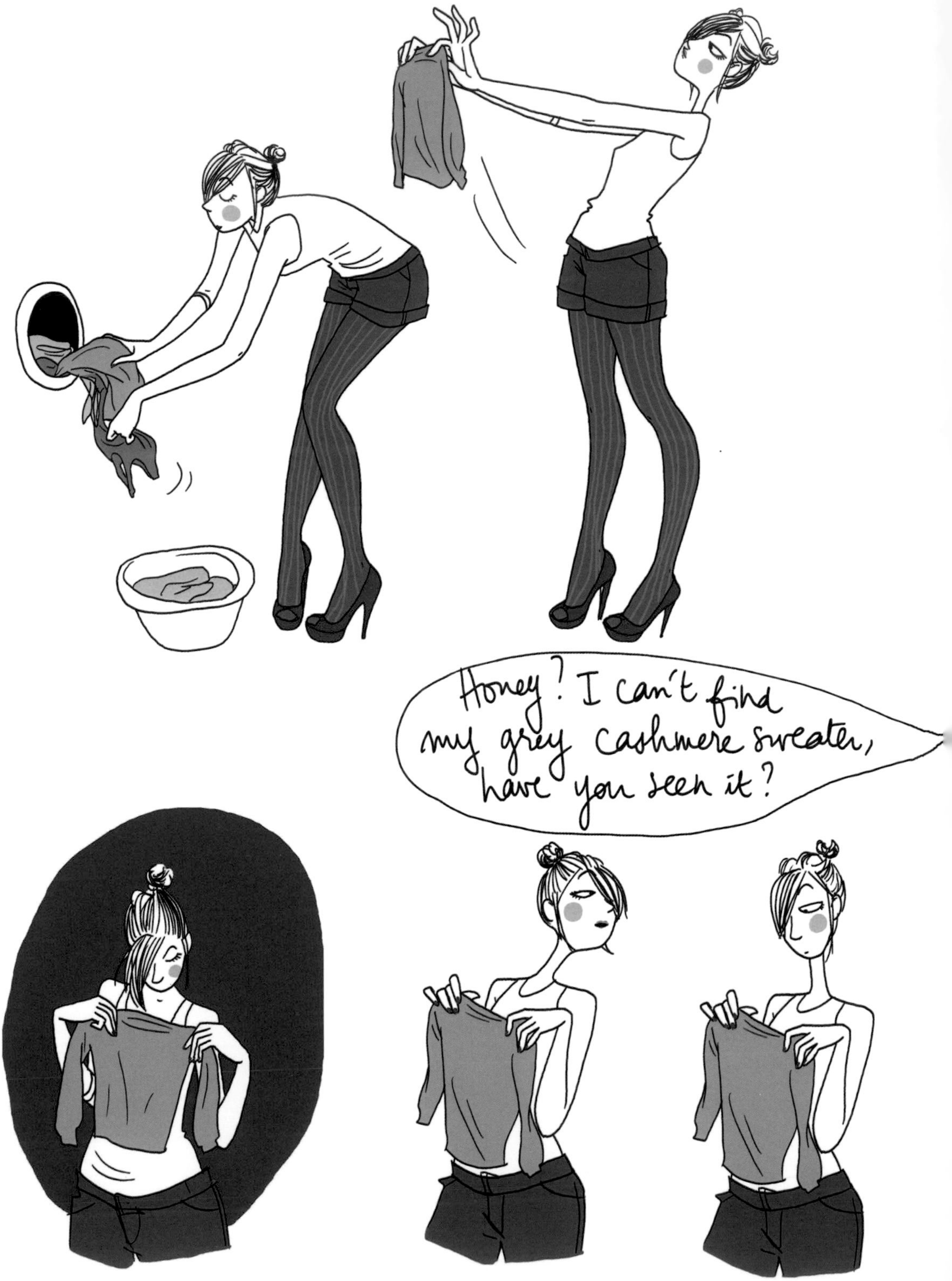
Honey? I can't find my grey cashmere sweater, have you seen it?

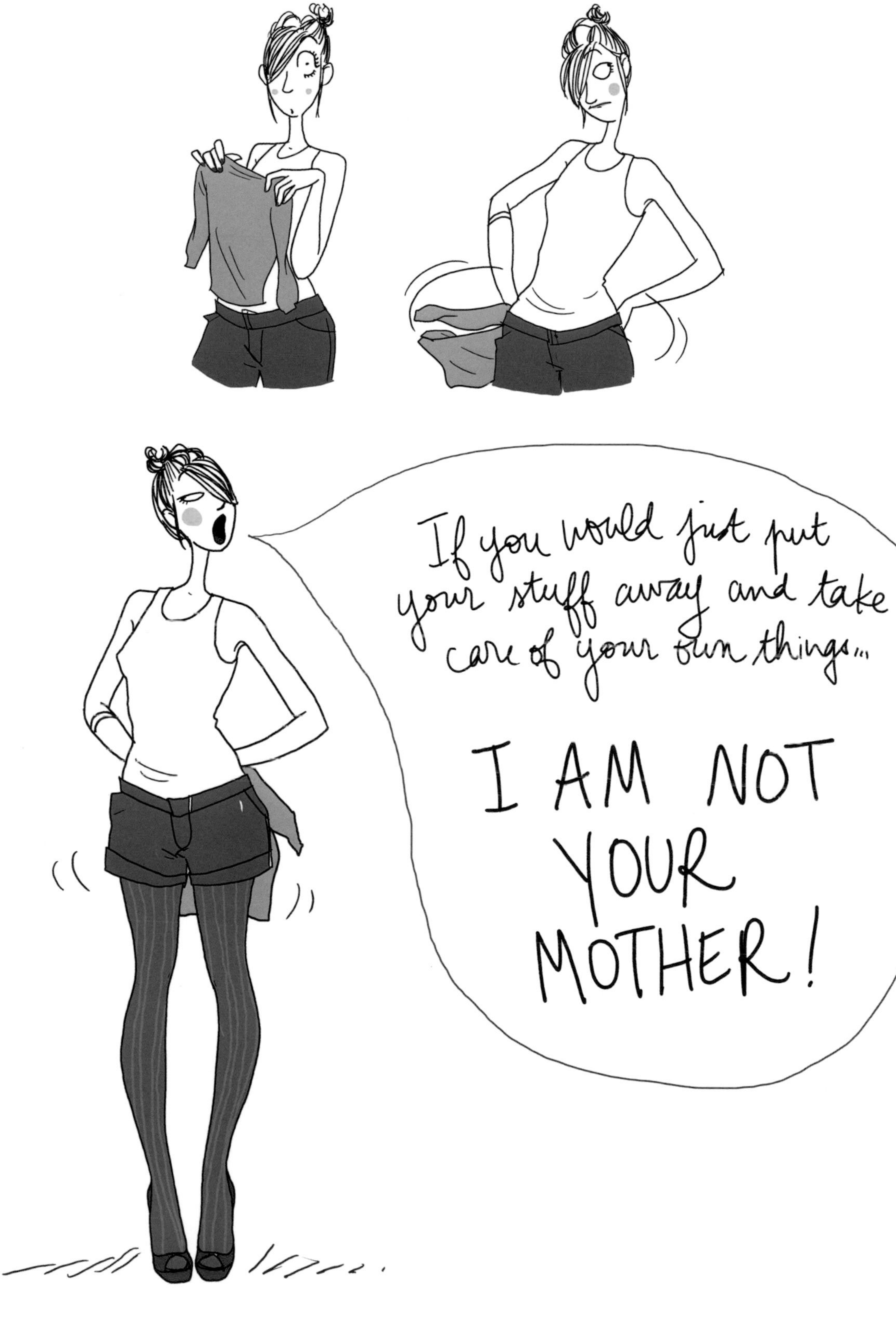
If you would just put your stuff away and take care of your own things...
I AM NOT YOUR MOTHER!

Bad girls are always more believable with backup

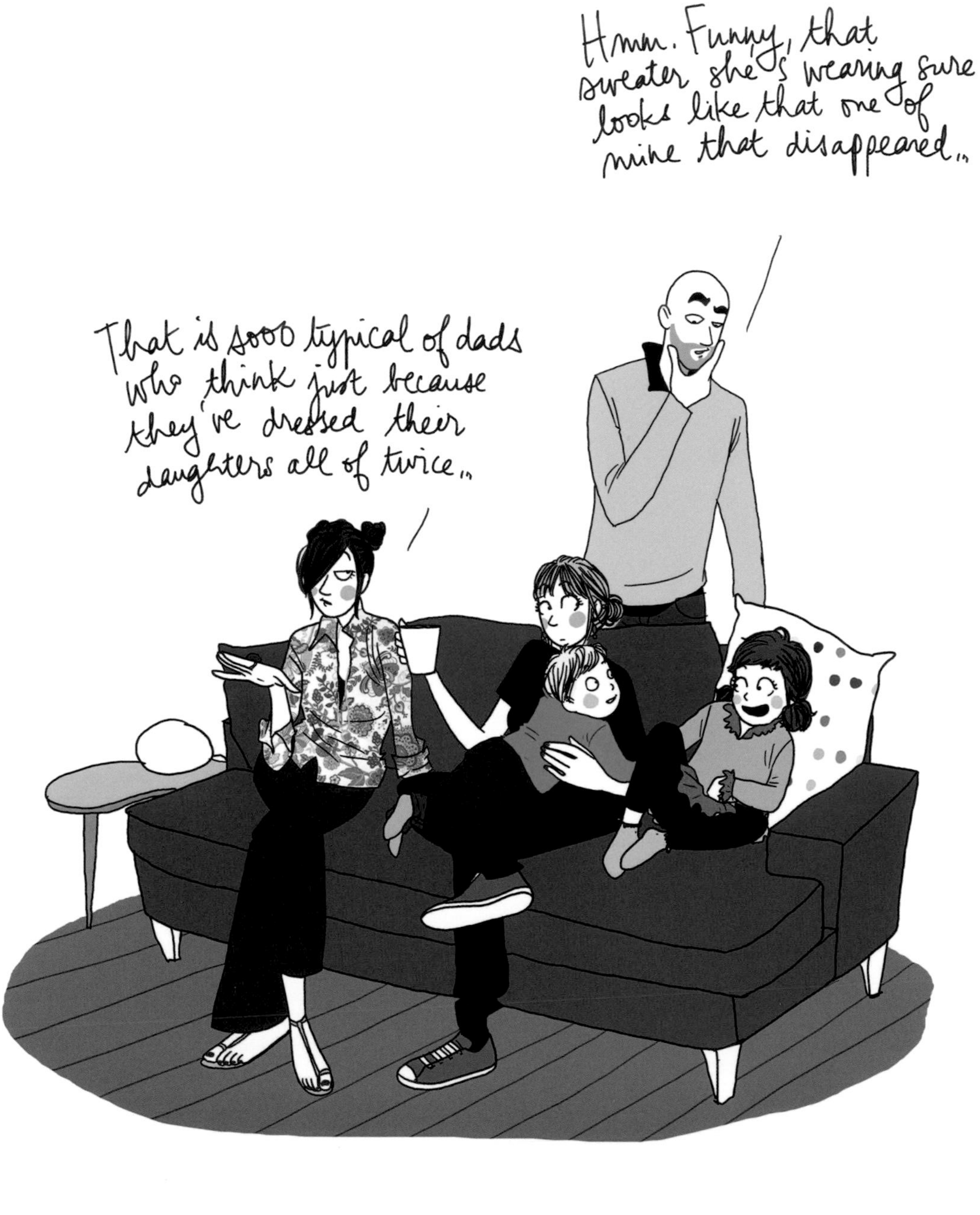
That is sooo typical of dads who think just because they've dressed their daughters all of twice...
Hmm. Funny, that sweater she's wearing sure looks like that one of mine that disappeared...

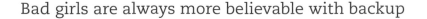

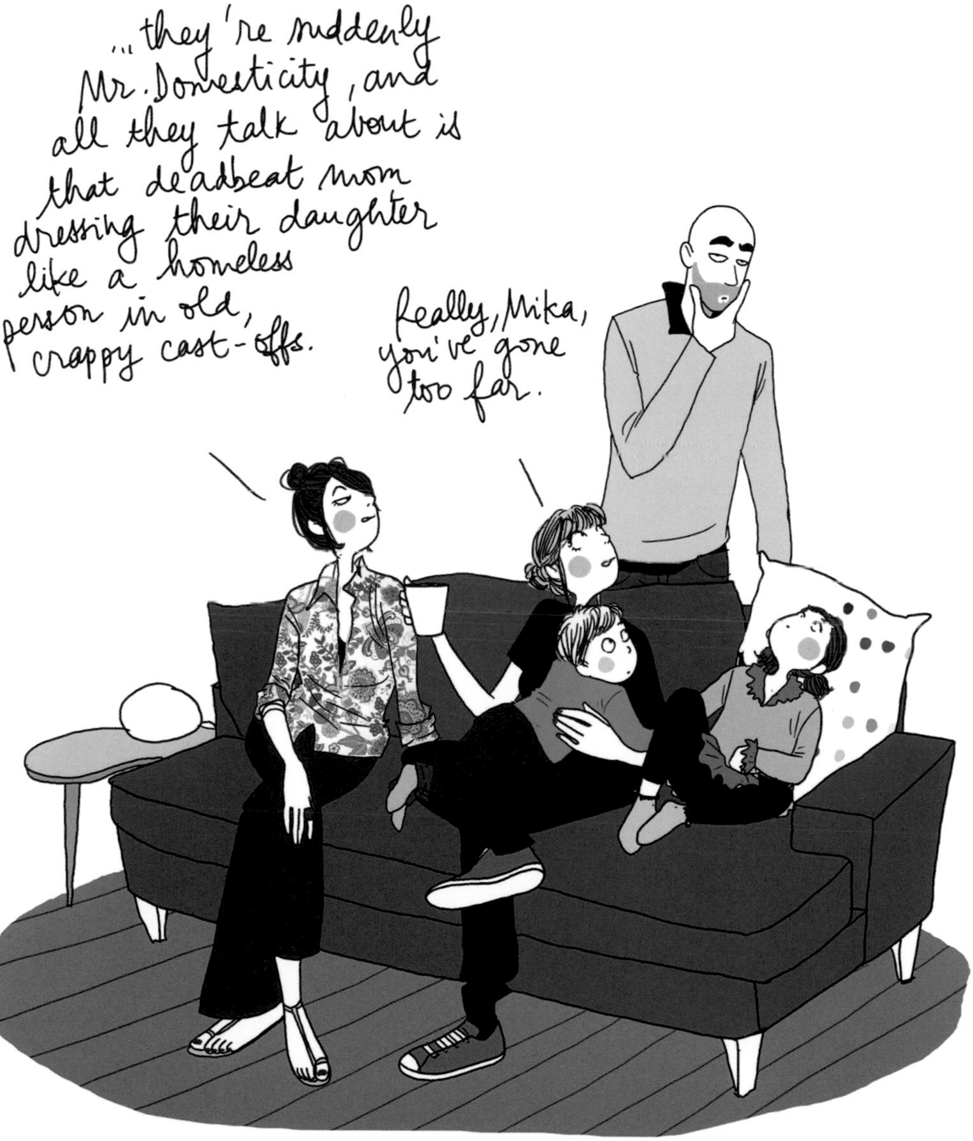
...they're suddenly Mr. Domesticity, and all they talk about is that deadbeat mom dressing their daughter like a homeless person in old, crappy cast-offs.
Really, Mika, you've gone too far.

Some things you don't say to a soldier coming back from the front

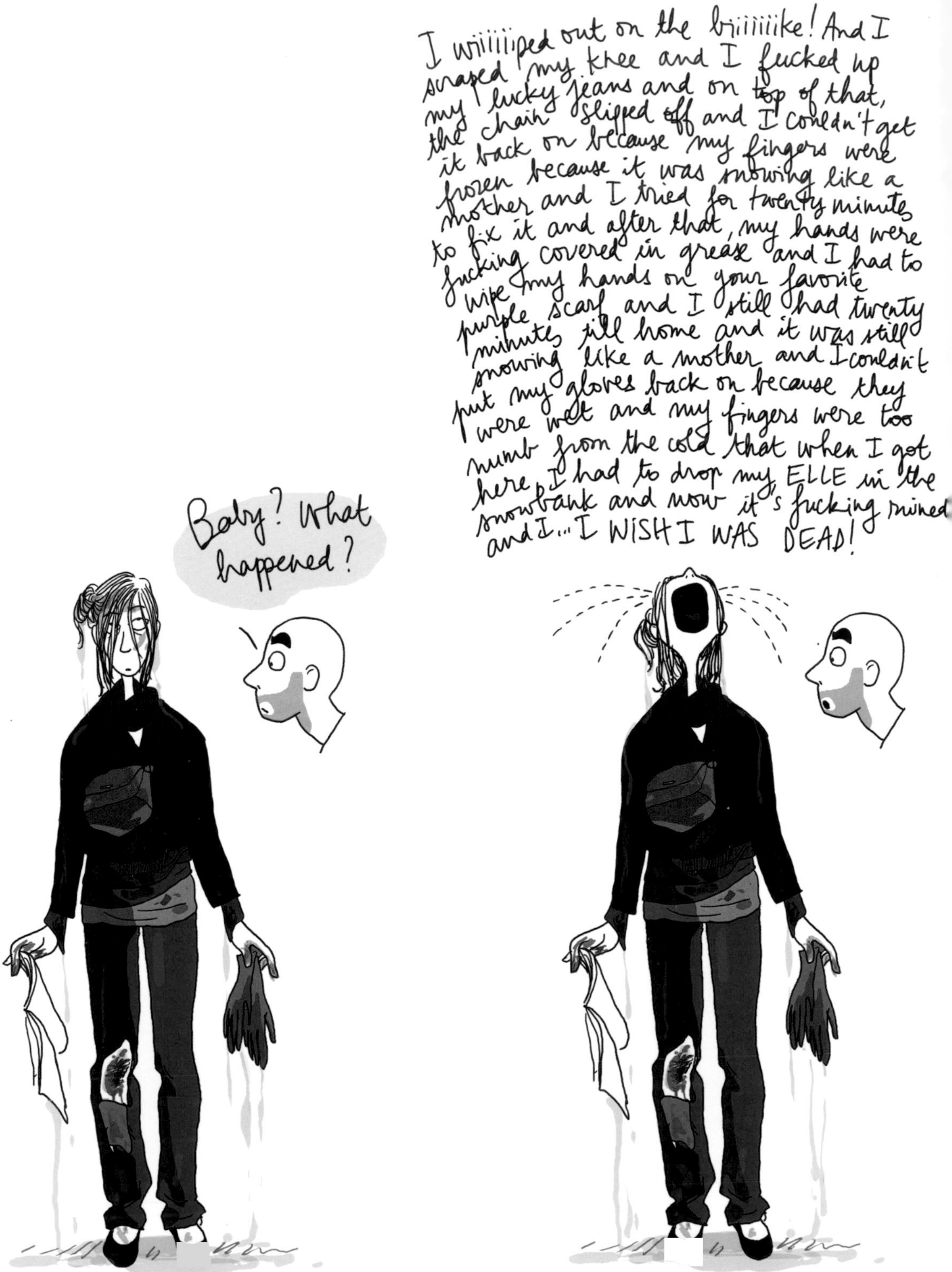
Baby? What happened?
I wriiiiiped out on the briiiiiike! And I scraped my knee and I fucked up my lucky jeans and on top of that, the chain slipped off and I couldn't get it back on because my fingers were frozen because it was snowing like a mother and I tried for twenty minutes to fix it and after that, my hands were fucking covered in grease and I had to wipe my hands on your favorite purple scarf and I still had twenty minutes till home and it was still snowing like a mother and I couldn't put my gloves back on because they were wet and my fingers were too numb from the cold that when I got here, I had to drop my ELLE in the snowbank and now it's fucking ruined and I... I WISH I WAS DEAD!

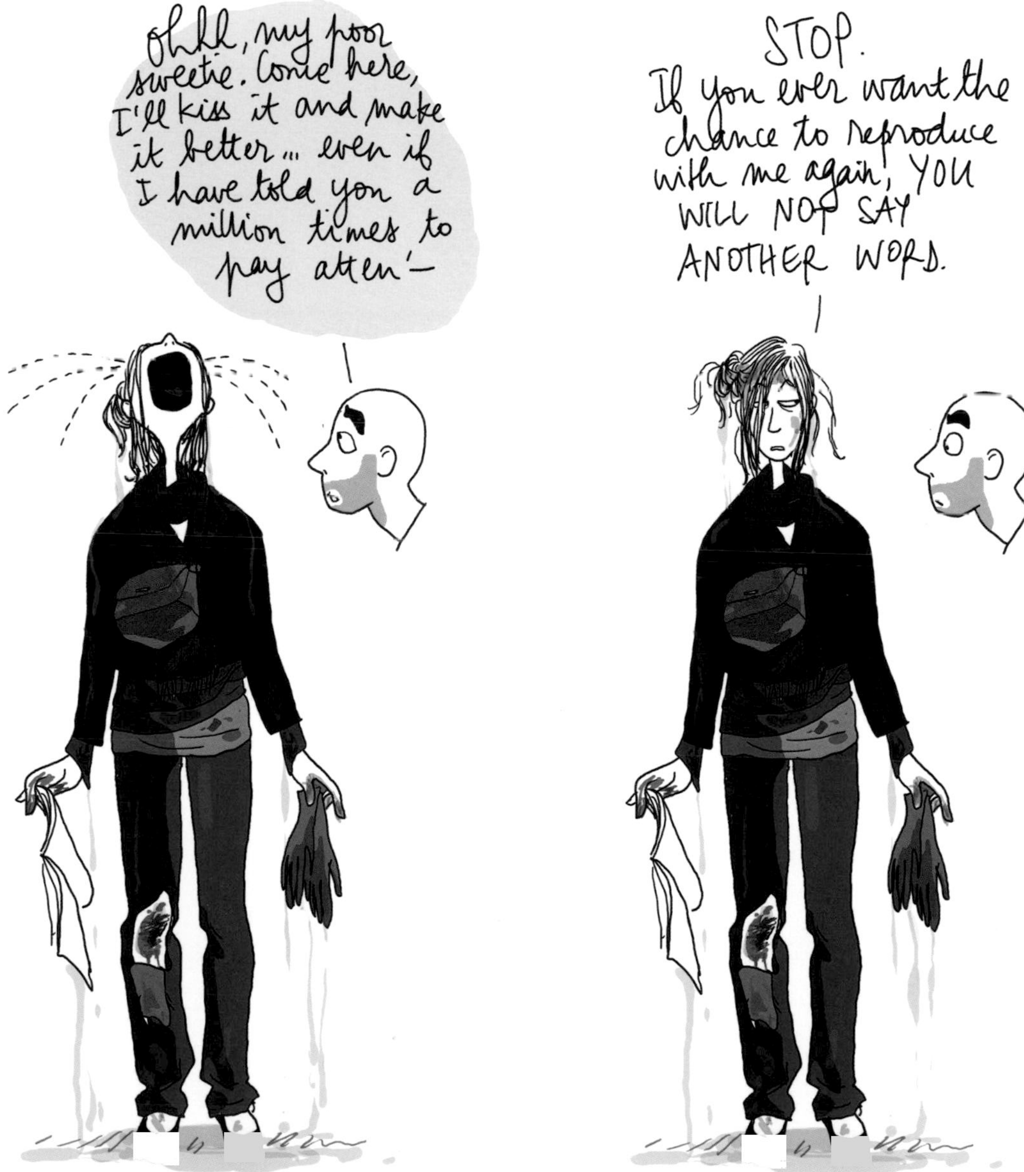
Ohhh, my poor sweetie. Come here, I'll kiss it and make it better... even if I have told you a million times to pay atten'–
STOP.
If you ever want the chance to reproduce with me again, YOU WILL NOT SAY ANOTHER WORD.

The art of the *mot juste*

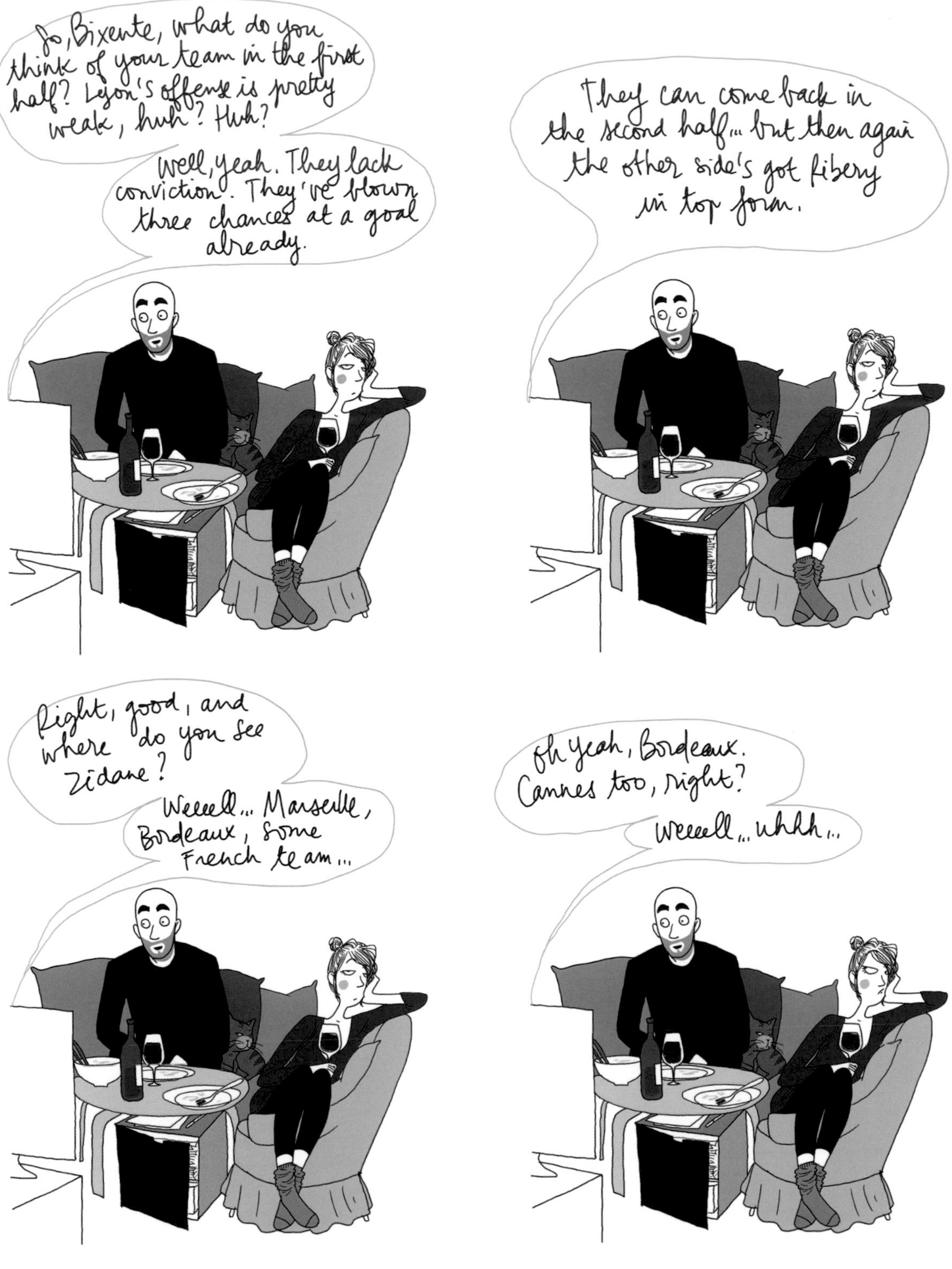
So, Bixente, what do you think of your team in the first half? Lyon's offense is pretty weak, huh? Huh?
Well, yeah. They lack conviction. They've blown three chances at a goal already.
They can come back in the second half... but then again the other side's got Ribery in top form.
Right, good, and where do you see Zidane?
Weeeell... Marseille, Bordeaux, some French team...
Oh yeah, Bordeaux. Cannes too, right?
Weeeell... uhhh...

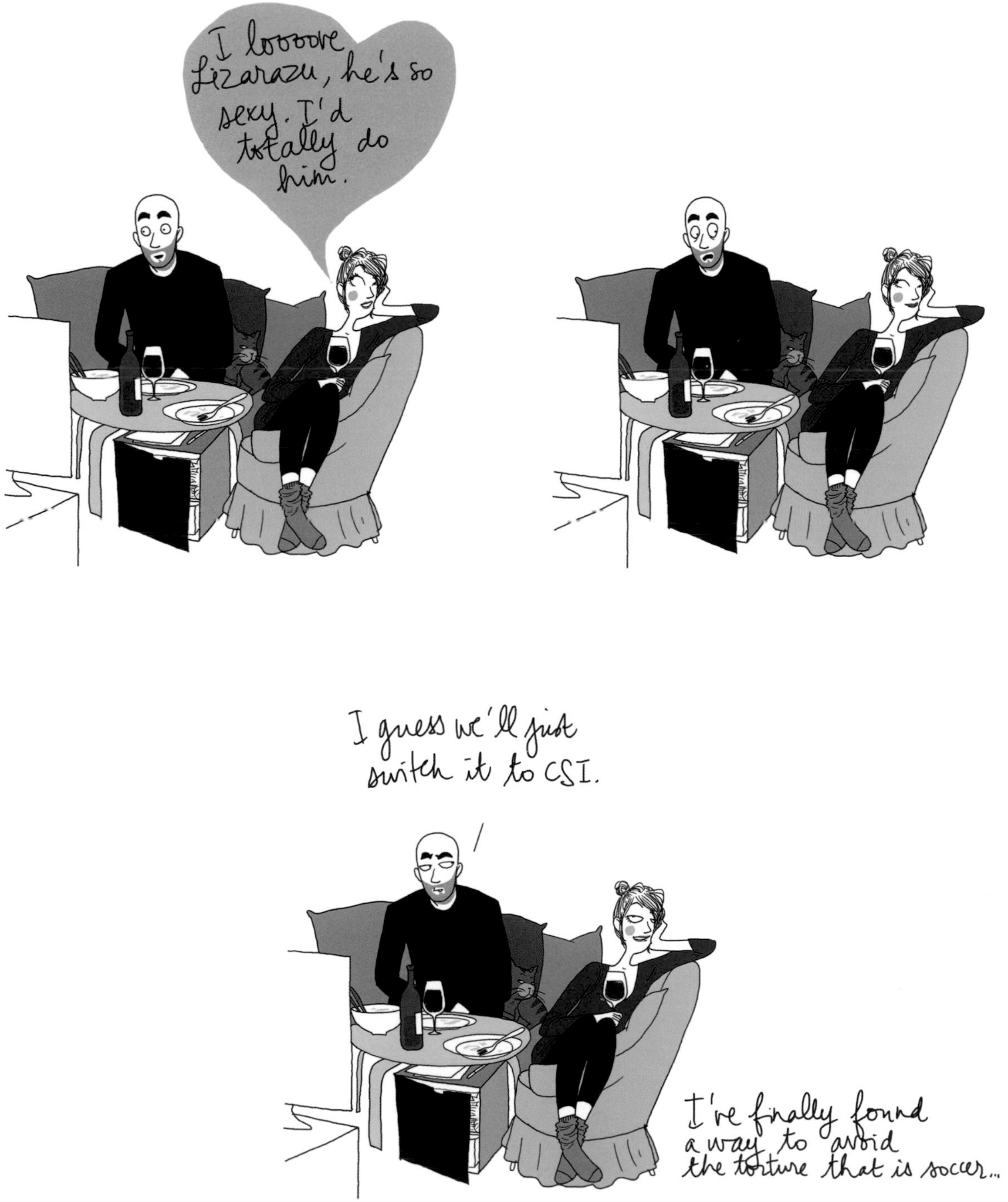
I looooove Lizarazu, he's so sexy. I'd totally do him.
I guess we'll just switch it to CSI.
I've finally found a way to avoid the torture that is soccer...

Is that really what you want? Huh? HUH?

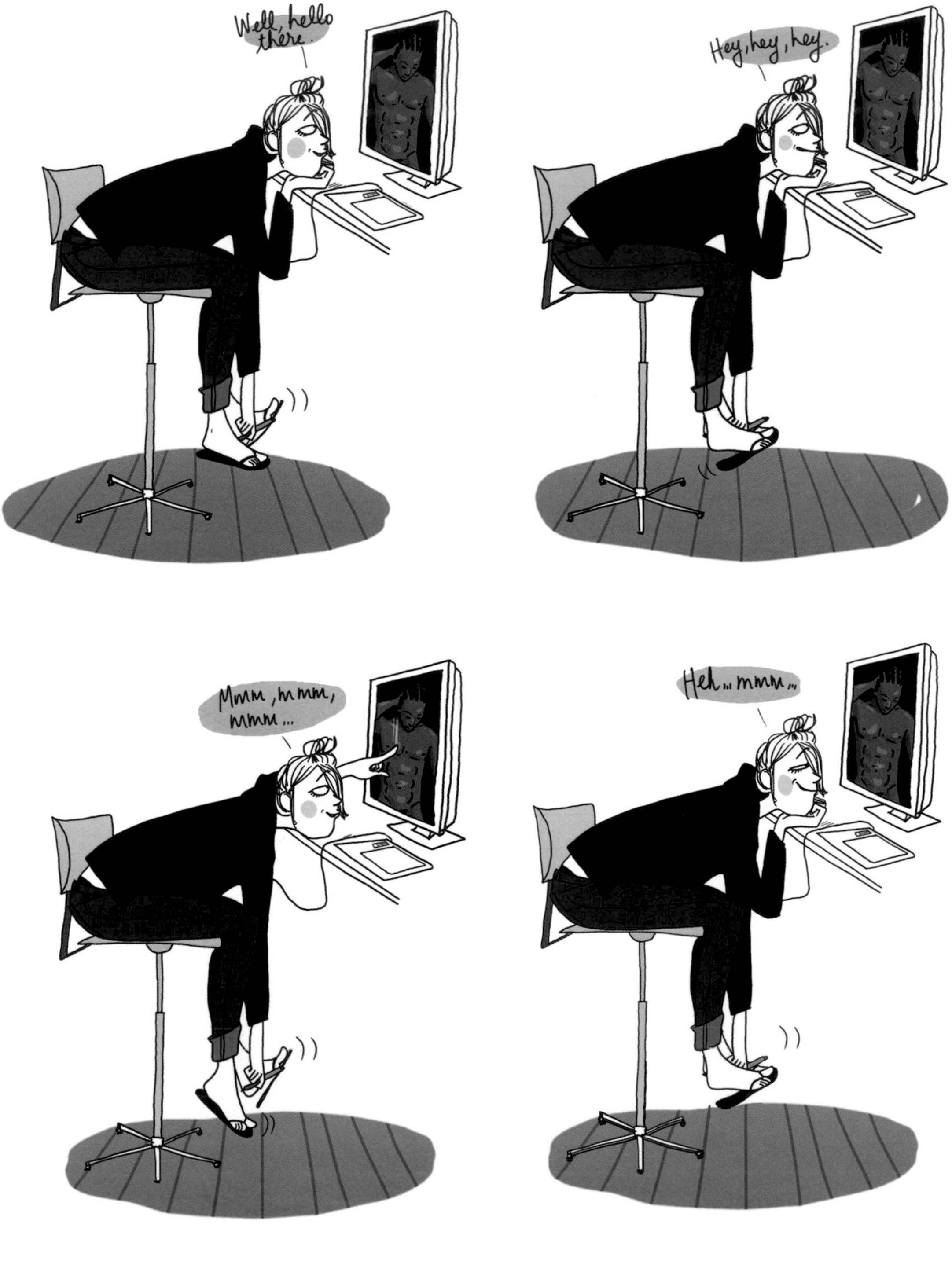
Well, hello there.
Hey, hey, hey.
Mmm, mmm, mmm...
Heh... mmm...

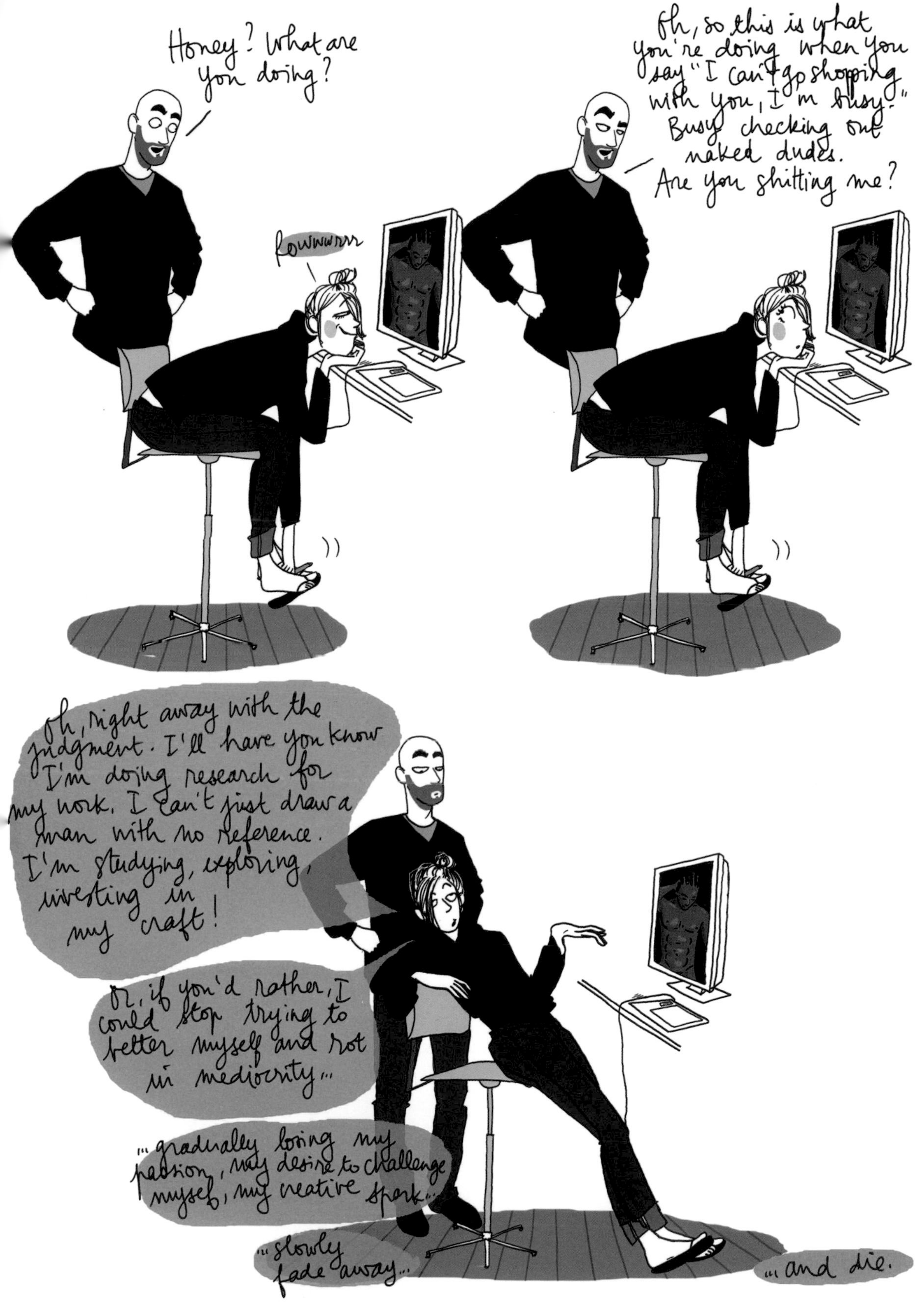
Honey? What are you doing?
Rowwwrrr
Oh, so this is what you're doing when you say "I can't go shopping with you, I'm busy." Busy checking out naked dudes. Are you shitting me?
Oh, right away with the judgment. I'll have you know I'm doing research for my work. I can't just draw a man with no reference. I'm studying, exploring, investing in my craft!
Or, if you'd rather, I could stop trying to better myself and rot in mediocrity...
...gradually losing my passion, my desire to challenge myself, my creative spark...
...slowly fade away...
...and die.

Because, in 36 days, it's my birthday...

... and because the last few Christmases have demonstrated that the male does not get my subliminal messages – discreet allusions/excited squee-ing before the coveted object/magazines left open to a page with aforementioned object highlighted and "I want you" in marker underneath...

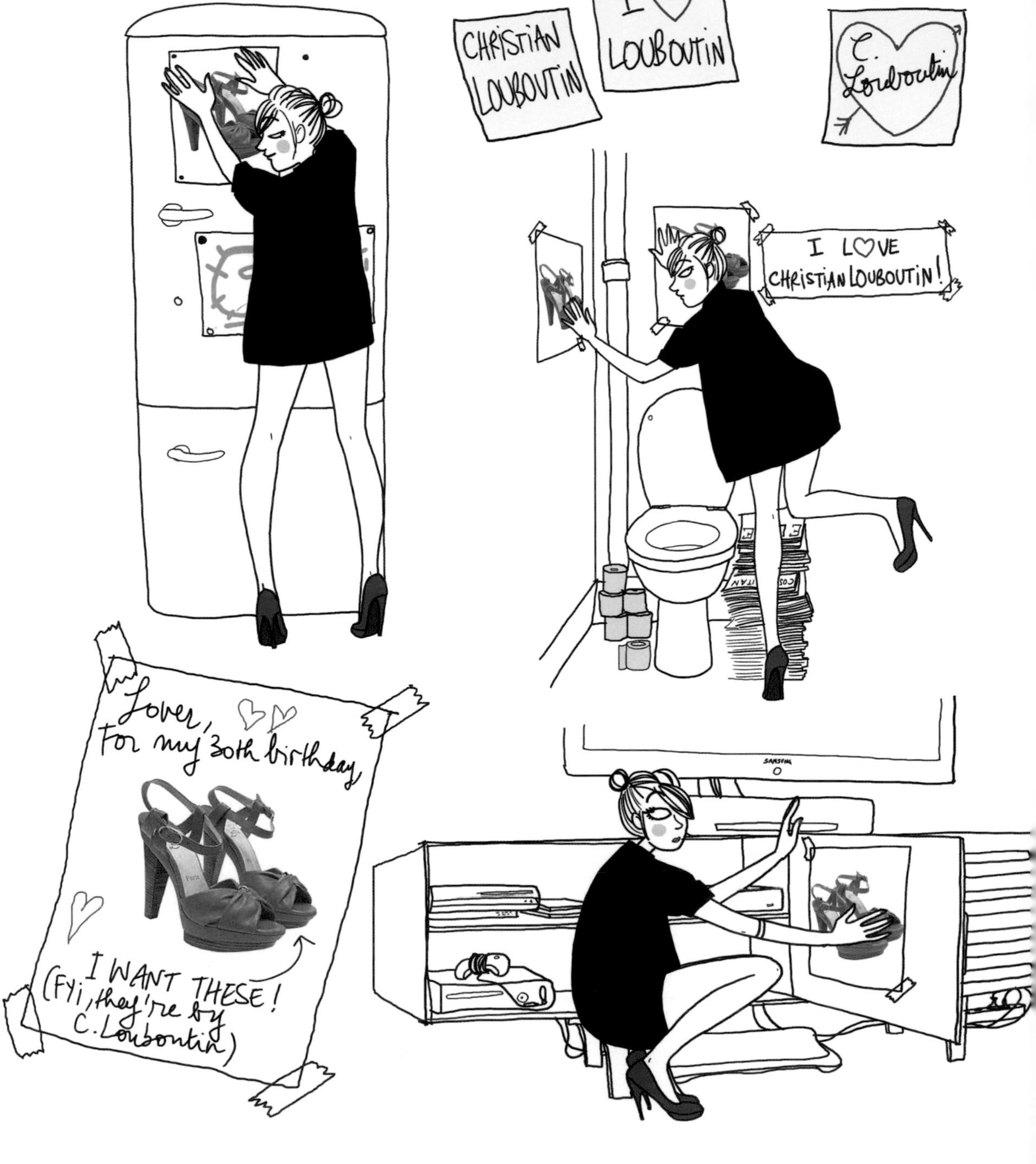

CHRISTIAN LOUBOUTIN
I ♡ LOUBOUTIN
C. Louboutin
I L♡VE CHRISTIAN LOUBOUTIN!
Lover,
For my 30th birthday
I WANT THESE!
(FYI, they're by C. Louboutin)

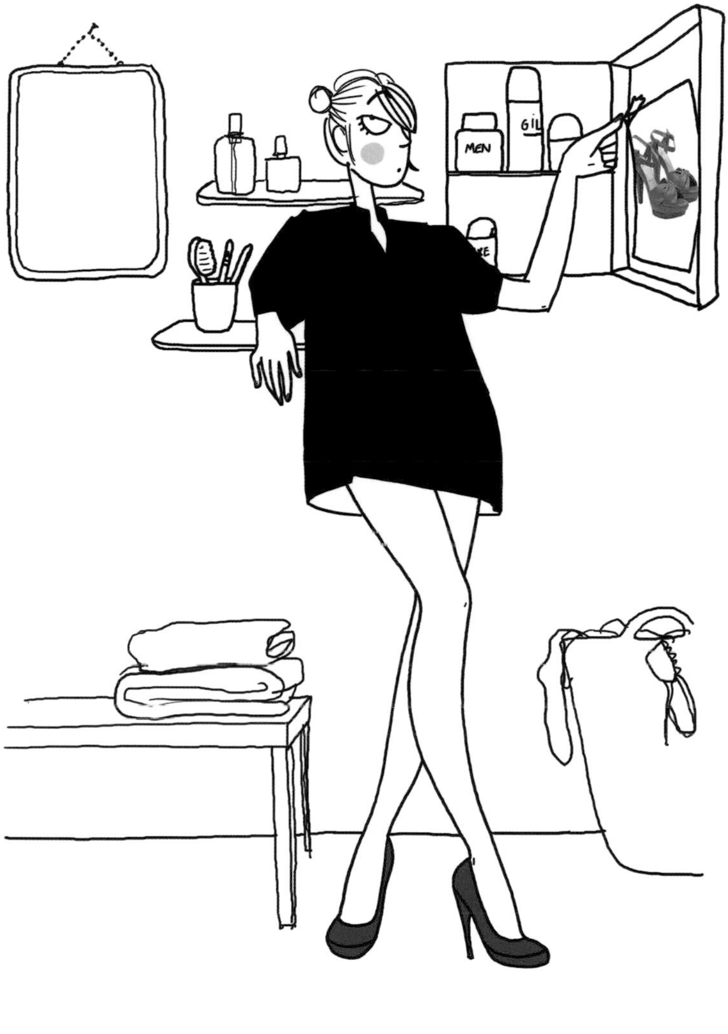
MEN
GIL

... I've decided to cool it with the subtle verbal hints.

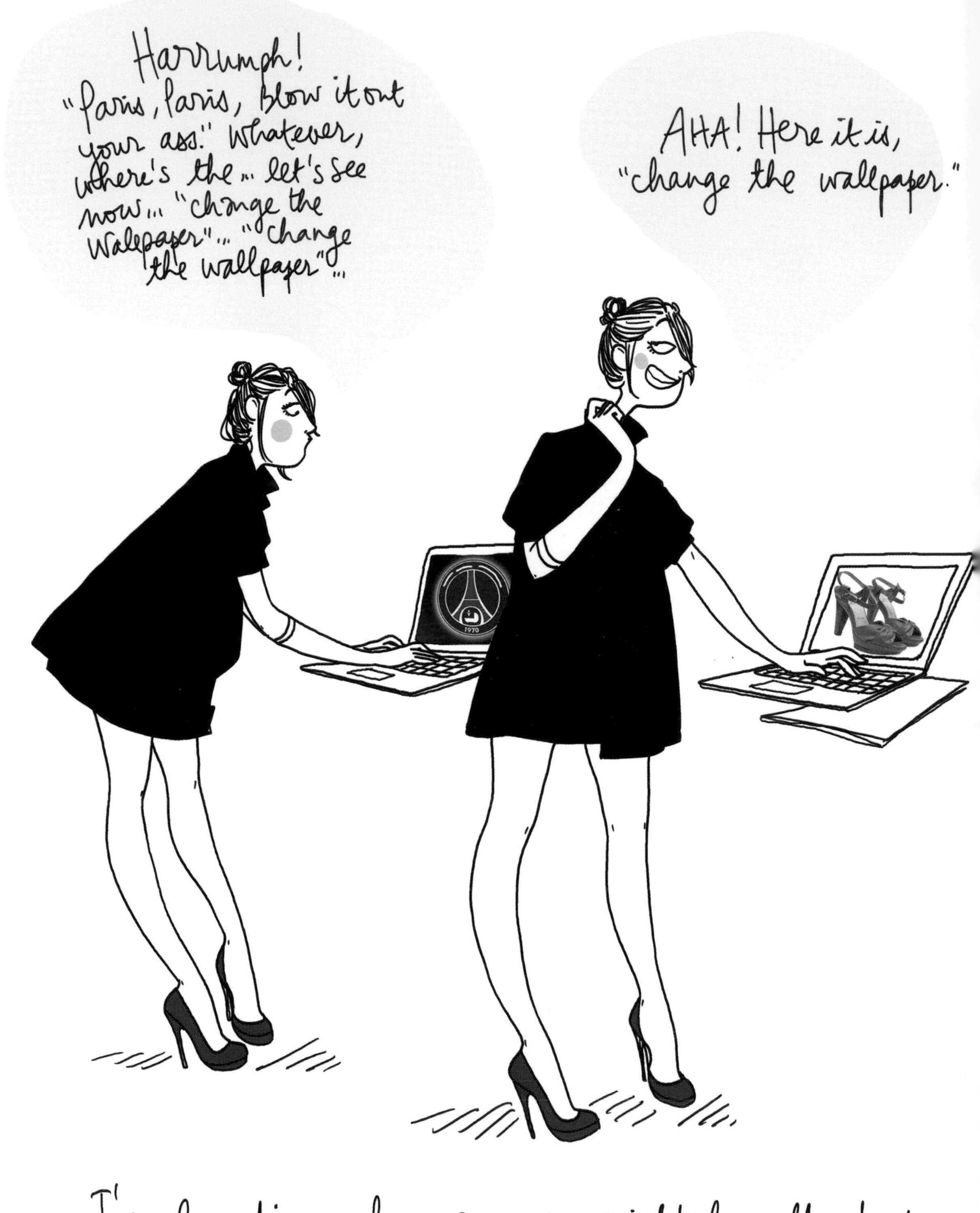
Harrumph! "Paris, Paris, blow it out your ass." Whatever, where's the... let's see now... "change the walepaper"... "change the wallpaper"...
AHA! Here it is, "change the wallpaper."

I'm launching a huge campaign right from the start.

OK, but meanwhile...
the male of the species makes war, chops wood, eats bloody steak, is hairy... and so if, on top of all that, you want him to pay attention to signs and plan ahead, then...

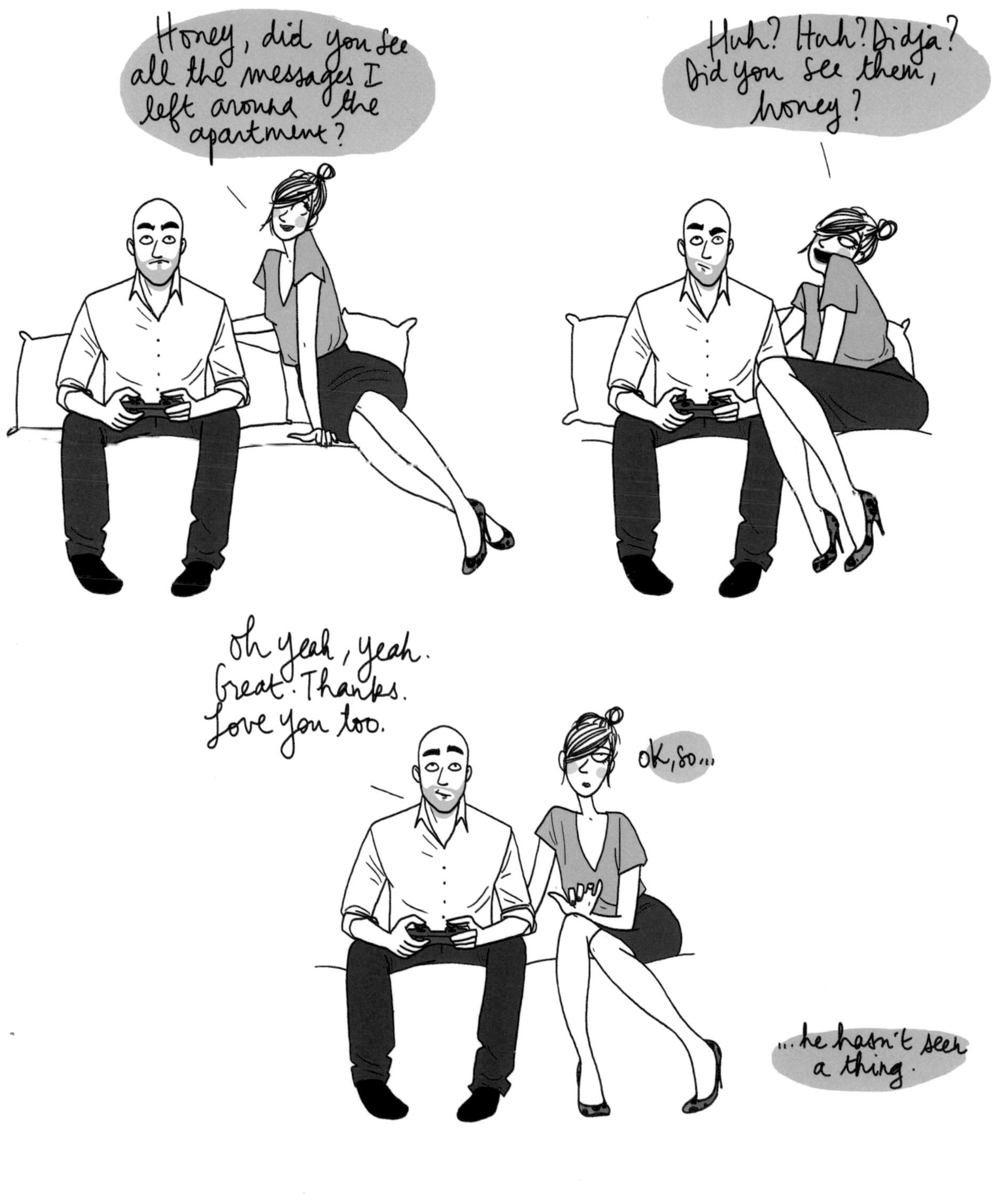
Honey, did you see all the messages I left around the apartment?
Huh? Huh? Didja? Did you see them, honey?
Oh yeah, yeah. Great. Thanks. Love you too.
OK, so...
...he hasn't seen a thing.

All things considered

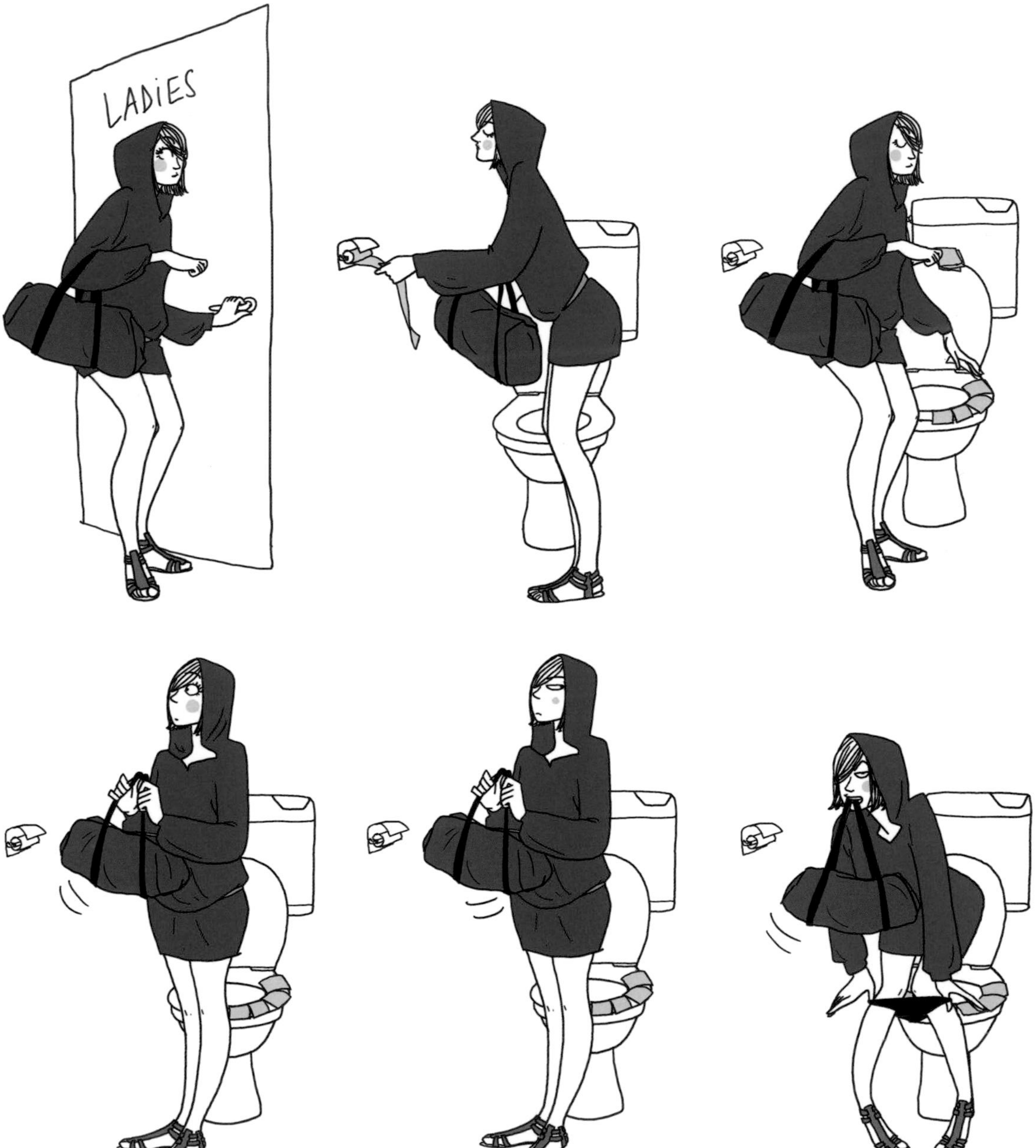
LADIES

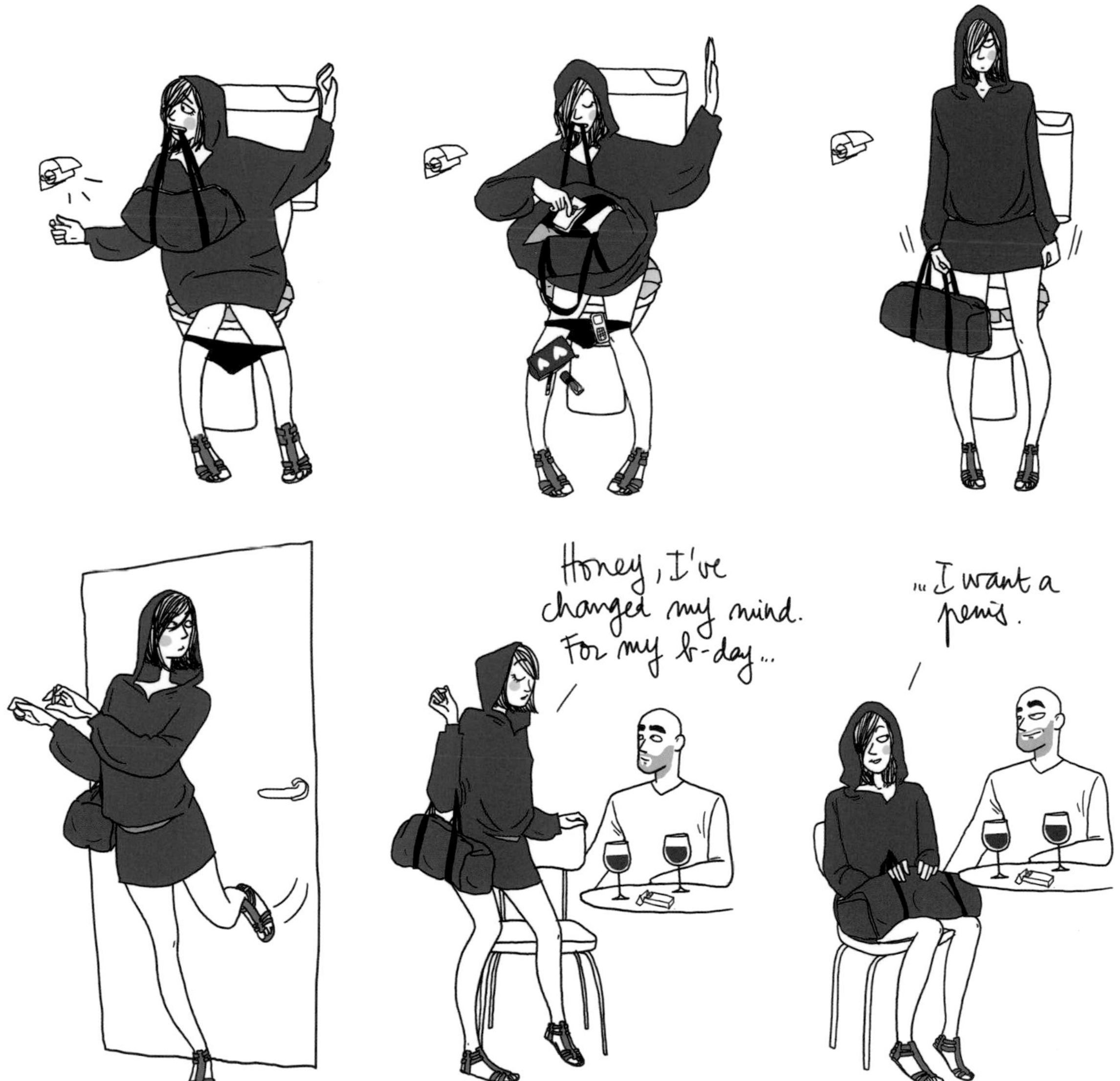
Honey, I've changed my mind. For my b-day...
... I want a penis.

With their young absent, the adults occasionally abandon all common sense...

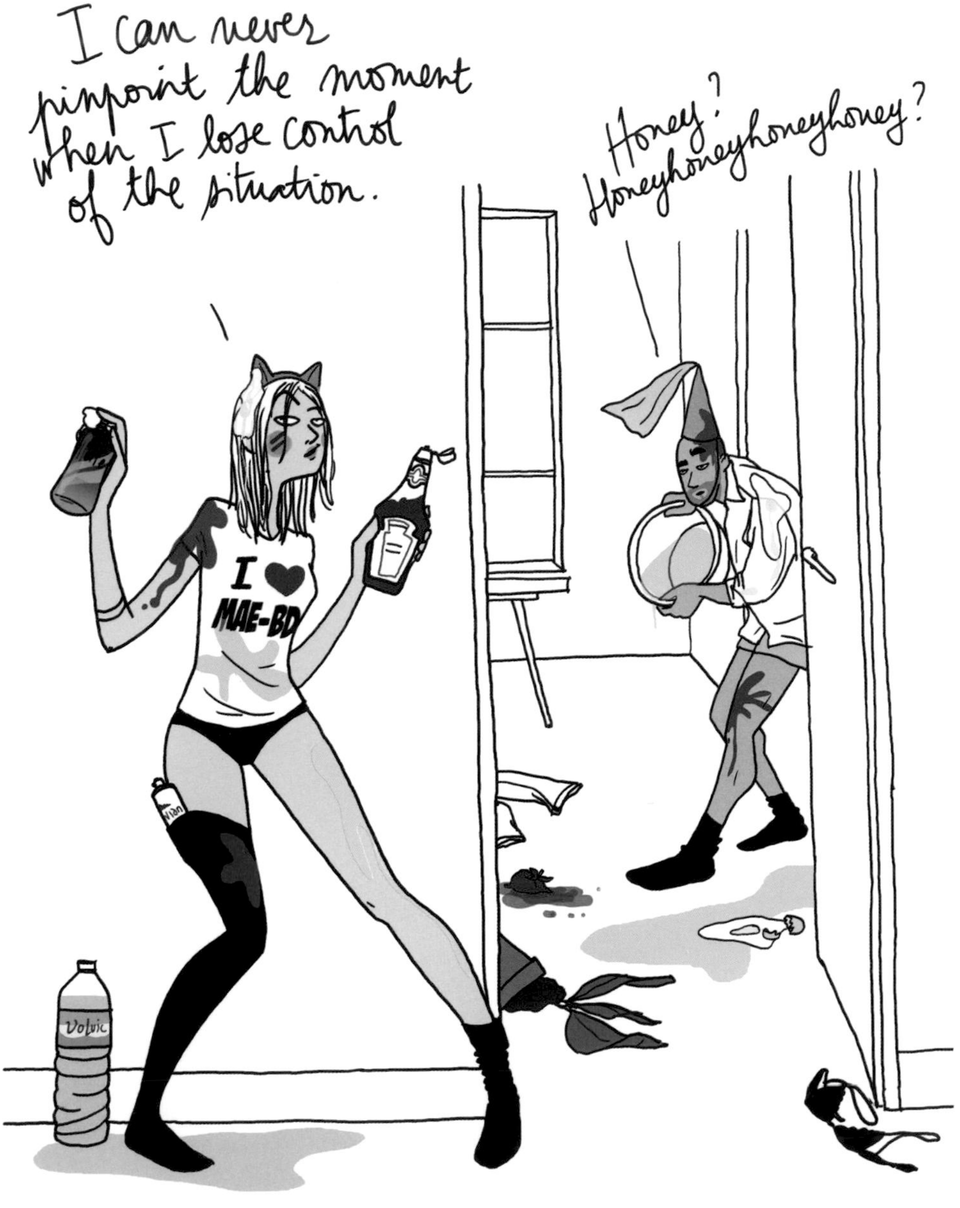
I can never pinpoint the moment when I lose control of the situation.
Honey? Honeyhoneyhoneyhoney?
I ♥ MAE-BD
Volvic

Note to self:

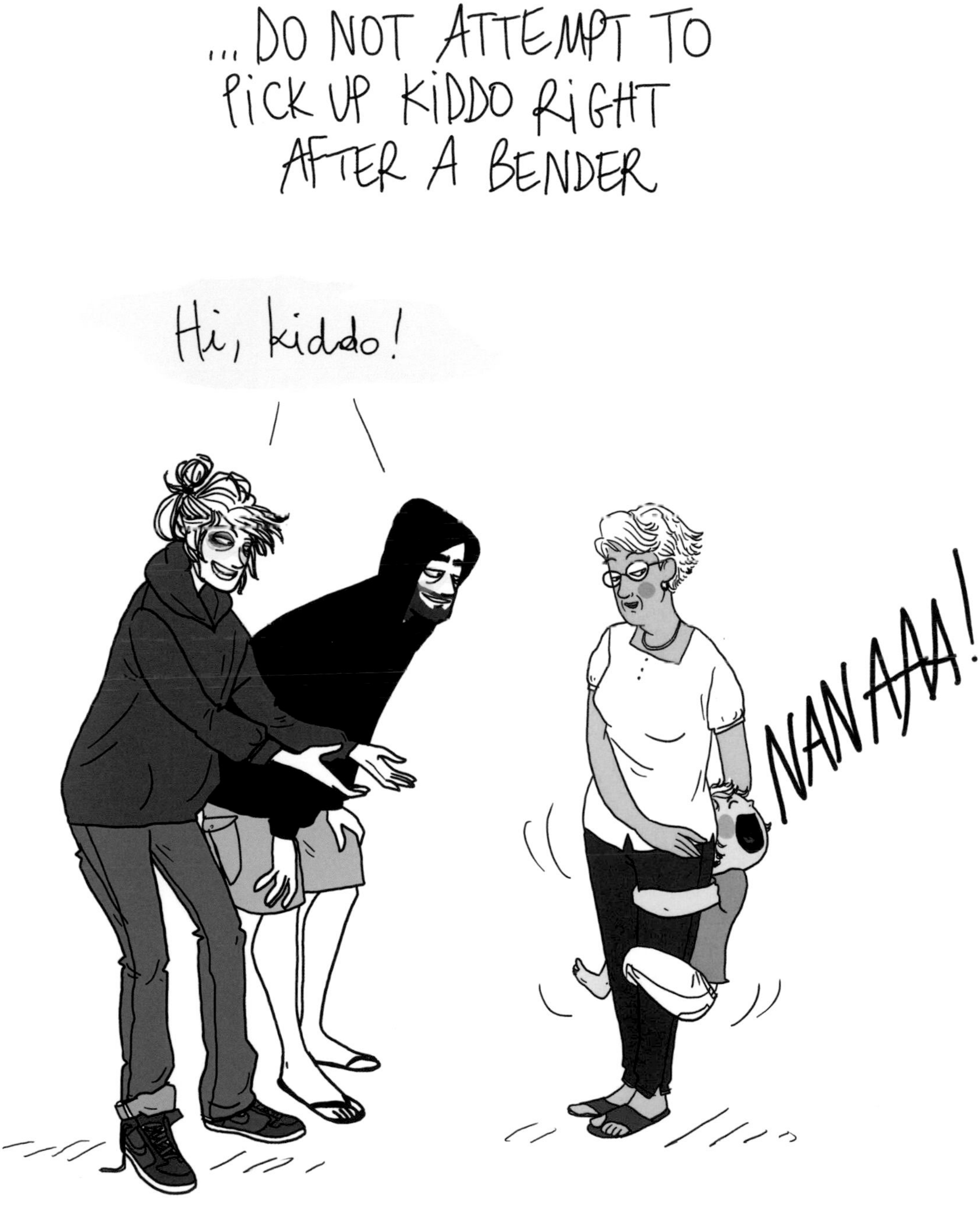
...DO NOT ATTEMPT TO PICK UP KIDDO RIGHT AFTER A BENDER
Hi, kiddo!
NANAAA!

I am crossing over to the dark side.

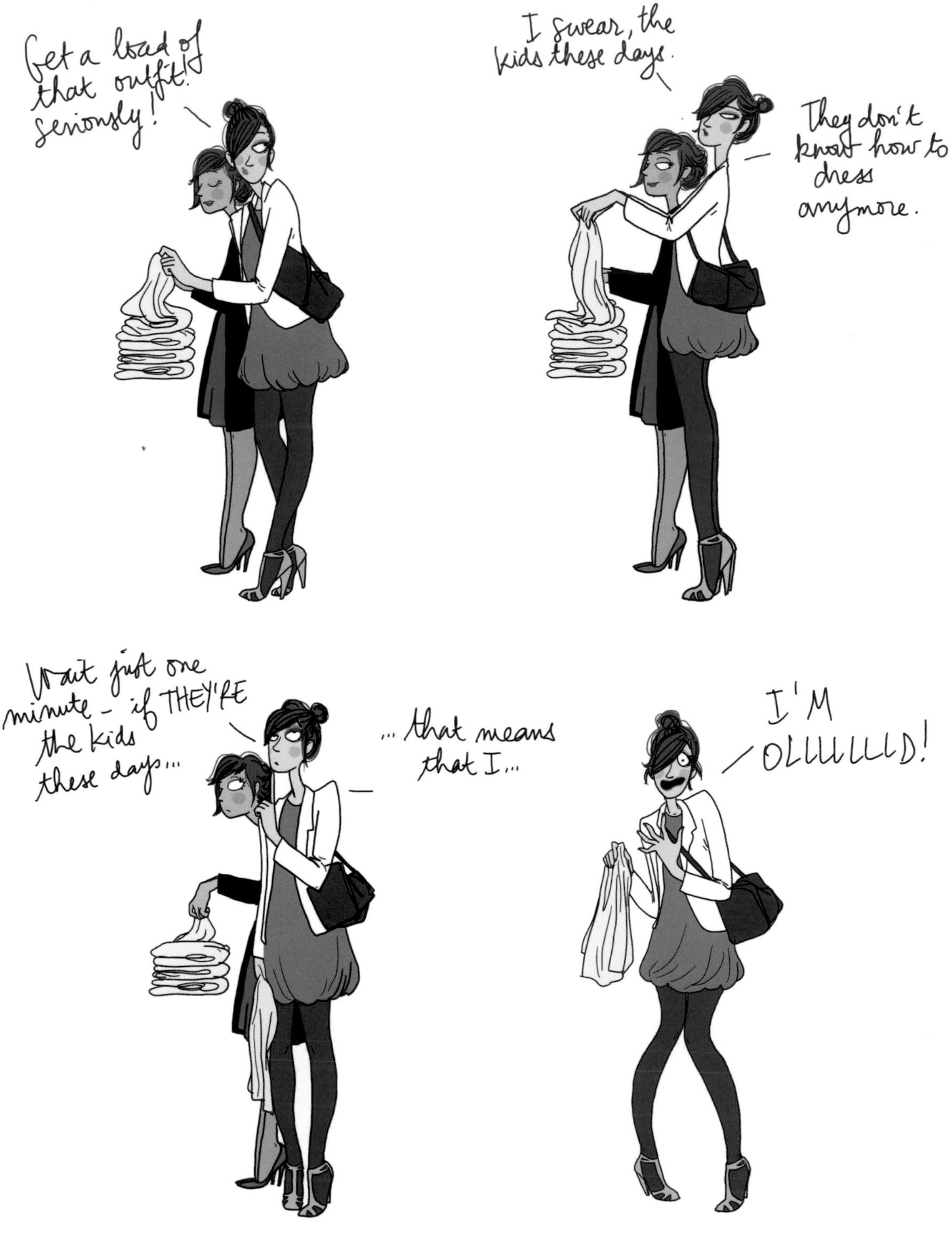
Get a load of that outfit! Seriously!
I swear, the kids these days.
They don't know how to dress anymore.
Wait just one minute - if THEY'RE the kids these days...
... that means that I...
I'M OLLLLLLD!

When a boy becomes independent

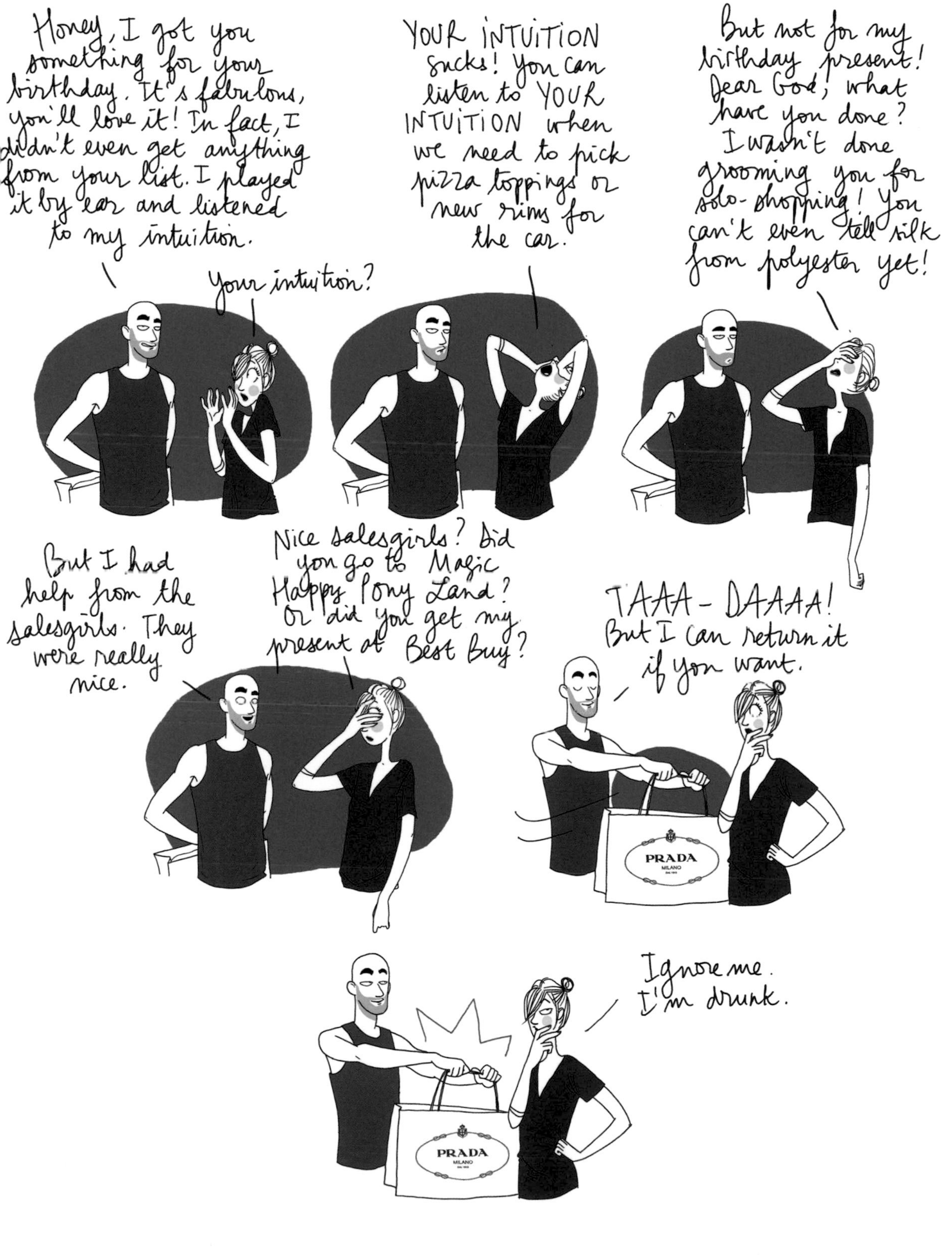
Honey, I got you something for your birthday. It's fabulous, you'll love it! In fact, I didn't even get anything from your list. I played it by ear and listened to my intuition.
Your intuition?
YOUR INTUITION sucks! You can listen to YOUR INTUITION when we need to pick pizza toppings or new rims for the car.
But not for my birthday present! Dear God, what have you done? I wasn't done grooming you for solo-shopping! You can't even tell silk from polyester yet!
But I had help from the salesgirls. They were really nice.
Nice salesgirls? Did you go to Magic Happy Pony Land? Or did you get my present at Best Buy?
TAAA-DAAAA! But I can return it if you want.
PRADA
MILANO
PRADA
MILANO
Ignore me. I'm drunk.

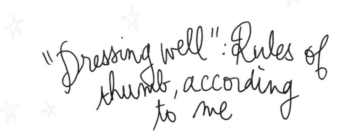

"Dressing well": Rules of thumb, according to me

RULE #1: A really, really cute bag can salvage a slightly shabby outfit...

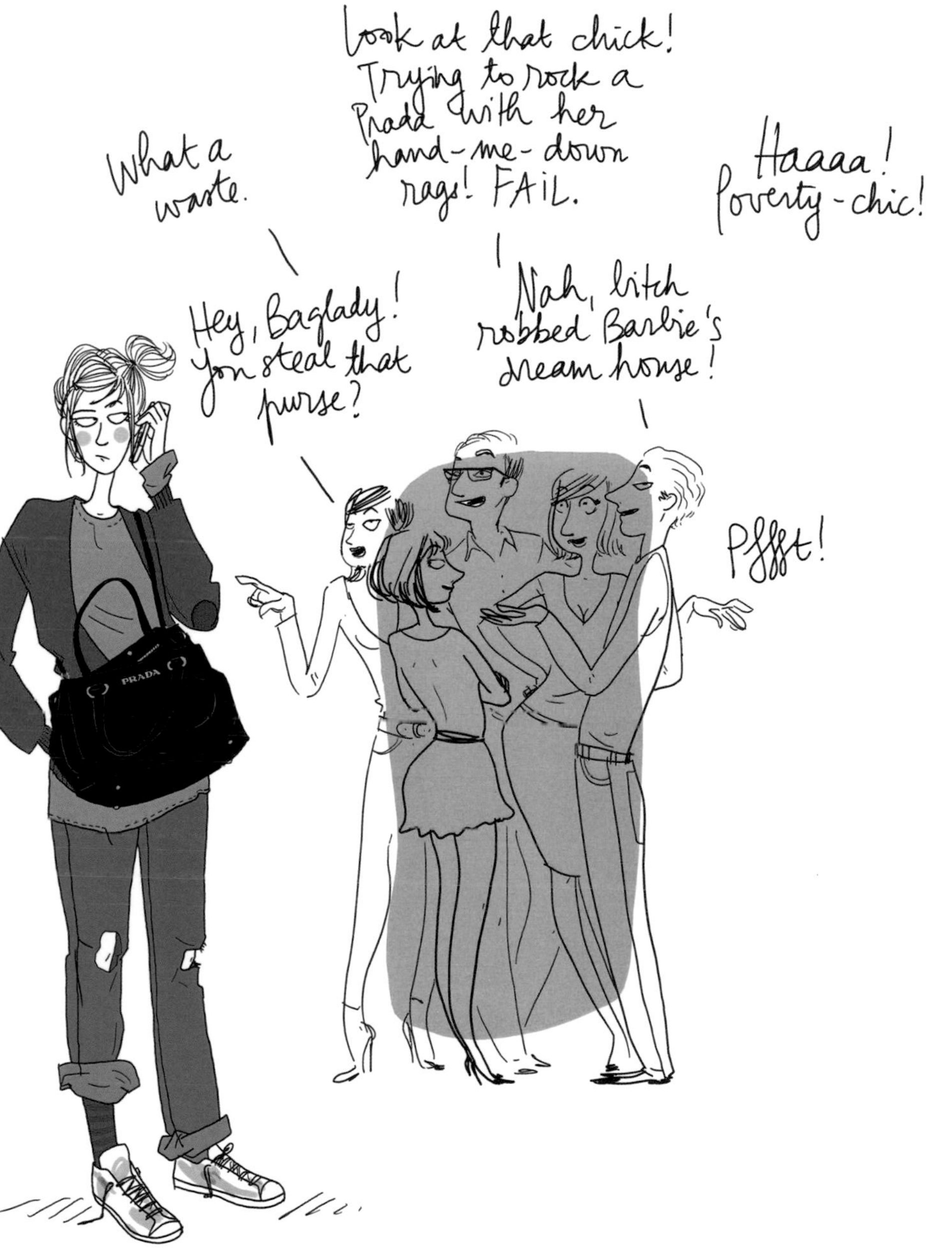
What a waste.
Look at that chick! Trying to rock a Prada with her hand-me-down rags! FAIL.
Haaaa! Poverty-chic!
Hey, Baglady! You steal that purse?
Nah, bitch robbed Barbie's dream house!
Pffft!
PRADA

… or not.

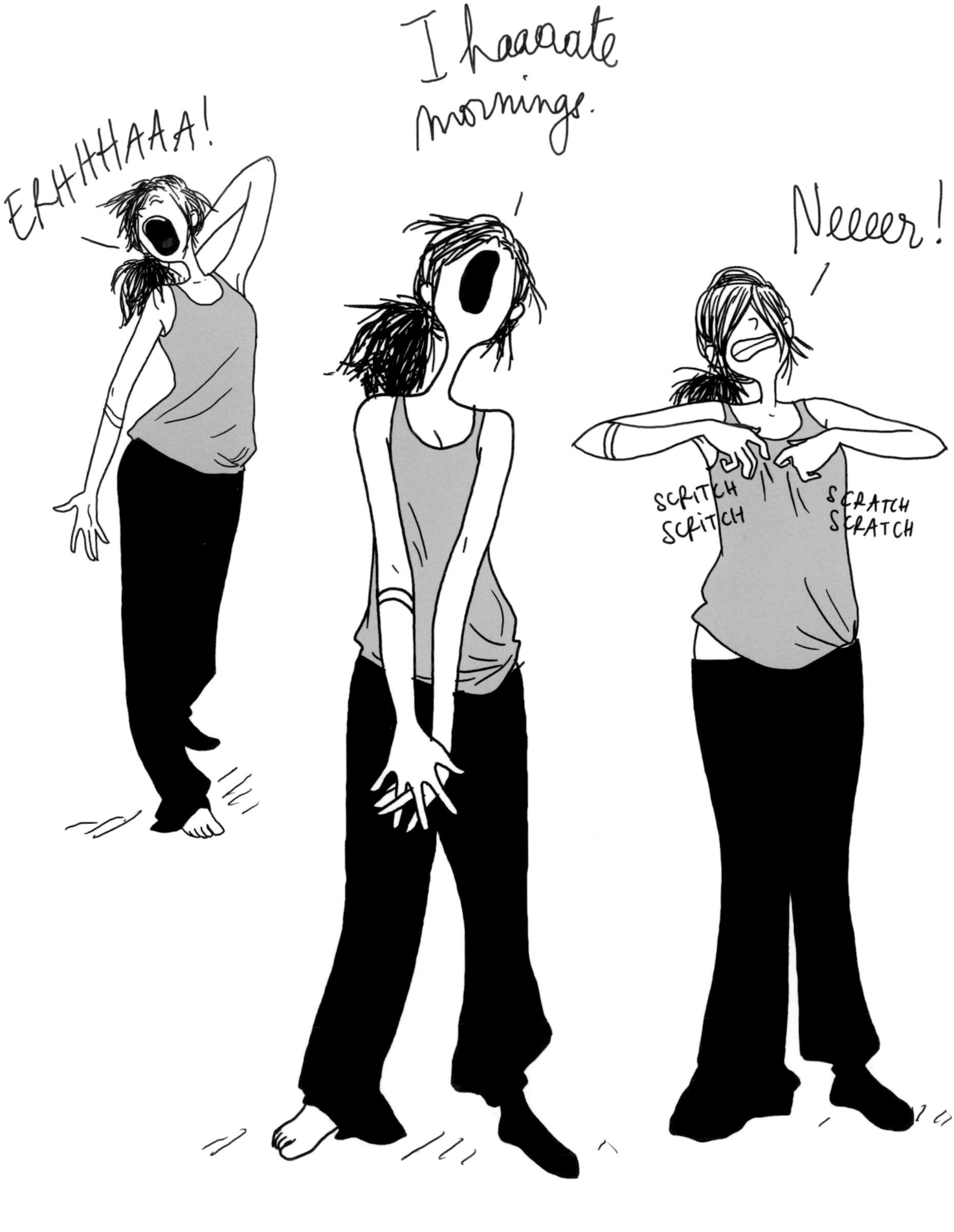
EHHHHAAA!
I haaaate mornings.
Neeeer!
SCRITCH SCRITCH
SCRATCH SCRATCH

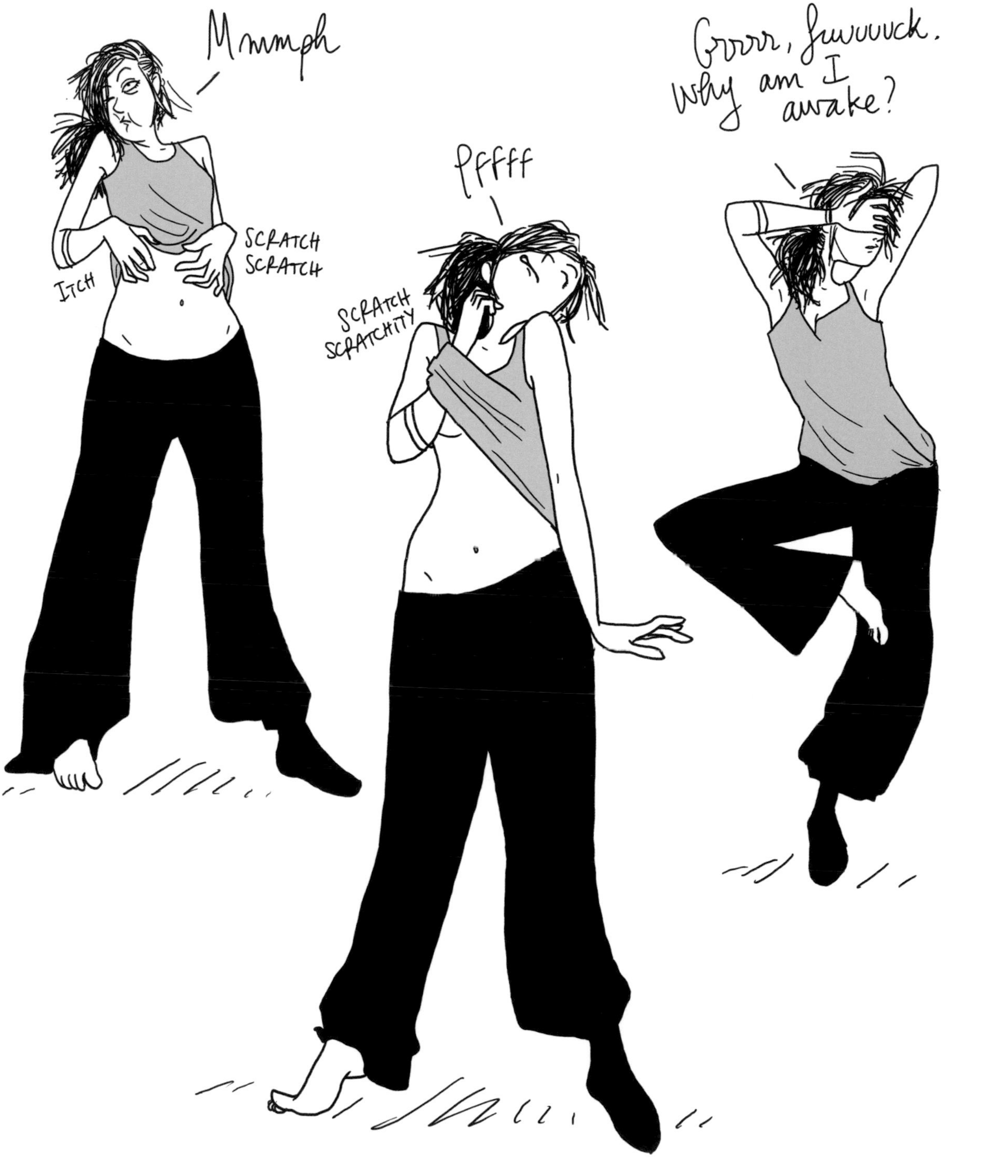
Mmmph
ITCH
SCRATCH
SCRATCH
Pffff
SCRATCH
SCRATCHITY
Grrrr, fuuuuck.
Why am I awake?

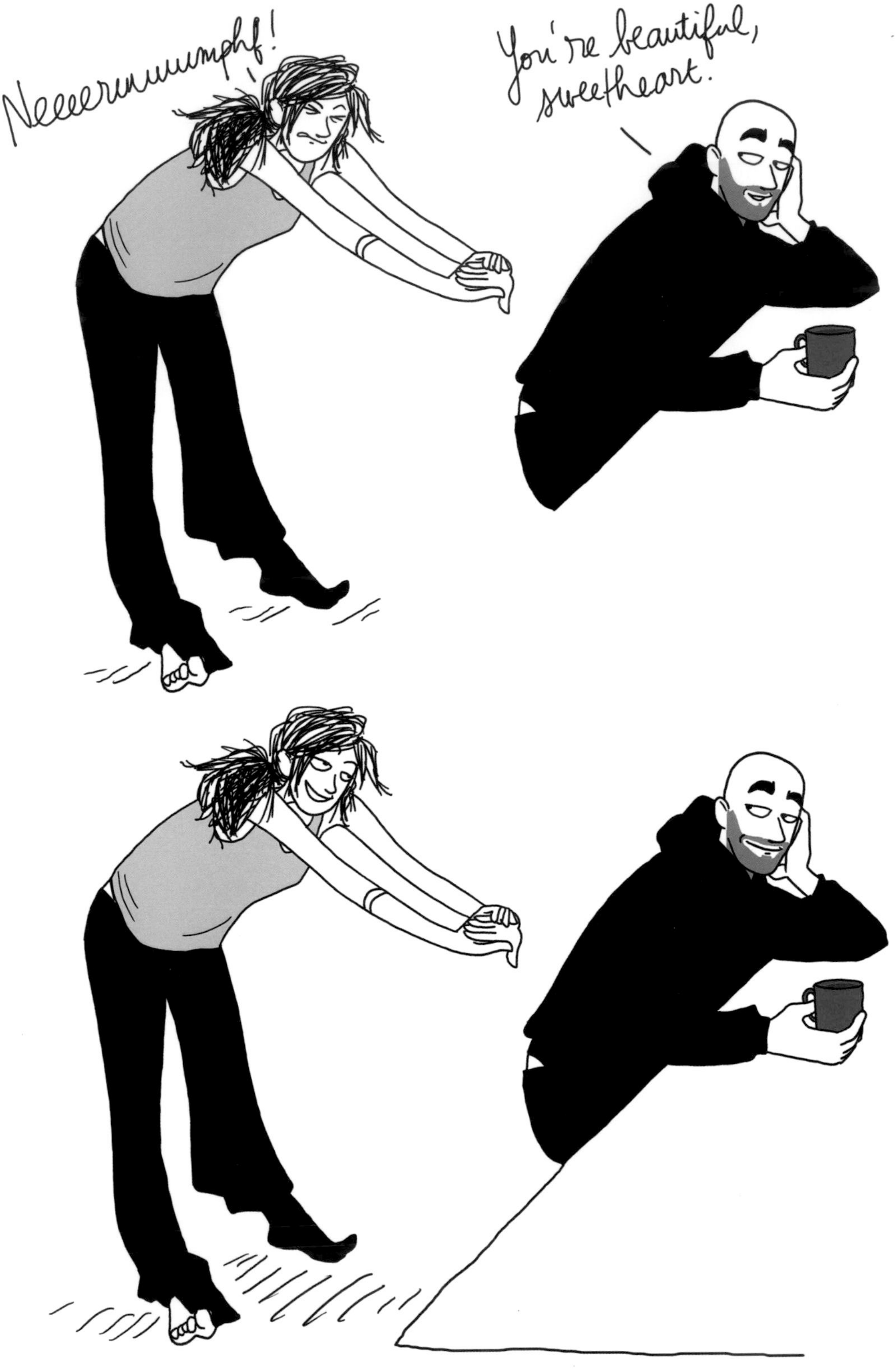
Neeeermmmmmphf!
You're beautiful, sweetheart.

It's totally better
(Though it is, quite possibly, blind).

Bunny solitaire

... a poker game ... at
Laurent's ... tonight ... you'll be back
late ... no, no, honey, that's perfect.
I really wanted to finish
"The Brothers Karamazov", so it's great ...

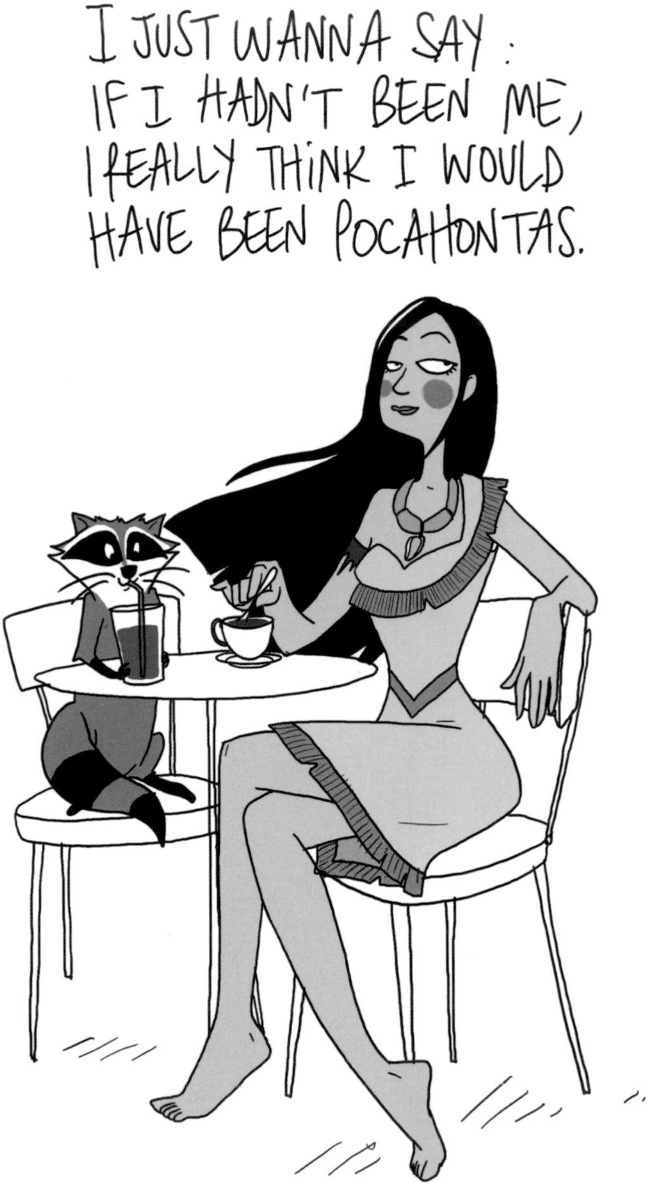
I JUST WANNA SAY:
IF I HADN'T BEEN ME,
I REALLY THINK I WOULD
HAVE BEEN POCAHONTAS.

OR CATWOMAN.

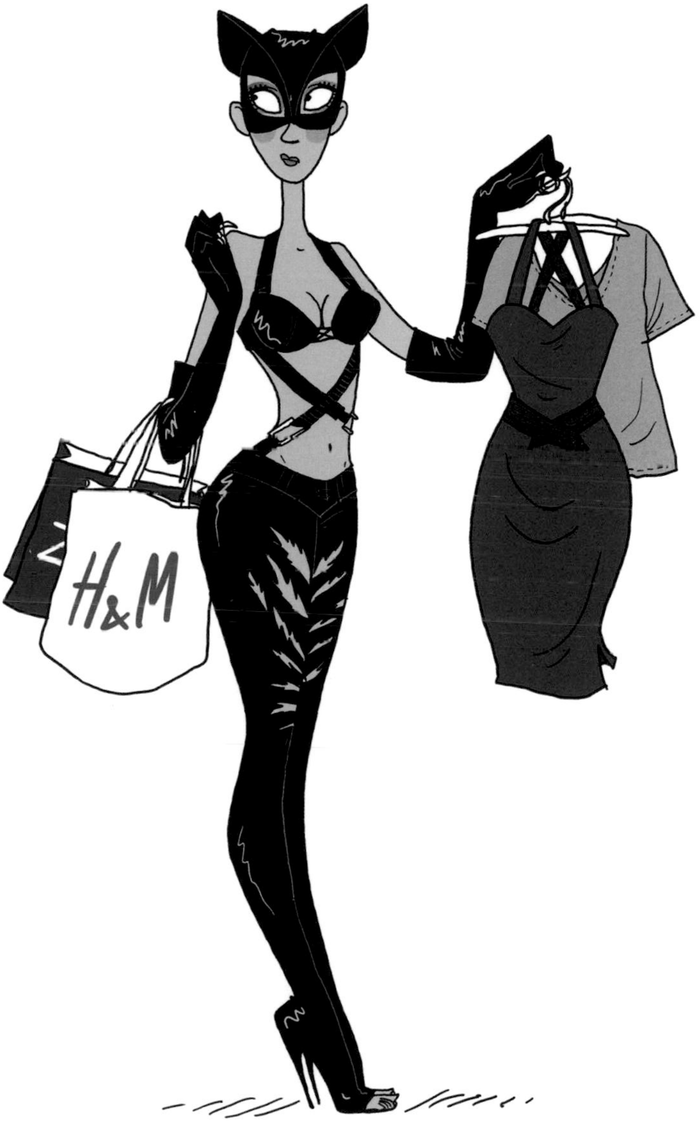
H&M

JUST TO CLARIFY.

"Dressing well": Rules of thumb, according to me

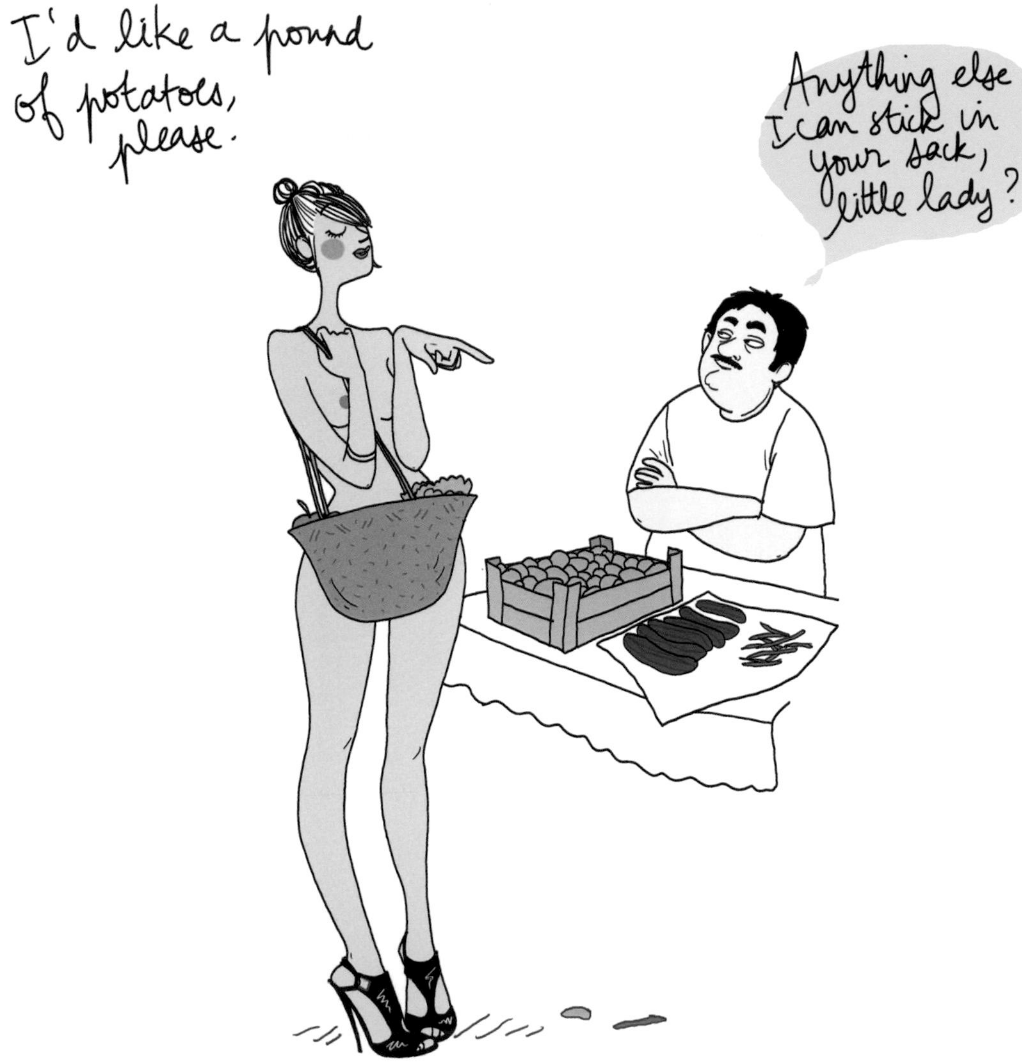

I'd like a pound of potatoes, please.
Anything else I can stick in your sack, little lady?

RULE #2: A beautiful pair of shoes is all you need!

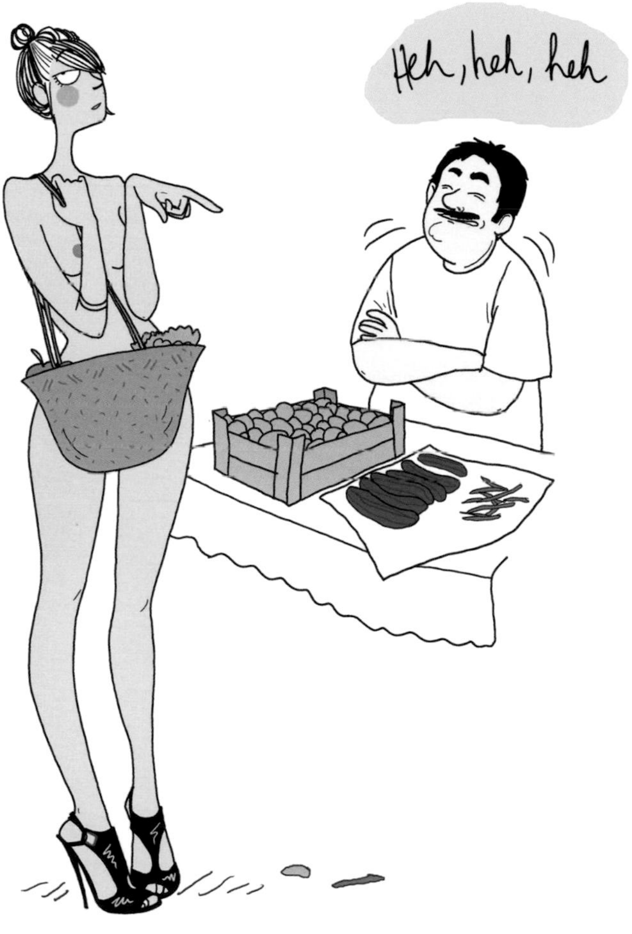
Heh, heh, heh

... or not.

Fashion addict

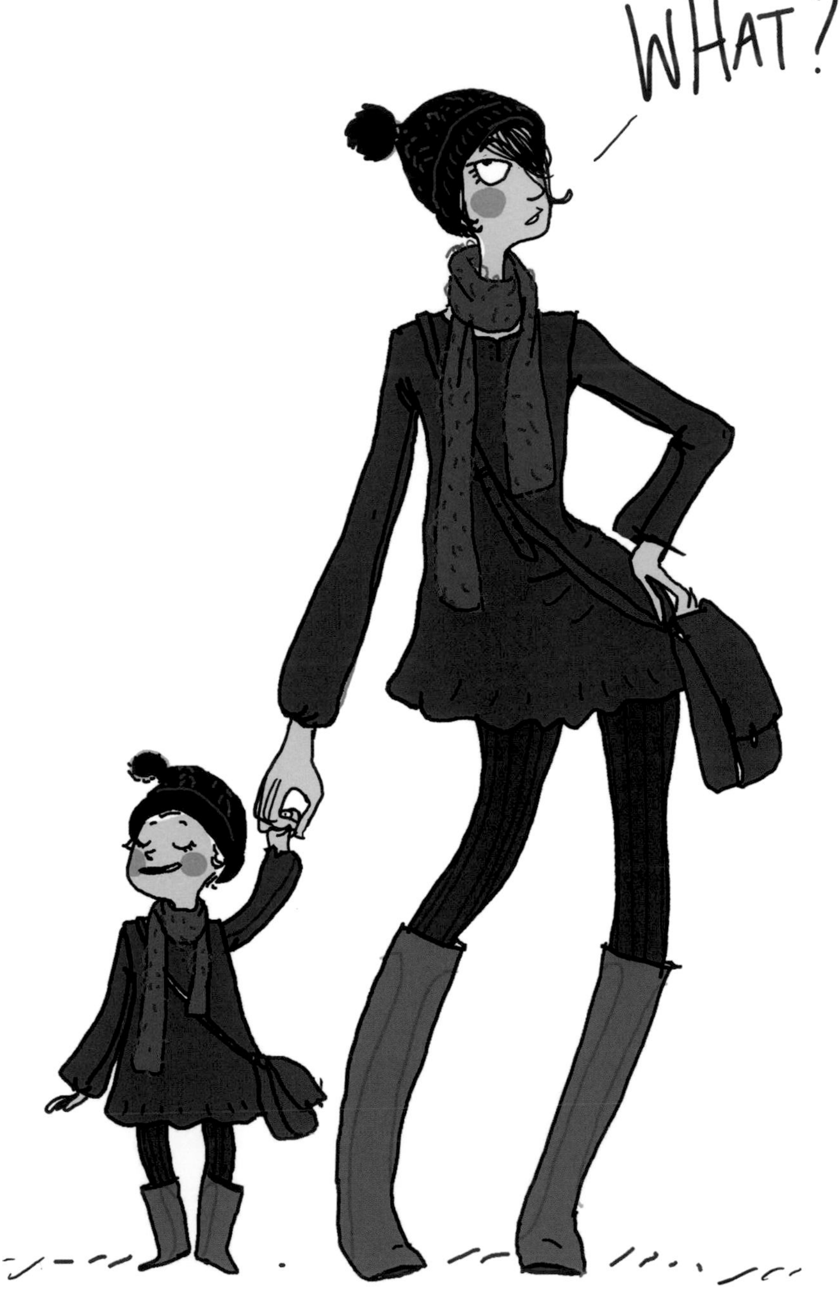
WHAT?

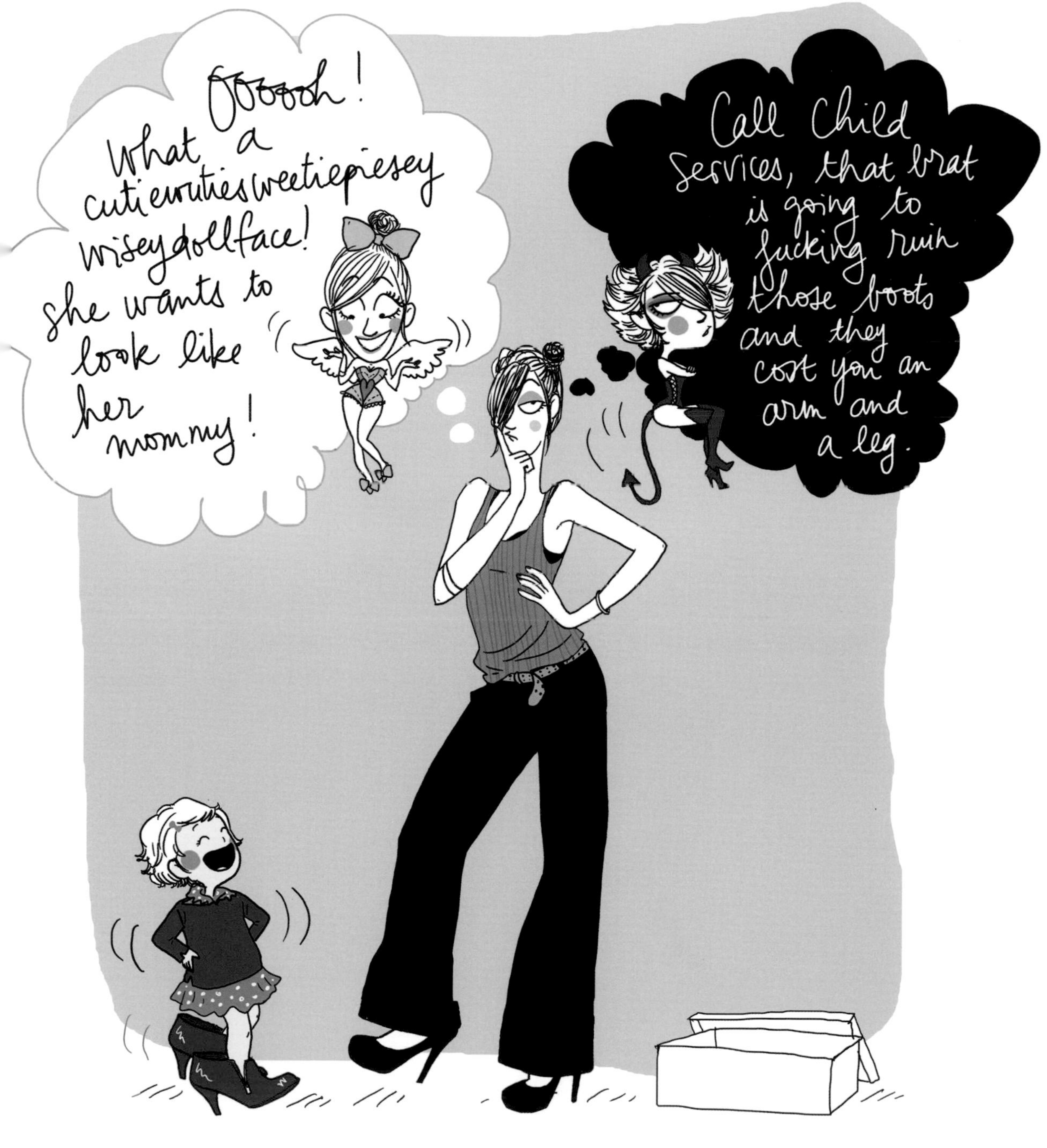
Ooooooh! What a cutiewutiesweetiepiesey wiseydollface! she wants to look like her mommy!
Call Child Services, that brat is going to fucking ruin those boots and they cost you an arm and a leg.

"Dressing well": Rules of thumb, according to me

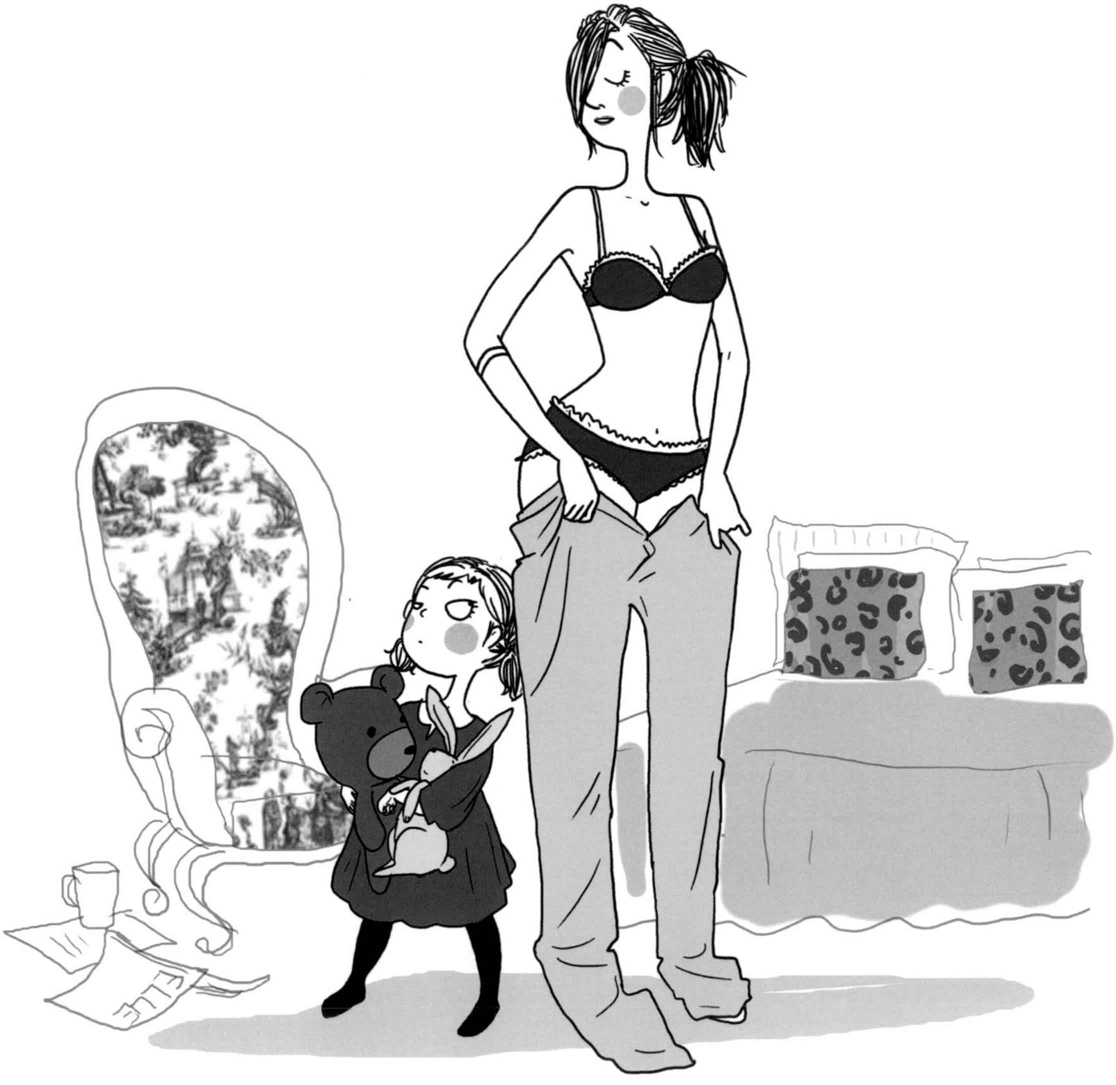

RULE #3: Like my mother always said: "Pretty underwear can save you a lot of embarrassment."

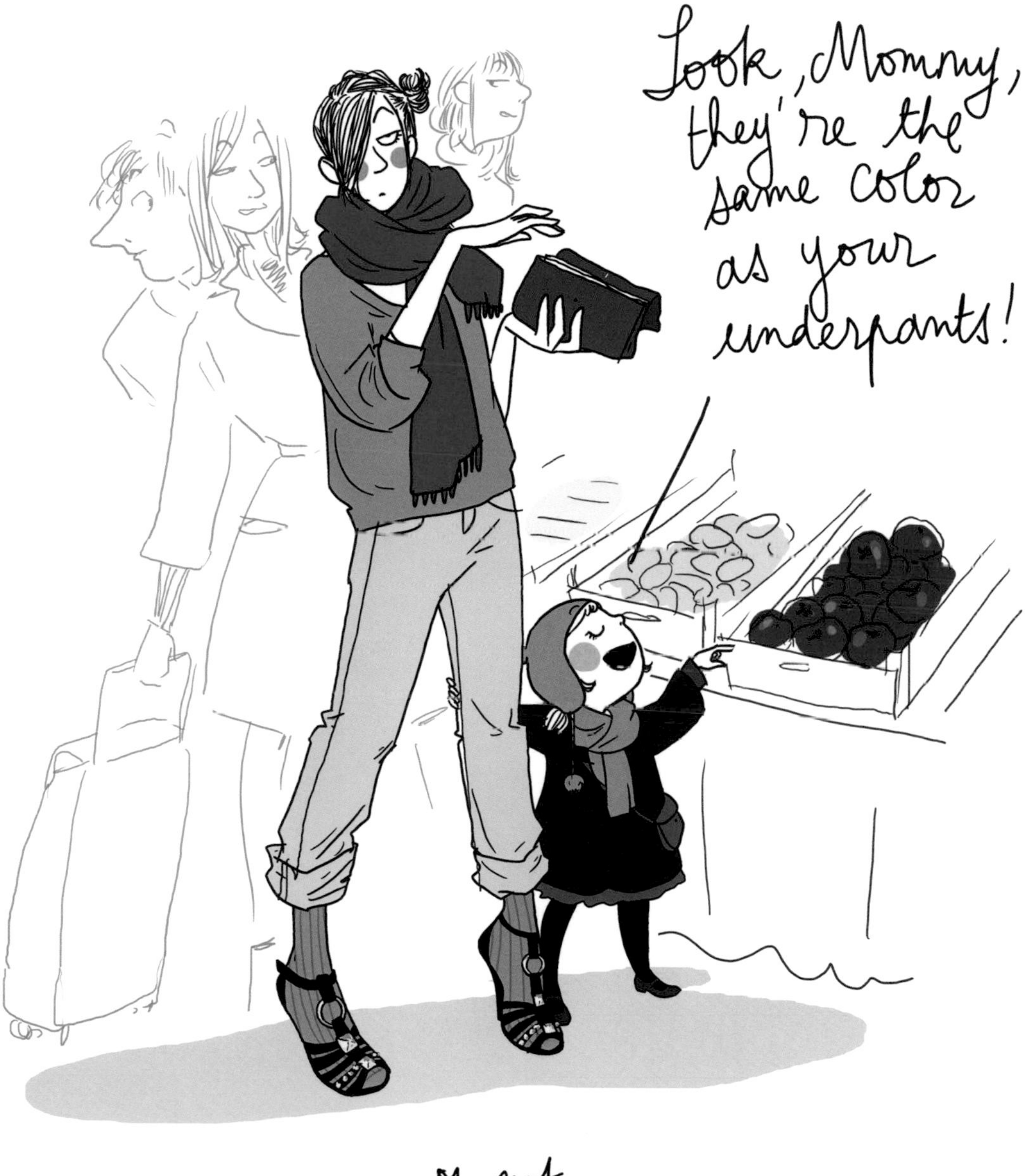
Look, Mommy, they're the same color as your underpants!

... or not.

(but my mother was thinking more about what if you get run down in the street and the firemen have to undress you in public to save your life...)

My mooooooother

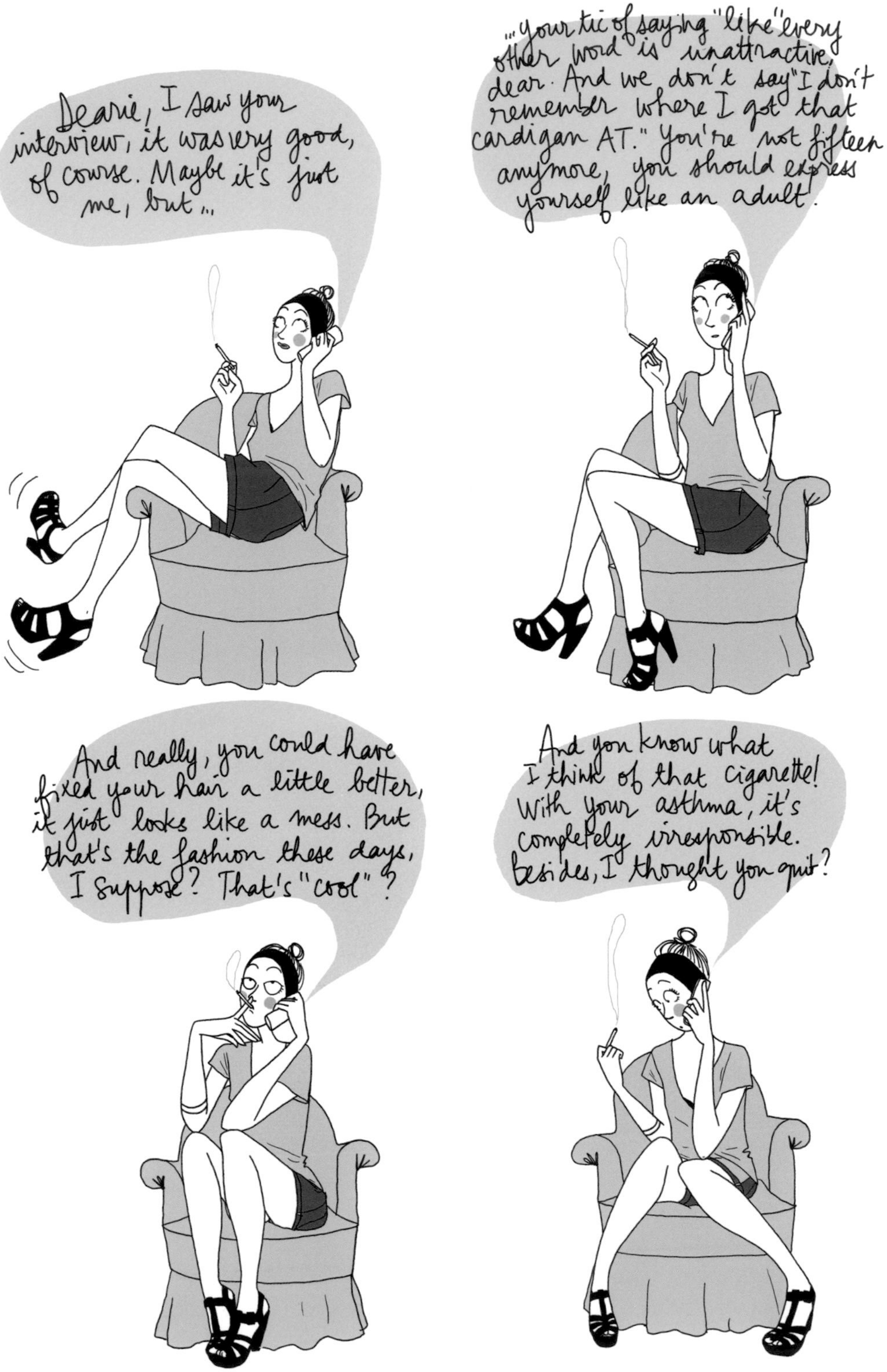
Dearie, I saw your interview, it was very good, of course. Maybe it's just me, but...
..."your tic of saying "like" every other word is unattractive, dear. And we don't say "I don't remember where I got that cardigan AT." You're not fifteen anymore, you should express yourself like an adult.
And really, you could have fixed your hair a little better, it just looks like a mess. But that's the fashion these days, I suppose? That's "cool"?
And you know what I think of that cigarette! With your asthma, it's completely irresponsible. Besides, I thought you quit?

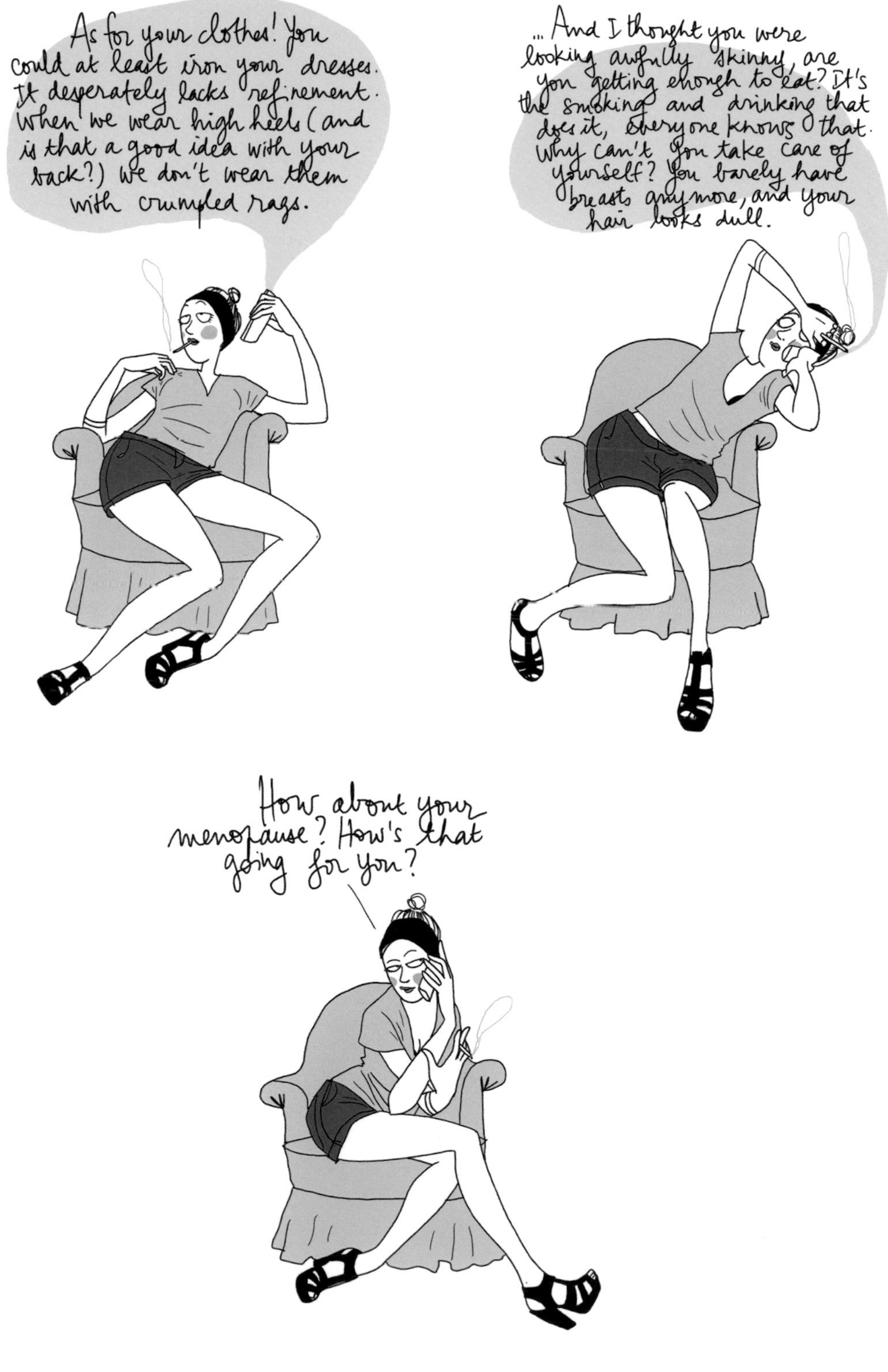
As for your clothes! You could at least iron your dresses. It desperately lacks refinement. When we wear high heels (and is that a good idea with your back?) we don't wear them with crumpled rags.
... And I thought you were looking awfully skinny, are you getting enough to eat? It's the smoking and drinking that does it, everyone knows that. Why can't you take care of yourself? You barely have breasts anymore, and your hair looks dull.
How about your menopause? How's that going for you?

There are some things only a daughter can do/say/think

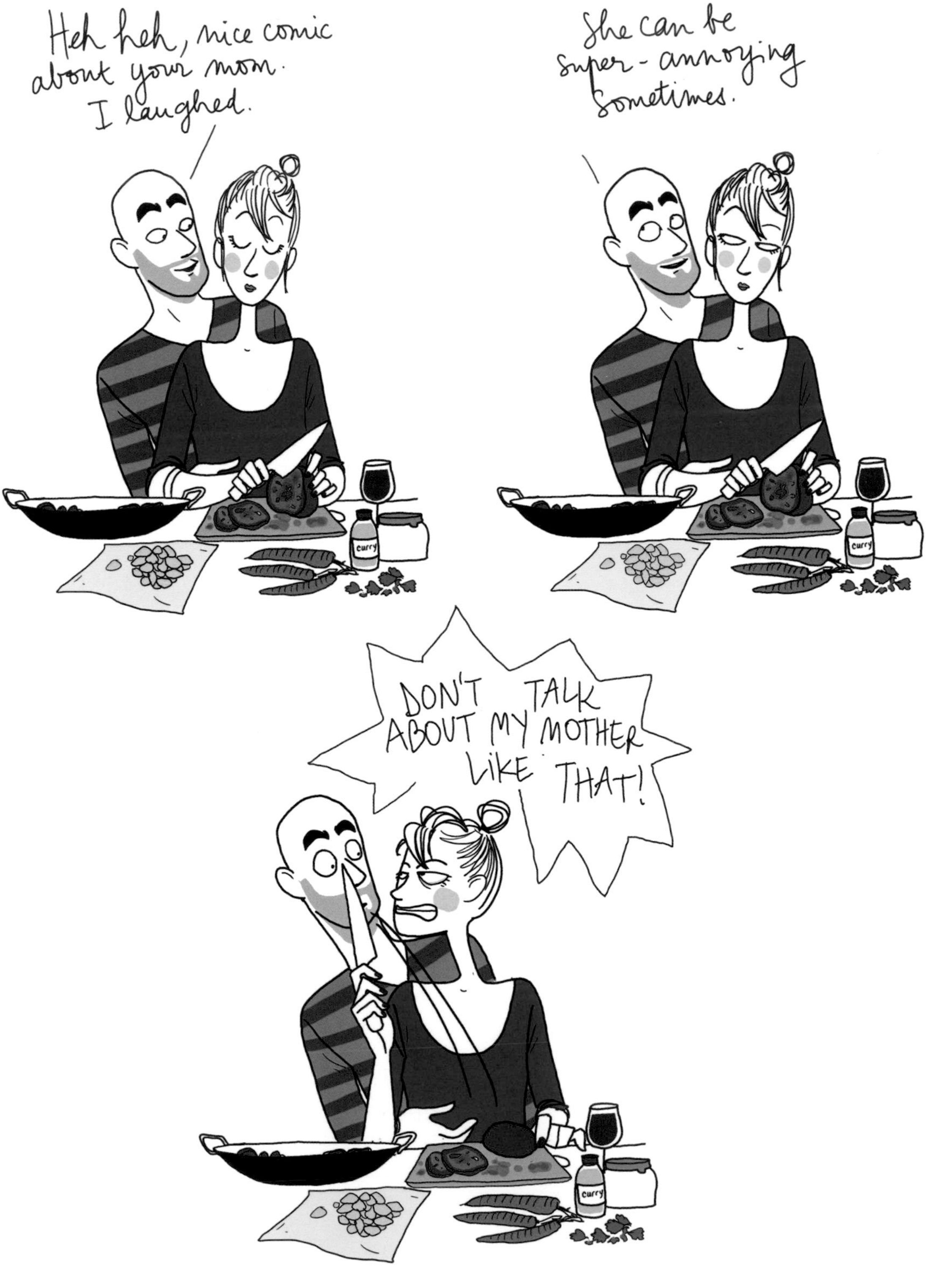
Heh heh, nice comic about your mom. I laughed.
She can be super-annoying sometimes.
DON'T TALK ABOUT MY MOTHER LIKE THAT!

The sister invasion: the arrival

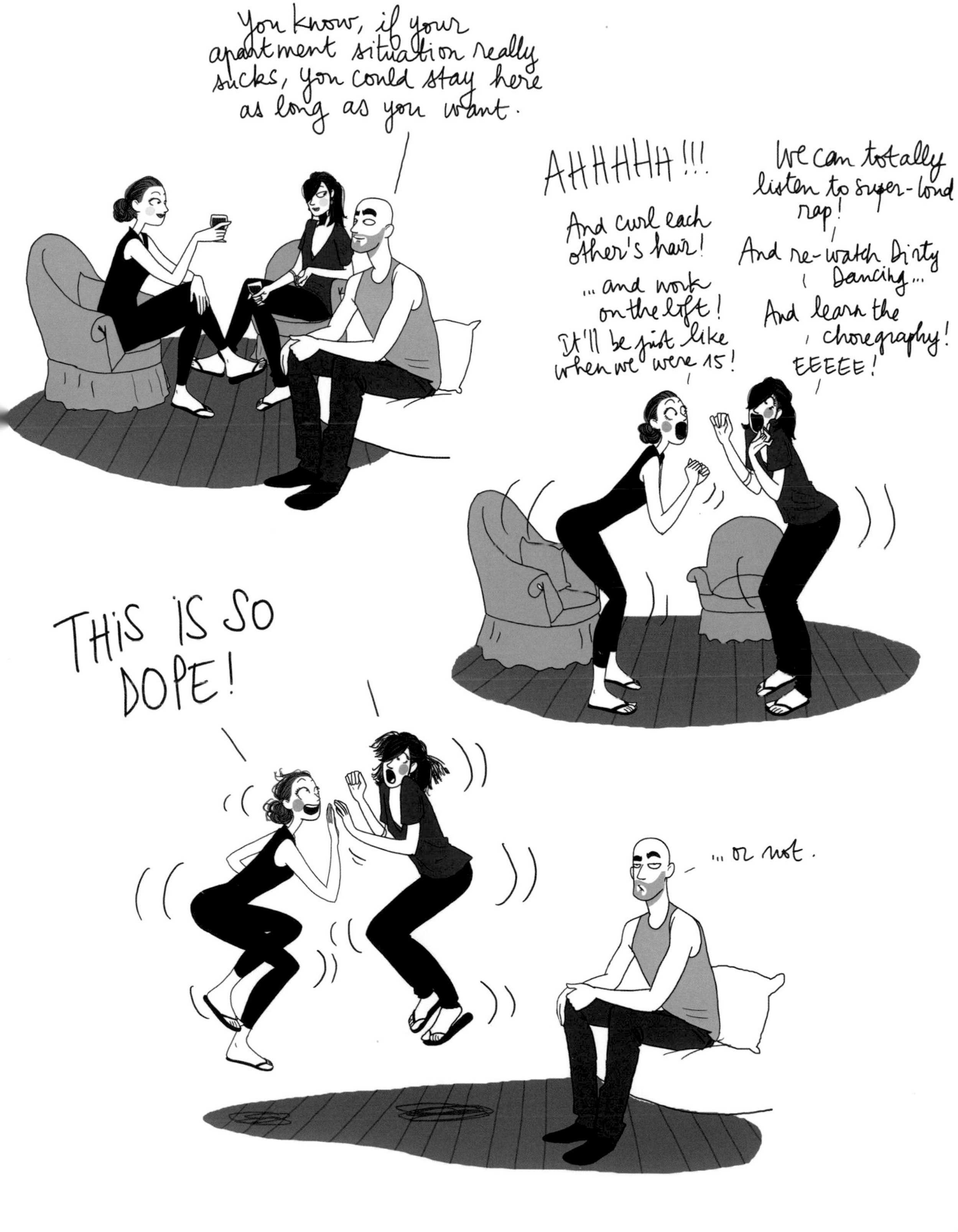
You know, if your apartment situation really sucks, you could stay here as long as you want.
AHHHHH!!!
And curl each other's hair!
... and work on the loft!
It'll be just like when we were 15!
We can totally listen to super-loud rap!
And re-watch Dirty Dancing...
And learn the choreography!
EEEEE!
THIS IS SO DOPE!
... or not.

The sister invasion: part 1

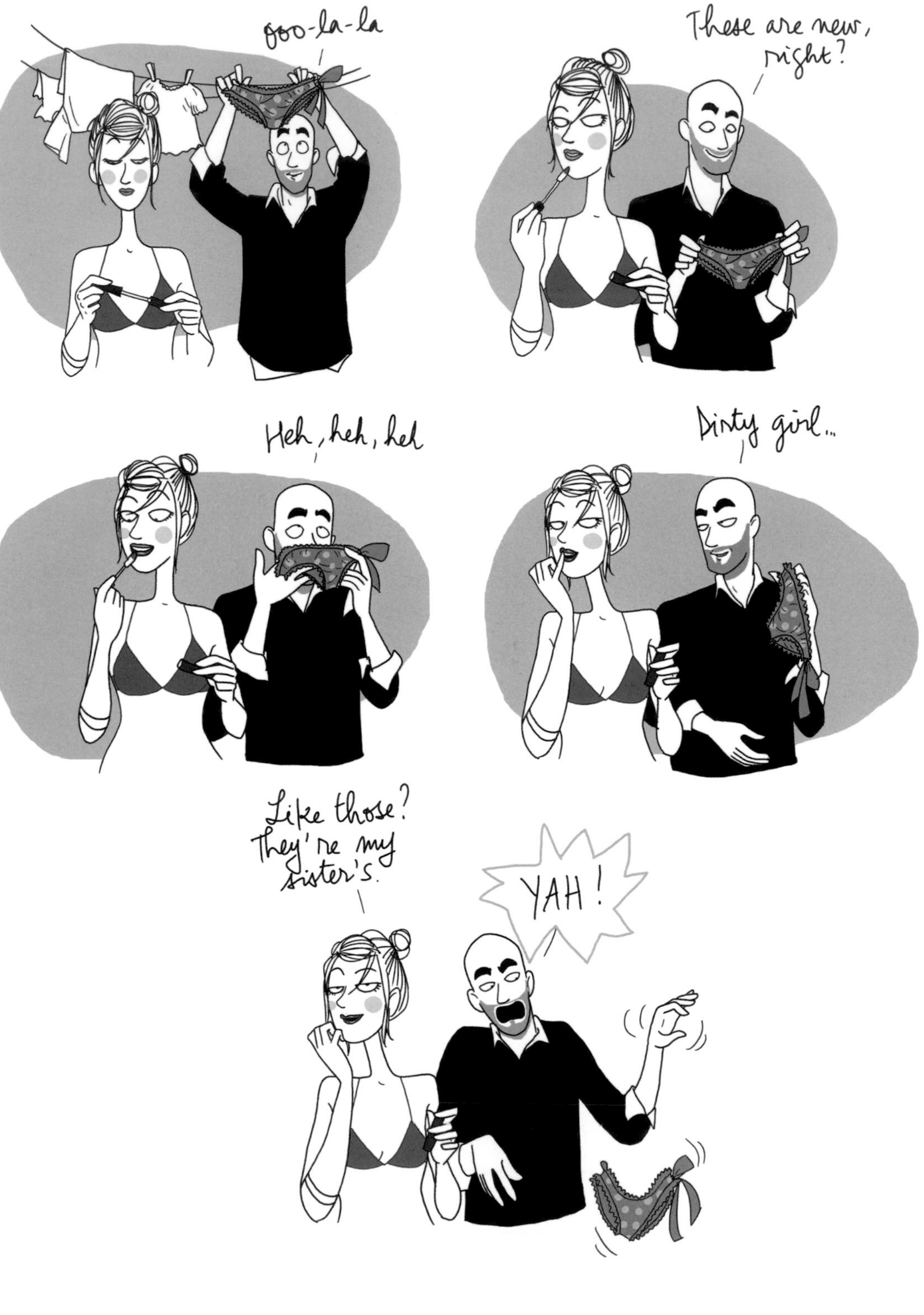

Ooo-la-la
These are new, right?
Heh, heh, heh
Dirty girl...
Like those? They're my sister's.
YAH!

The sister invasion: part 2

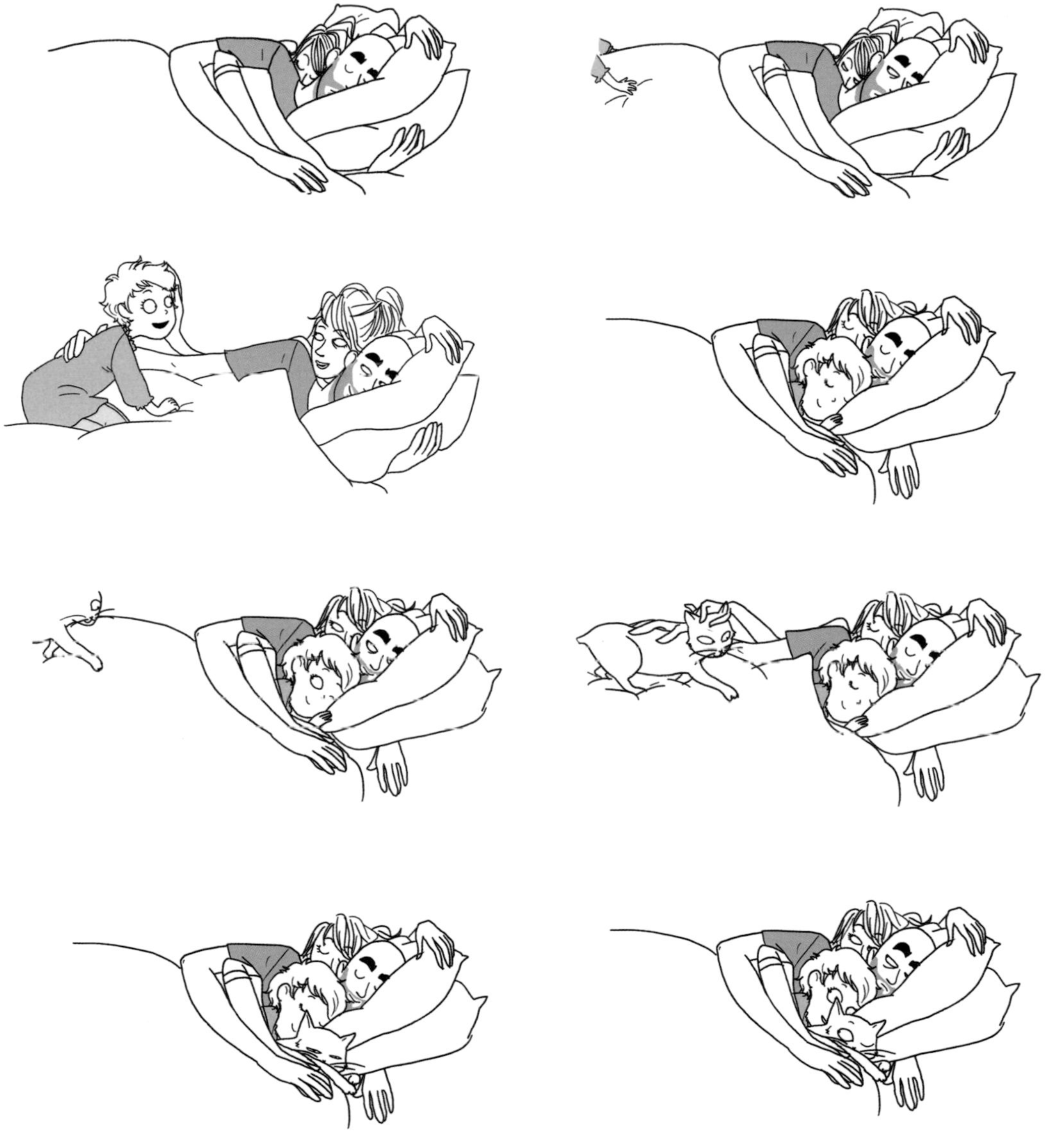

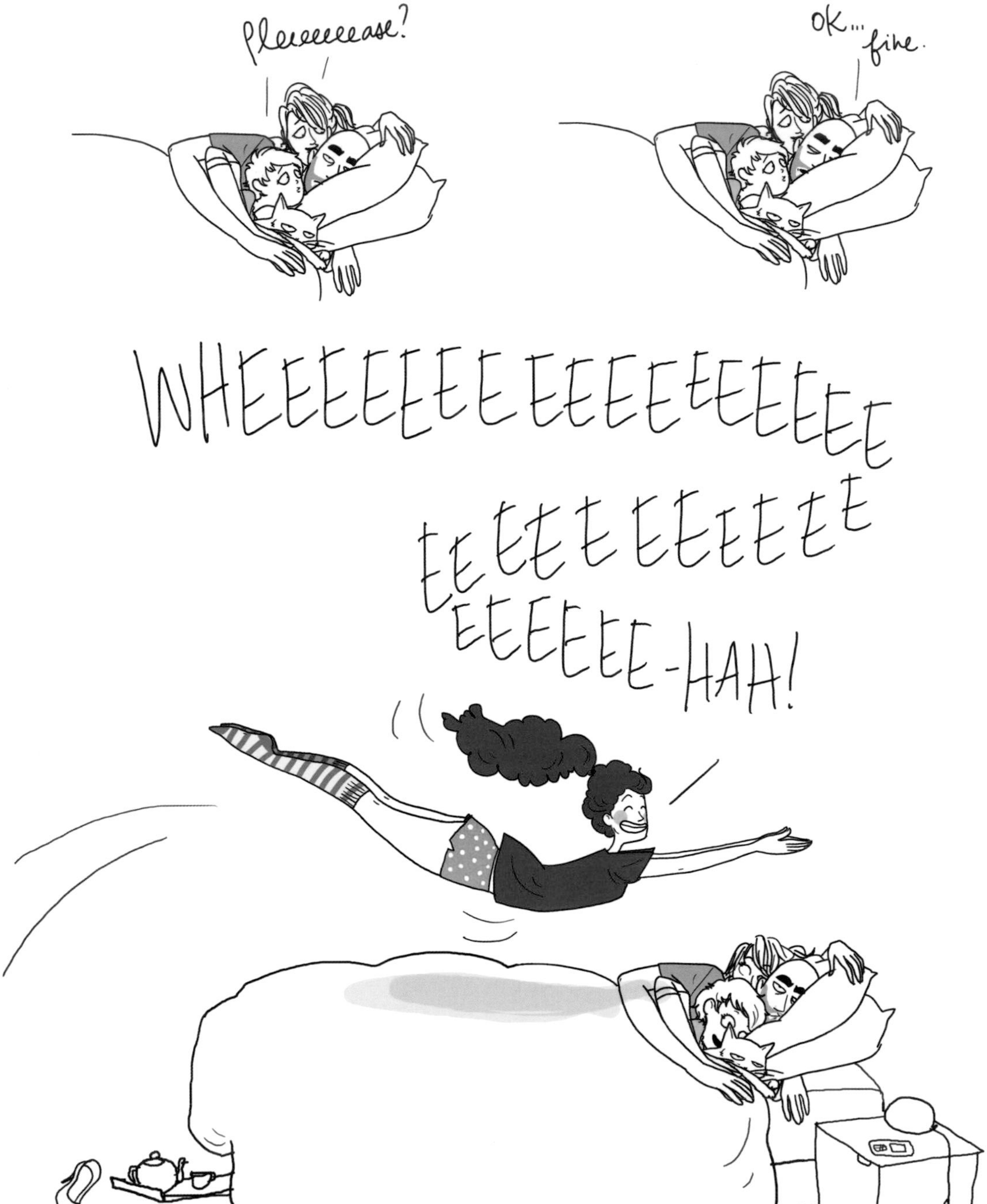
Pleeeeeease?
OK... fine.
WHEEEEEEEEEEEEEEEEE
EEEEEEEEEEE
EEEEEE-HAH!

The pernicious influence of my house-invading sister

I went shopping with my sister. At first I thought she was a tad monomaniacal with slight psychopathic tendencies, like obsessive behaviors and compulsive buying. Which was fine by me, because it made me look normal.

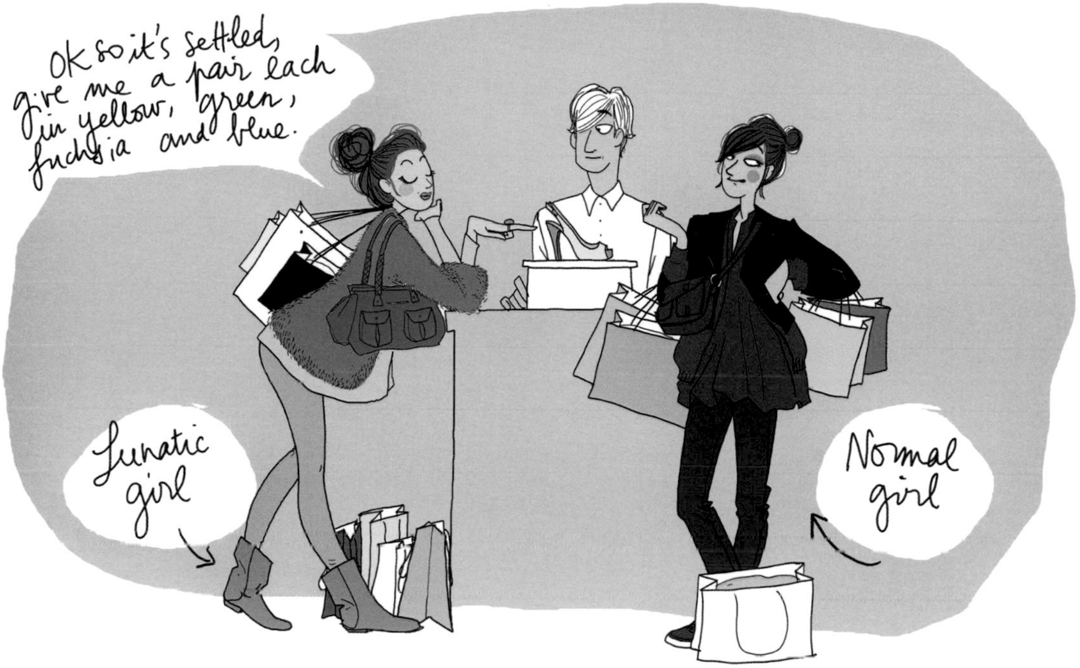
OK so it's settled, give me a pair each in yellow, green, fuchsia and blue.
Lunatic girl
Normal girl

Then the situation spiraled out of control.

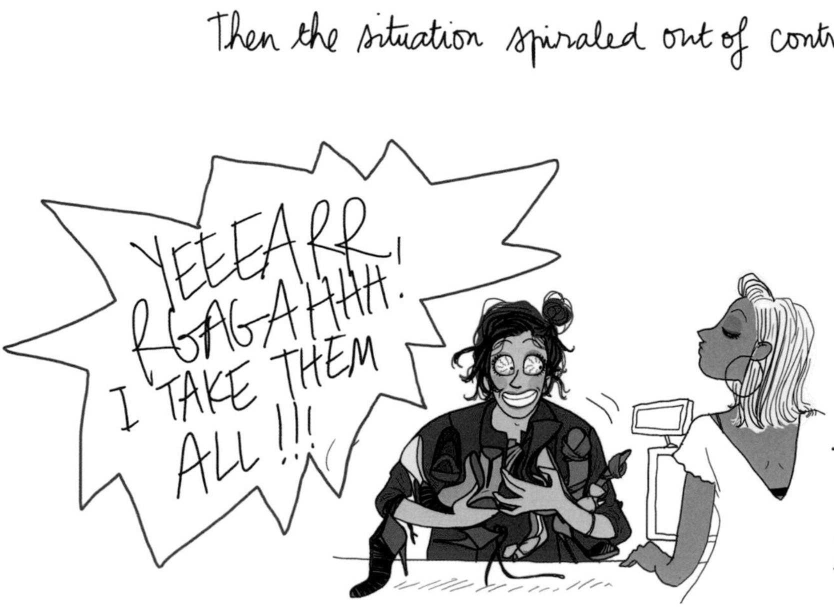
YEEEARR RGAGAHHH! I TAKE THEM ALL!!!

And my pathology is even more serious, when you consider that I spend my days alone in front of a computer in flip-flops.

God is love

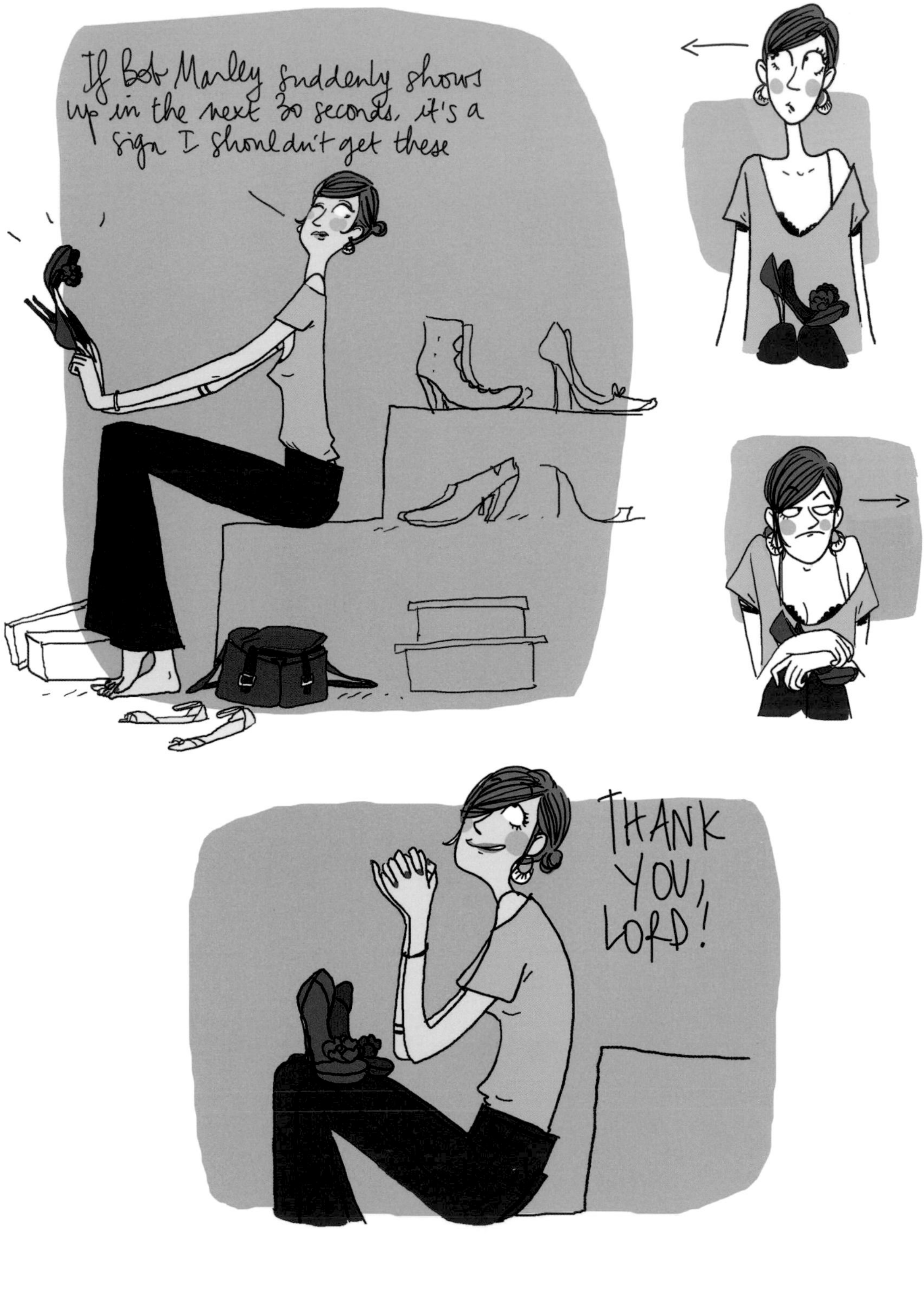
If Bob Marley suddenly shows up in the next 30 seconds, it's a sign I shouldn't get these
THANK YOU, LORD!

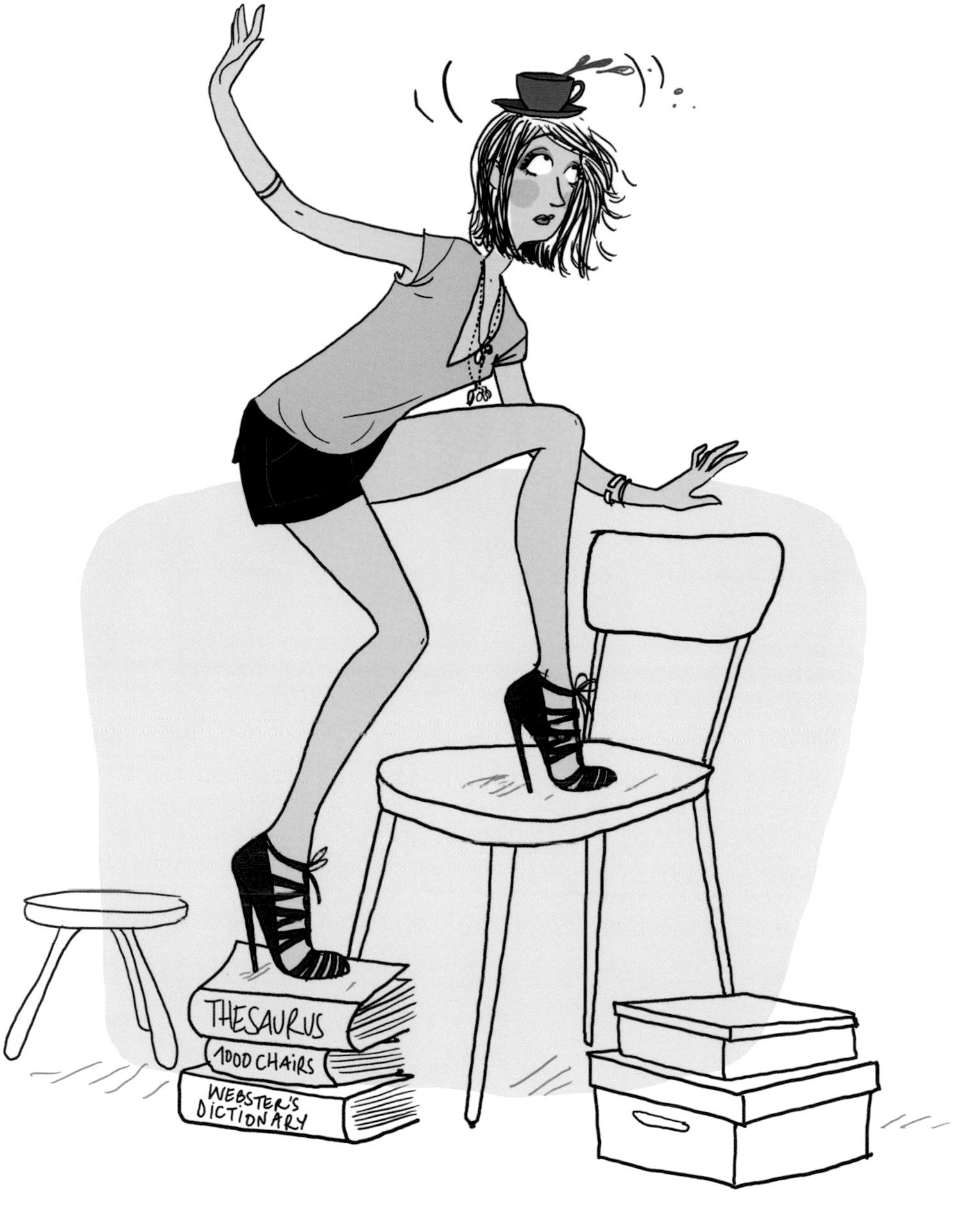
THESAURUS
1000 CHAIRS
WEBSTER'S DICTIONARY

Today: boot camp for girls who have just bought a great pair of hooker shoes with 14 inch heels... and don't know how to walk in them.

My father, the hero

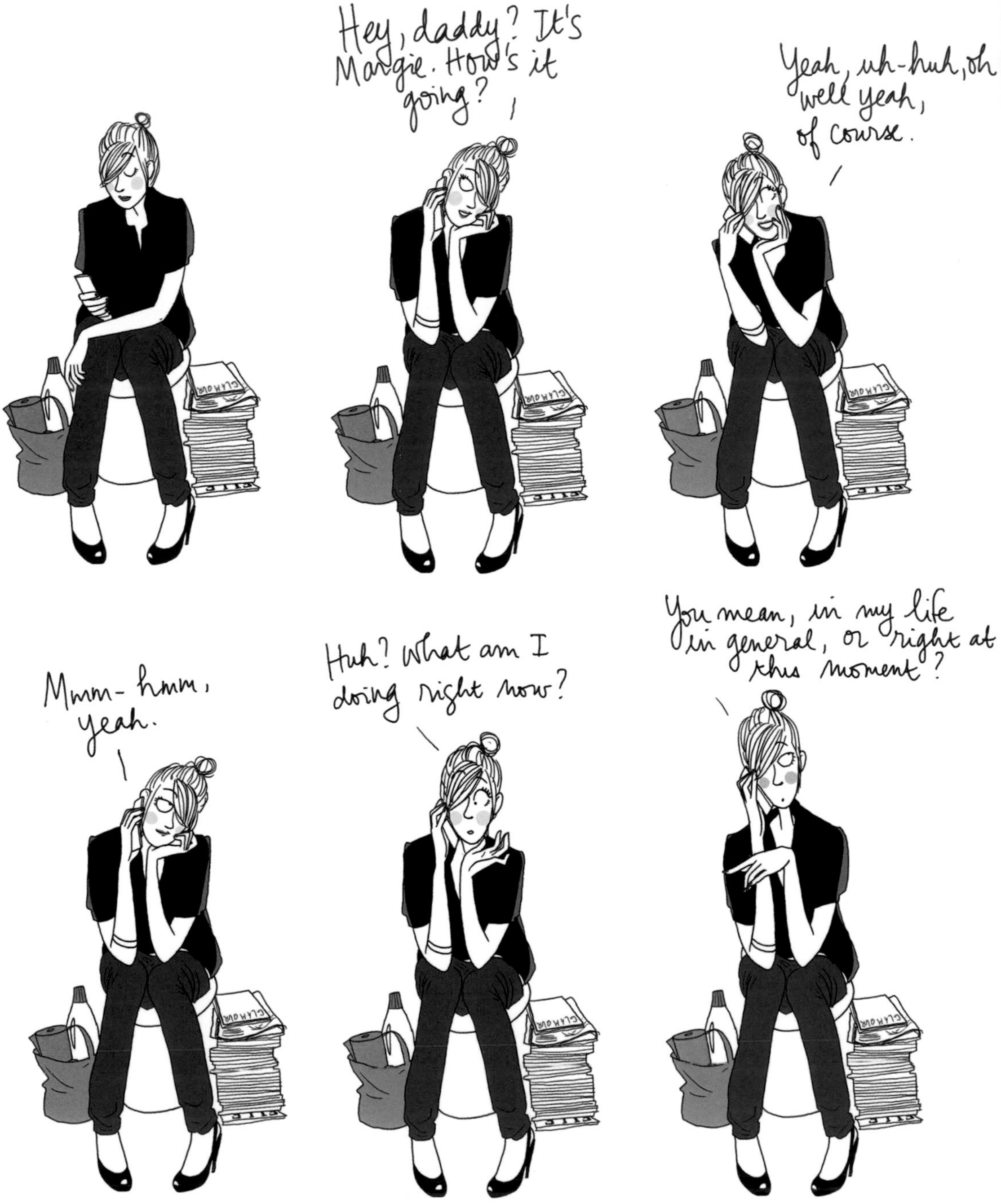
Hey, daddy? It's Margie. How's it going?
Yeah, uh-huh, oh well yeah, of course.
Mmm-hmm, yeah.
Huh? What am I doing right now?
You mean, in my life in general, or right at this moment?

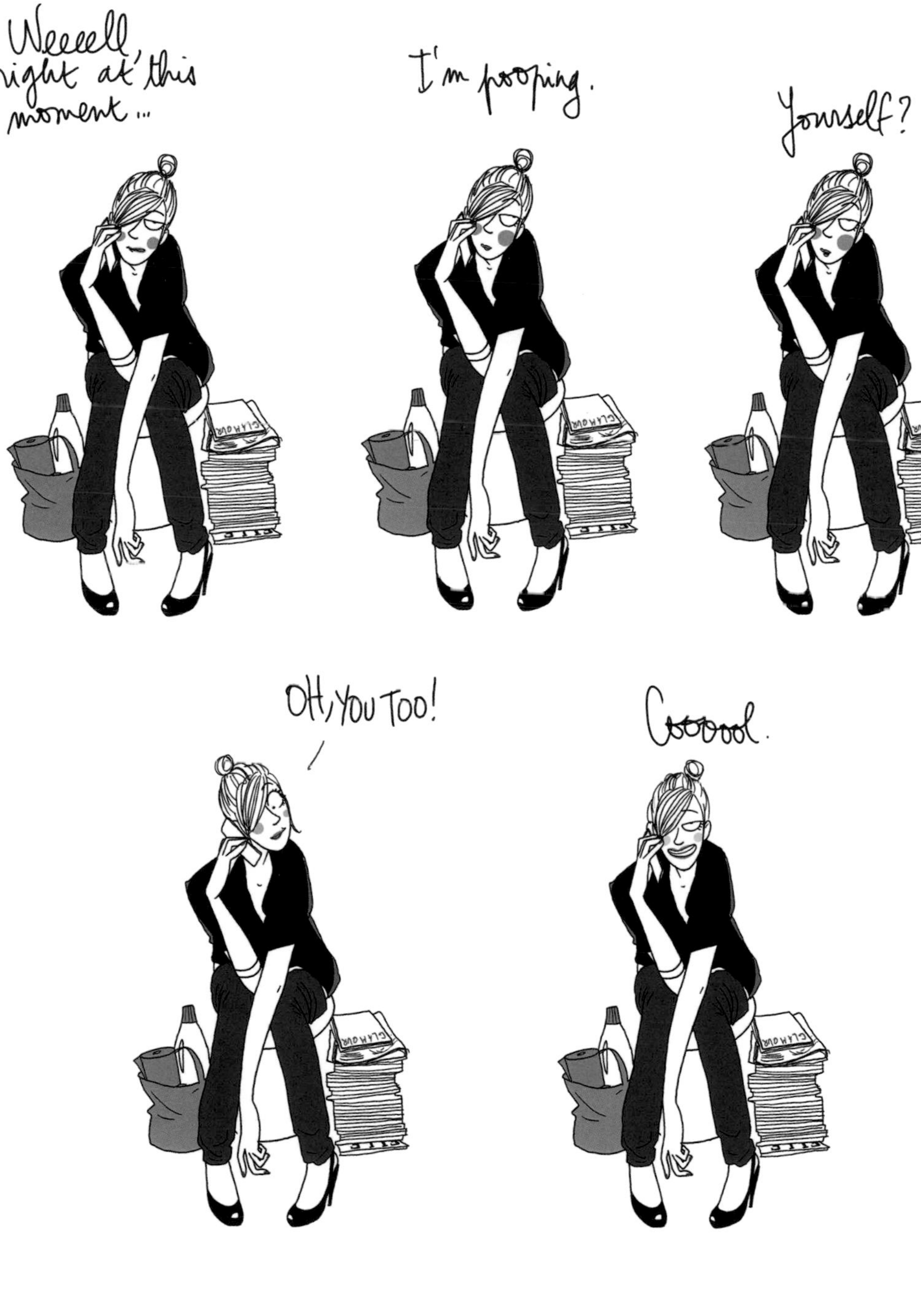
Weeeell, right at this moment...
I'm pooping.
Yourself?
OH, YOU TOO!
Cooool.

You can't fight genetics.

Clearly, the little wench has not mastered the
art of flattering the huge male ego

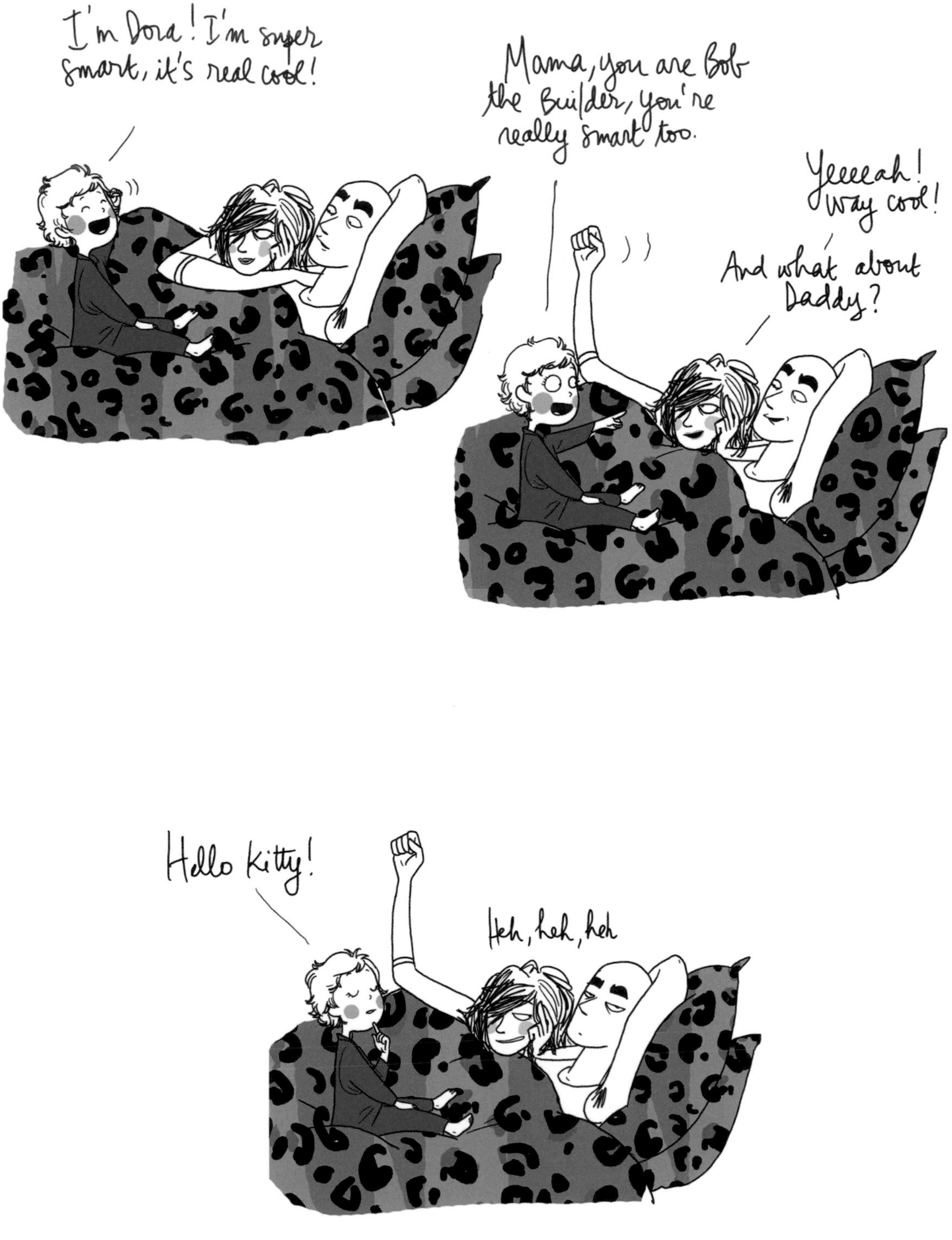
I'm Dora! I'm super smart, it's real cool!
Mama, you are Bob the Builder, you're really smart too.
Yeeeah! Way cool!
And what about Daddy?
Hello Kitty!
Heh, heh, heh

A mother's heart is a deep well, at the bottom of which lies forgiveness

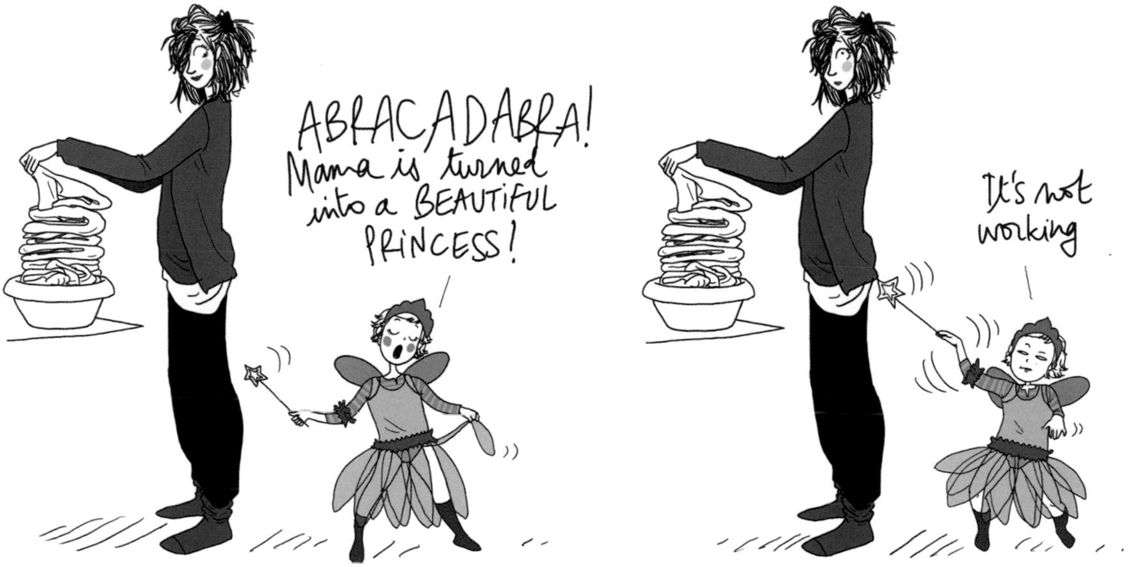
ABRACADABRA! Mama is turned into a BEAUTIFUL PRINCESS!
It's not working

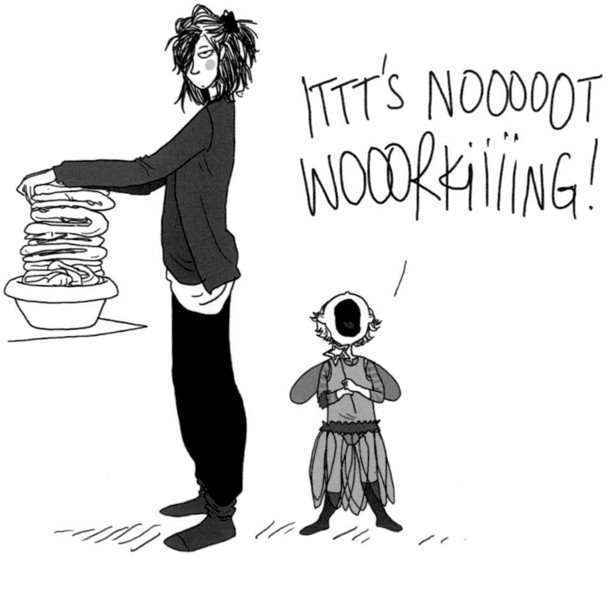
ITTT'S NOOOOOT WOOORKIIIING!

The joys of motherhood

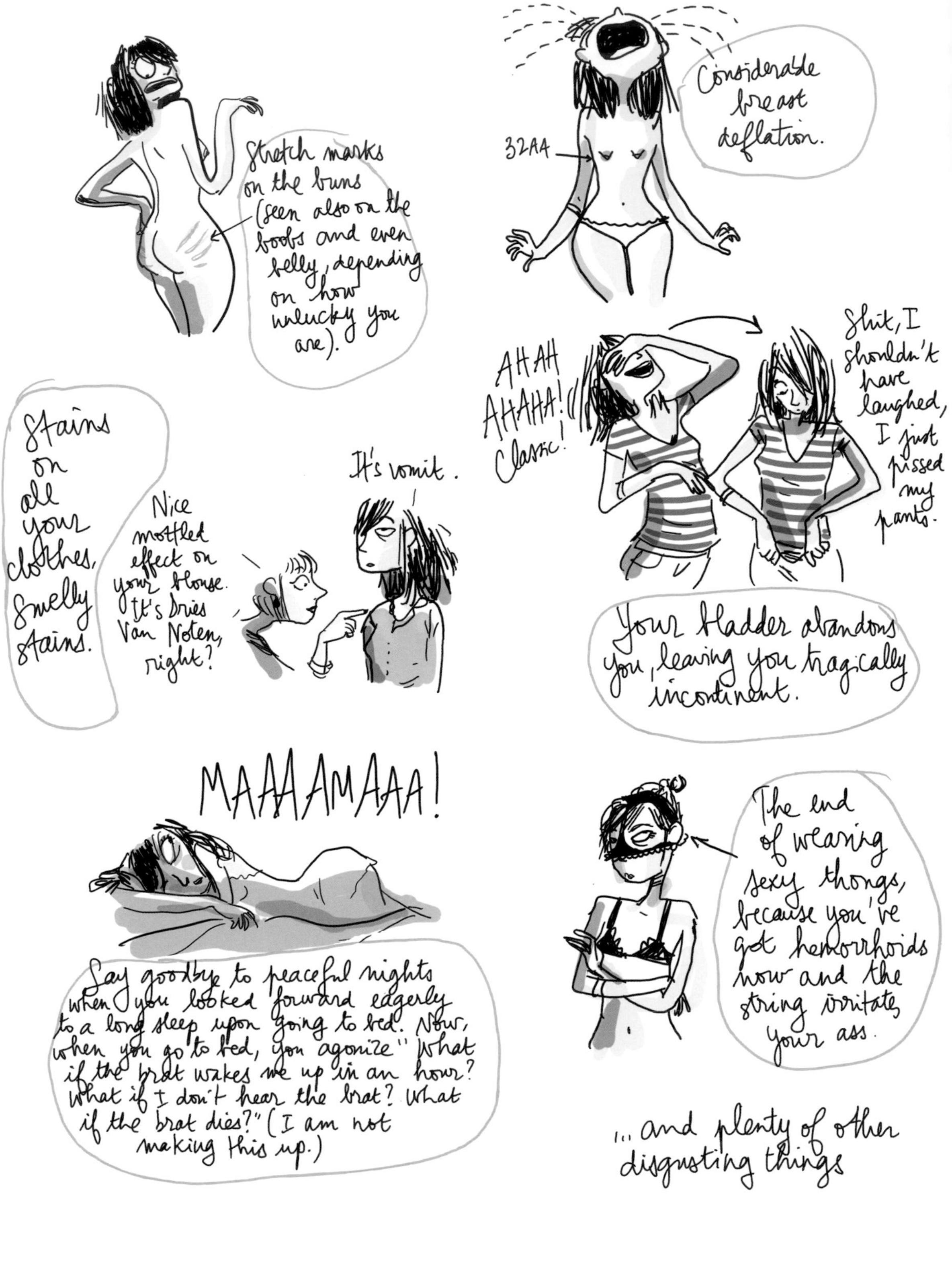
Stretch marks on the buns (seen also on the boobs and even belly, depending on how unlucky you are).
32AA
Considerable breast deflation.
Stains on all your clothes, smelly stains.
Nice mottled effect on your blouse. It's Dries Van Noten, right?
It's vomit.
AHAH AHAHA! Classic!
Shit, I shouldn't have laughed, I just pissed my pants.
Your bladder abandons you, leaving you tragically incontinent.
MAAAMAAA!
Say goodbye to peaceful nights when you looked forward eagerly to a long sleep upon going to bed. Now, when you go to bed, you agonize "What if the brat wakes me up in an hour? What if I don't hear the brat? What if the brat dies?" (I am not making this up.)
The end of wearing sexy thongs, because you've got hemorrhoids now and the string irritates your ass.
... and plenty of other disgusting things

And yet, all the chicks who already have babies keep telling first-timers

THE MOST FAMOUS TALL TALE IN THE UNIVERSE:

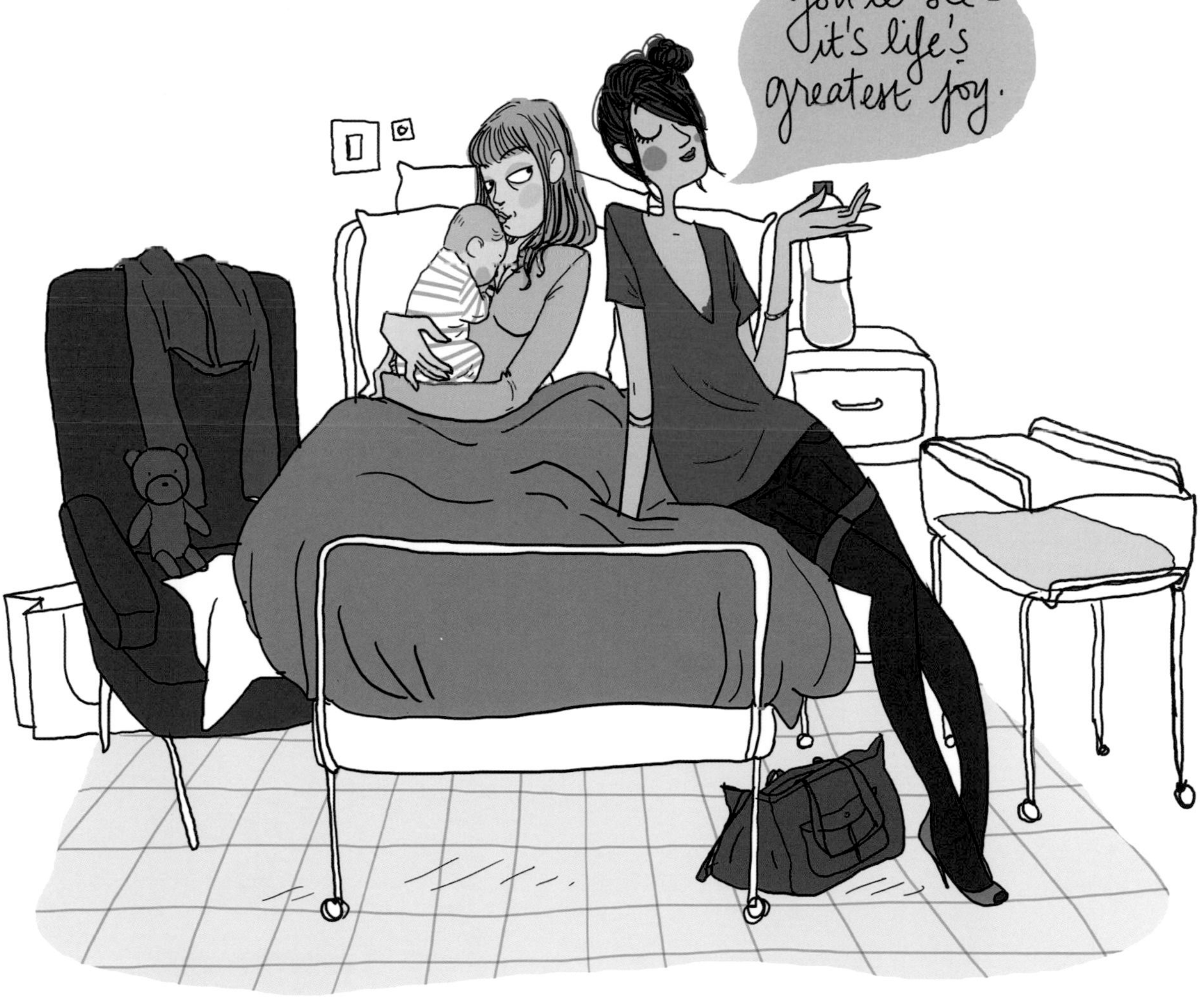
You'll see - it's life's greatest joy.

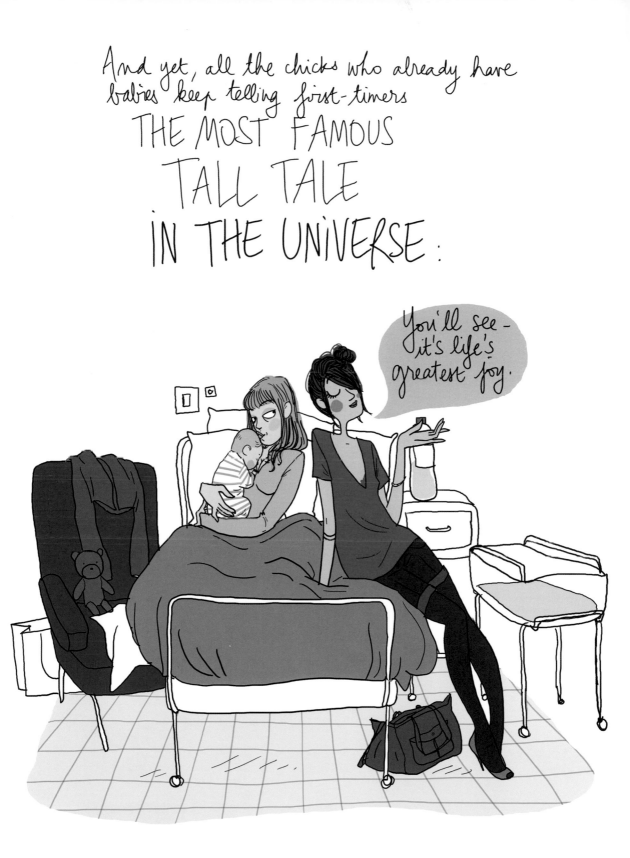

It's also called "karma"

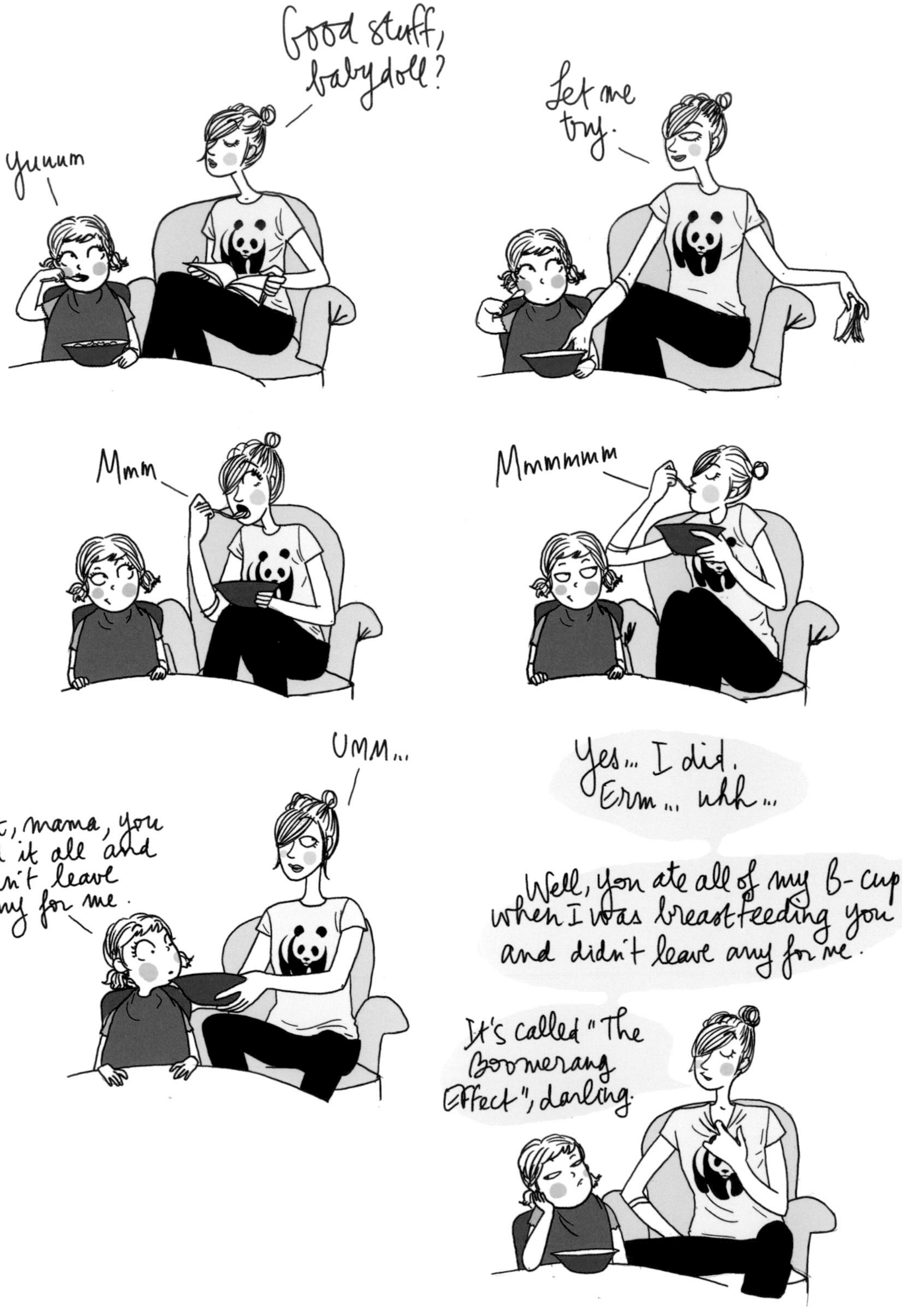

Yuuum
Good stuff, babydoll?
Let me try.
Mmm
Mmmmmm
But, mama, you ated it all and didn't leave any for me.
UMM...
Yes... I did. Erm... uhh...
Well, you ate all of my B-cup when I was breastfeeding you and didn't leave any for me.
It's called "The Boomerang Effect", darling.

Can't argue with the kid

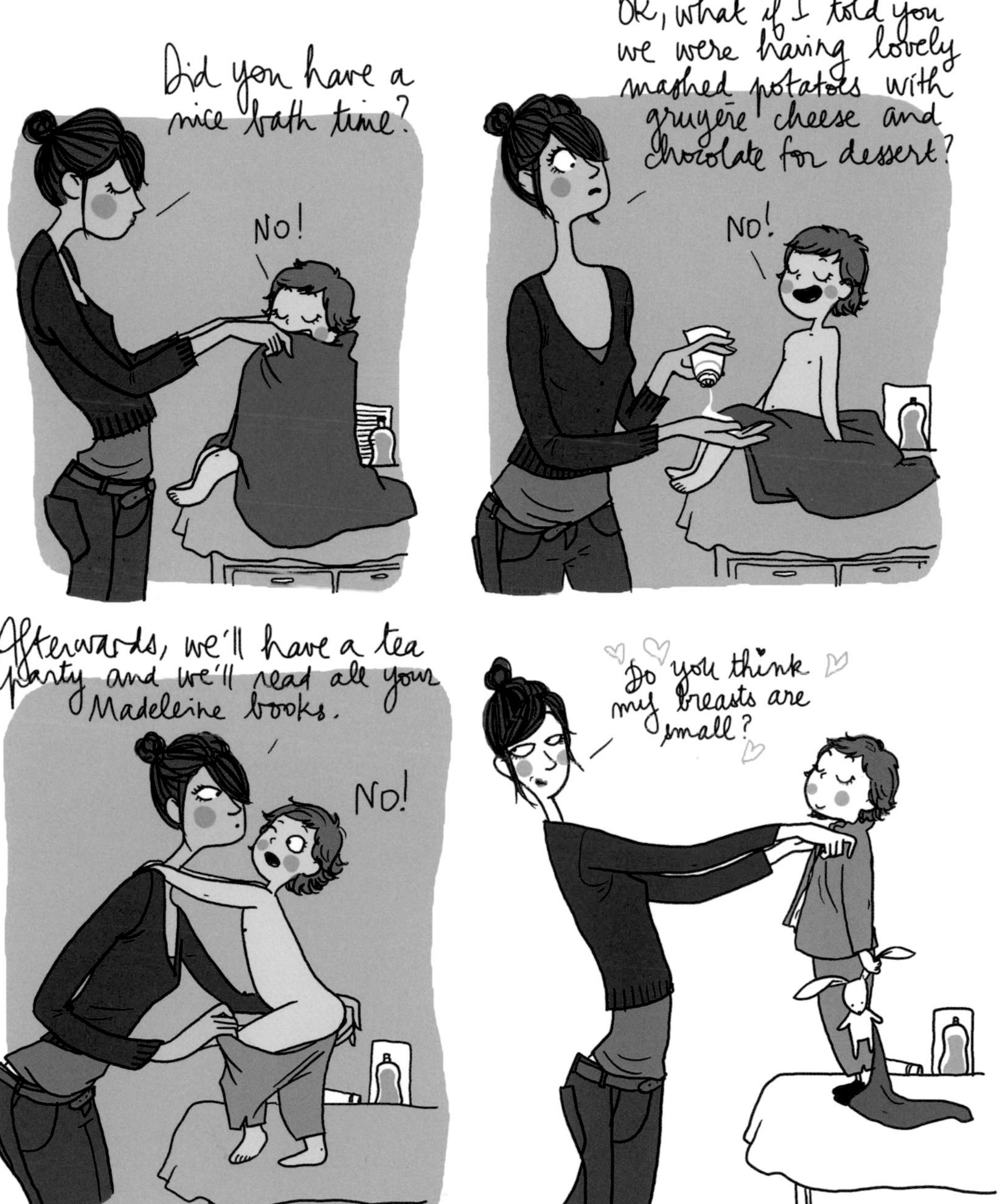
Did you have a nice bath time?
No!
Ok, what if I told you we were having lovely mashed potatoes with gruyère cheese and chocolate for dessert?
No!
Afterwards, we'll have a tea party and we'll read all your Madeleine books.
No!
Do you think my breasts are small?

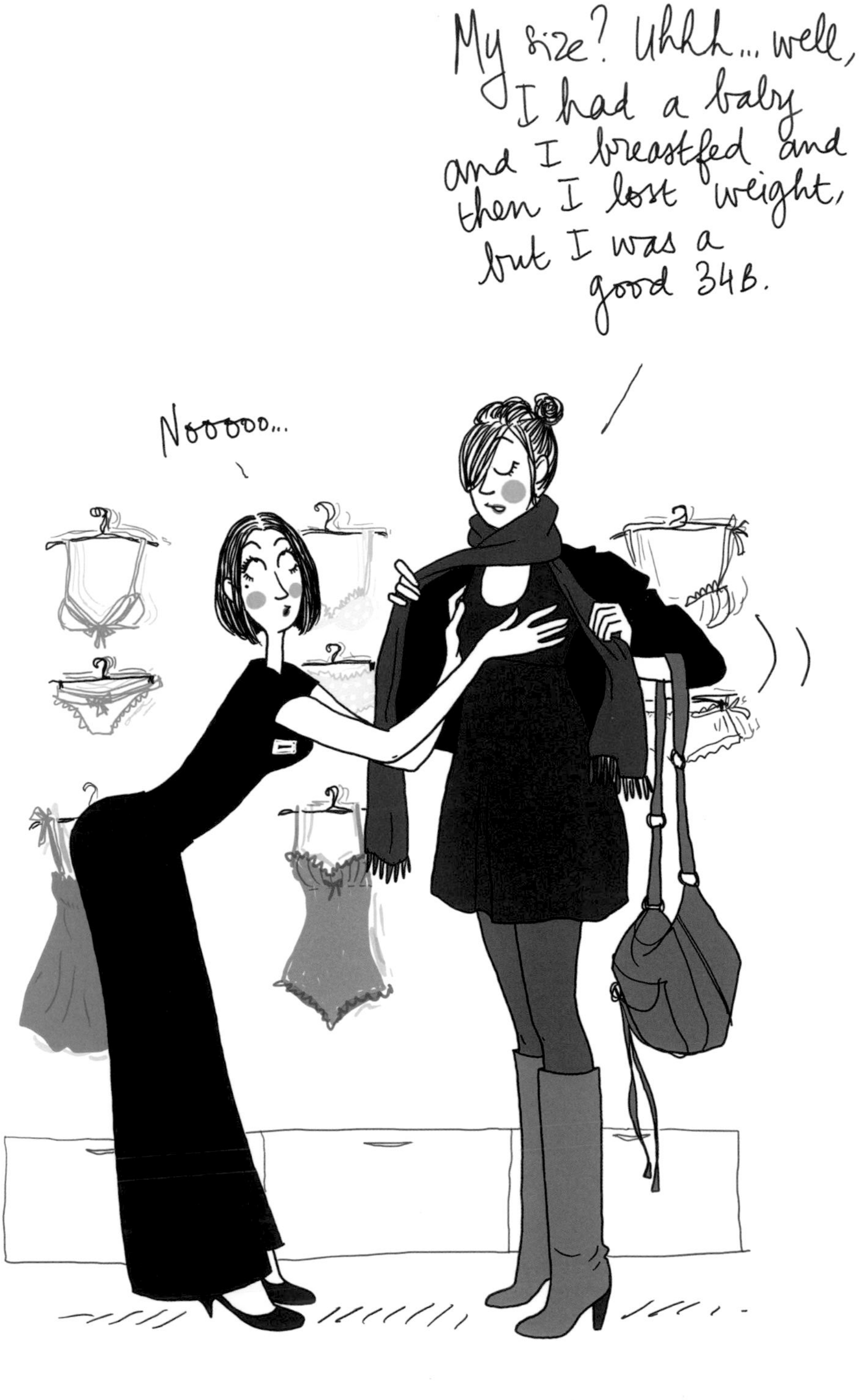
My size? Uhhh... well, I had a baby and I breastfed and then I lost weight, but I was a good 34B.
Nooooo...

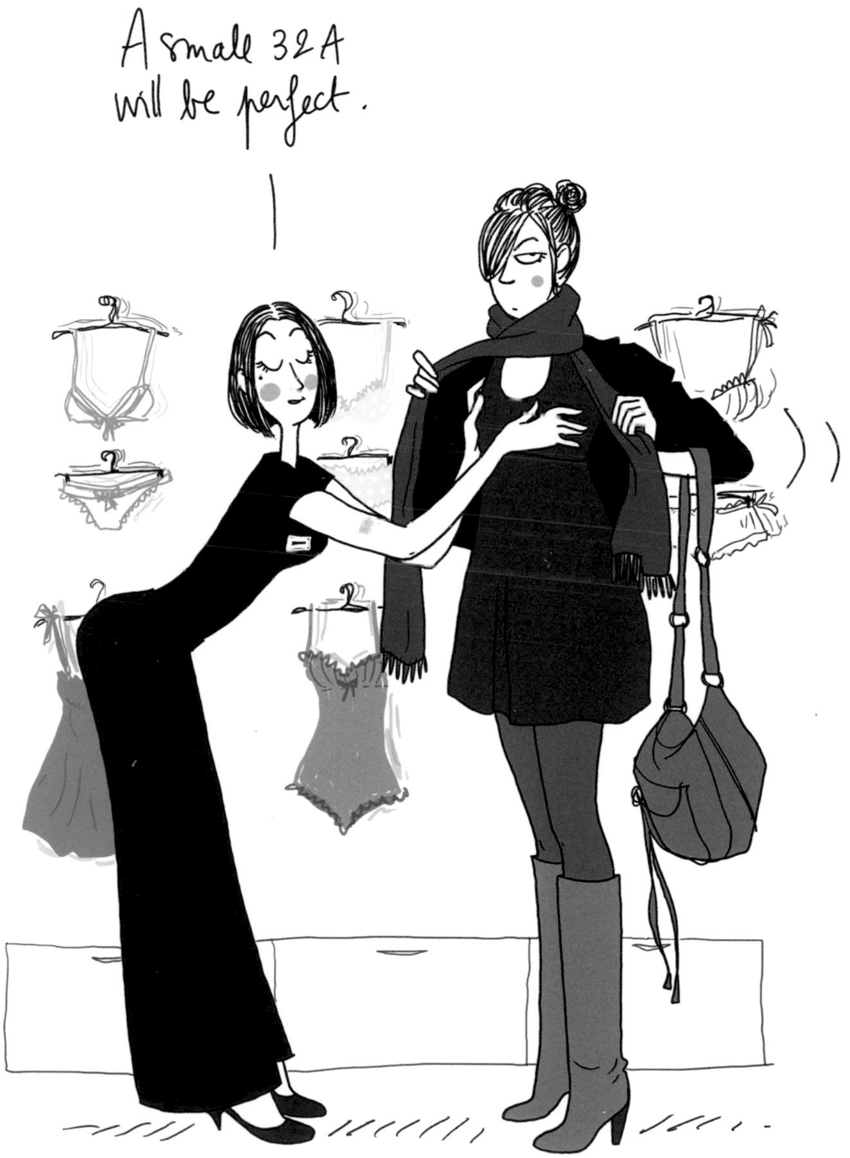
A small 32A will be perfect.

I have a scathing retort

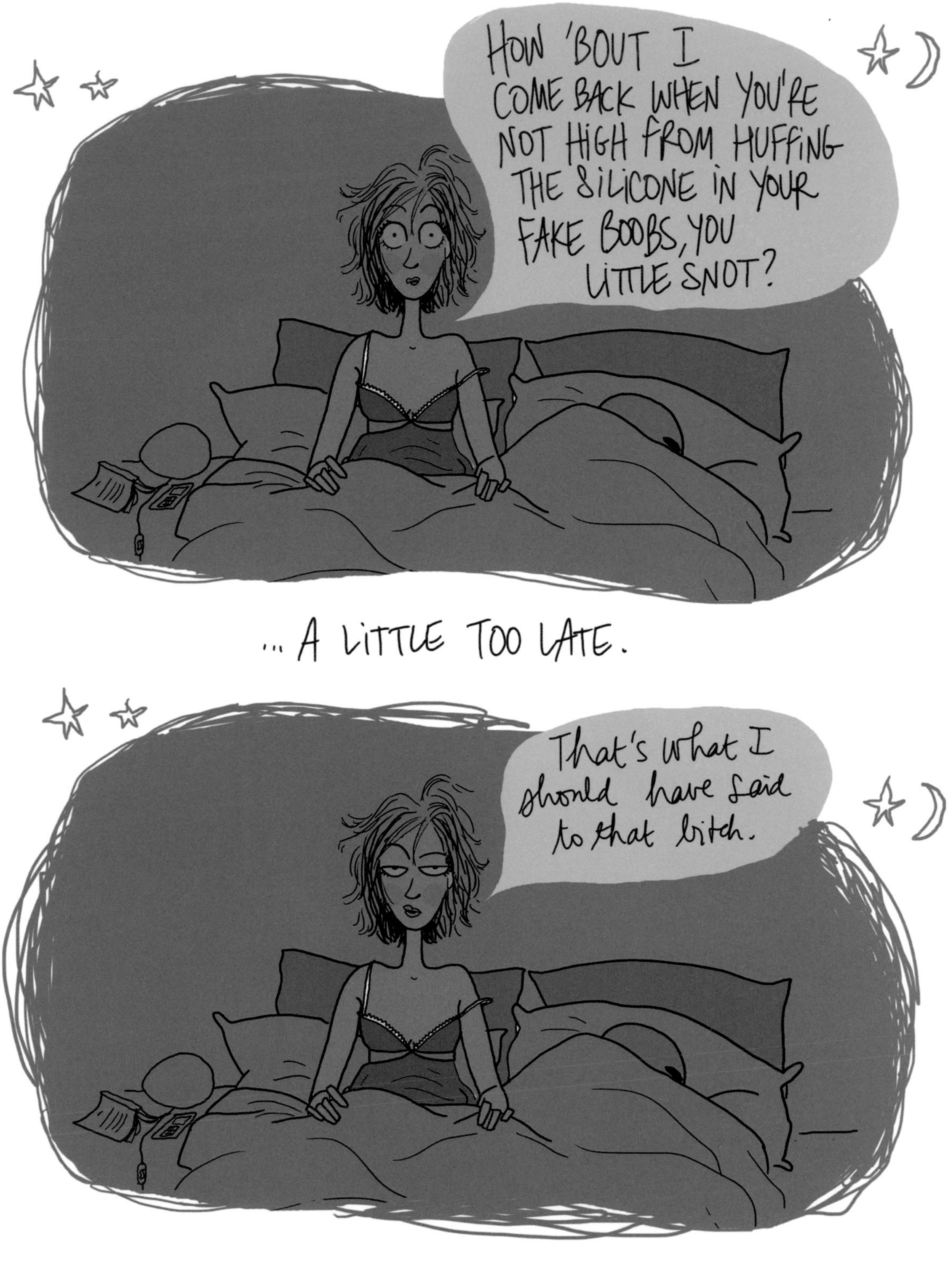
HOW 'BOUT I COME BACK WHEN YOU'RE NOT HIGH FROM HUFFING THE SILICONE IN YOUR FAKE BOOBS, YOU LITTLE SNOT?
... A LITTLE TOO LATE.
That's what I should have said to that bitch.

The magic of Christmas

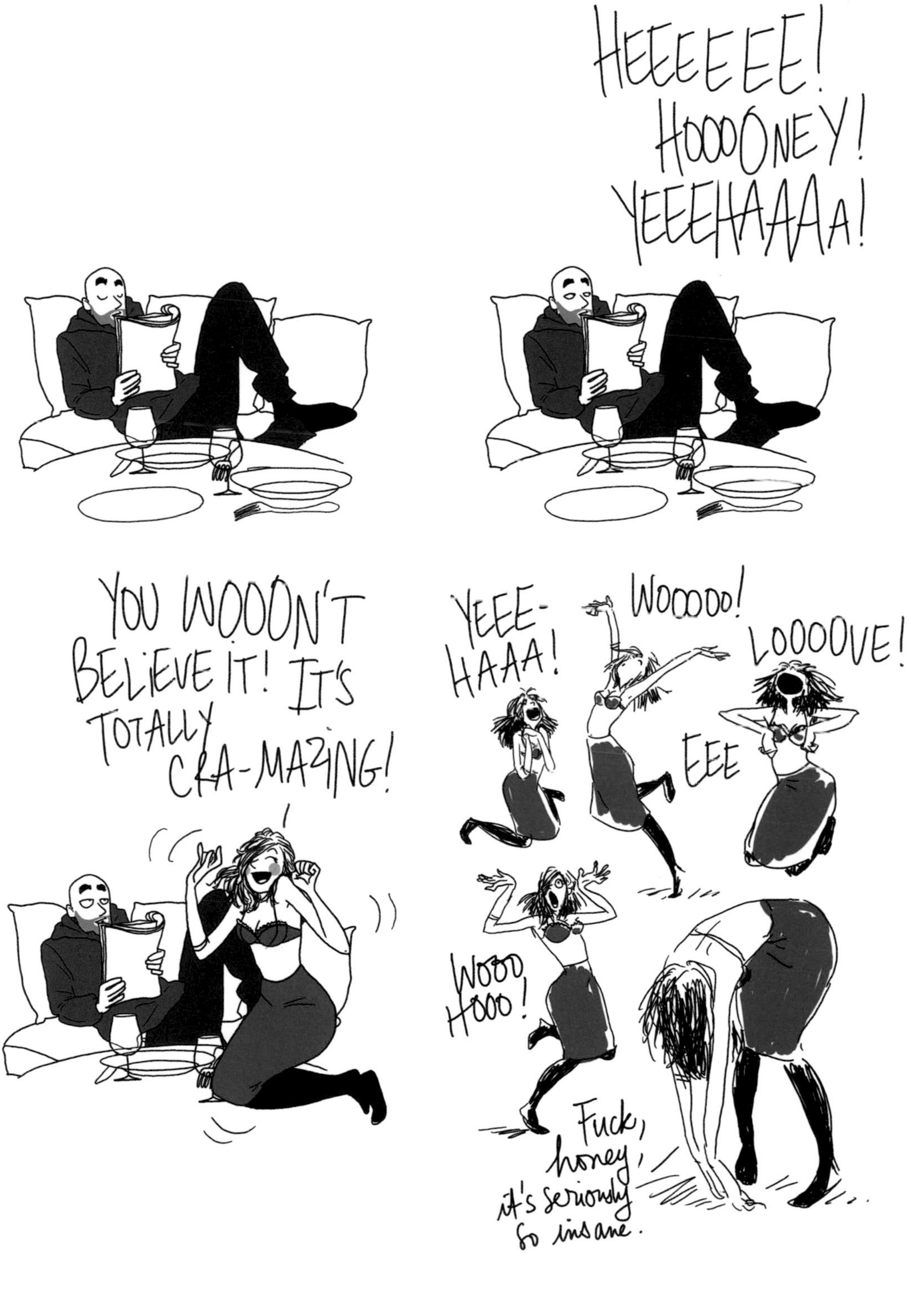
HEEEEEE! HOOOONEY! YEEEHAAAA!
YOU WOOON'T BELIEVE IT! IT'S TOTALLY CRA-MAZING!
YEEE-HAAA!
WOOOOO!
LOOOOVE!
EEE
WOOO HOOO!
Fuck, honey, it's seriously so insane.

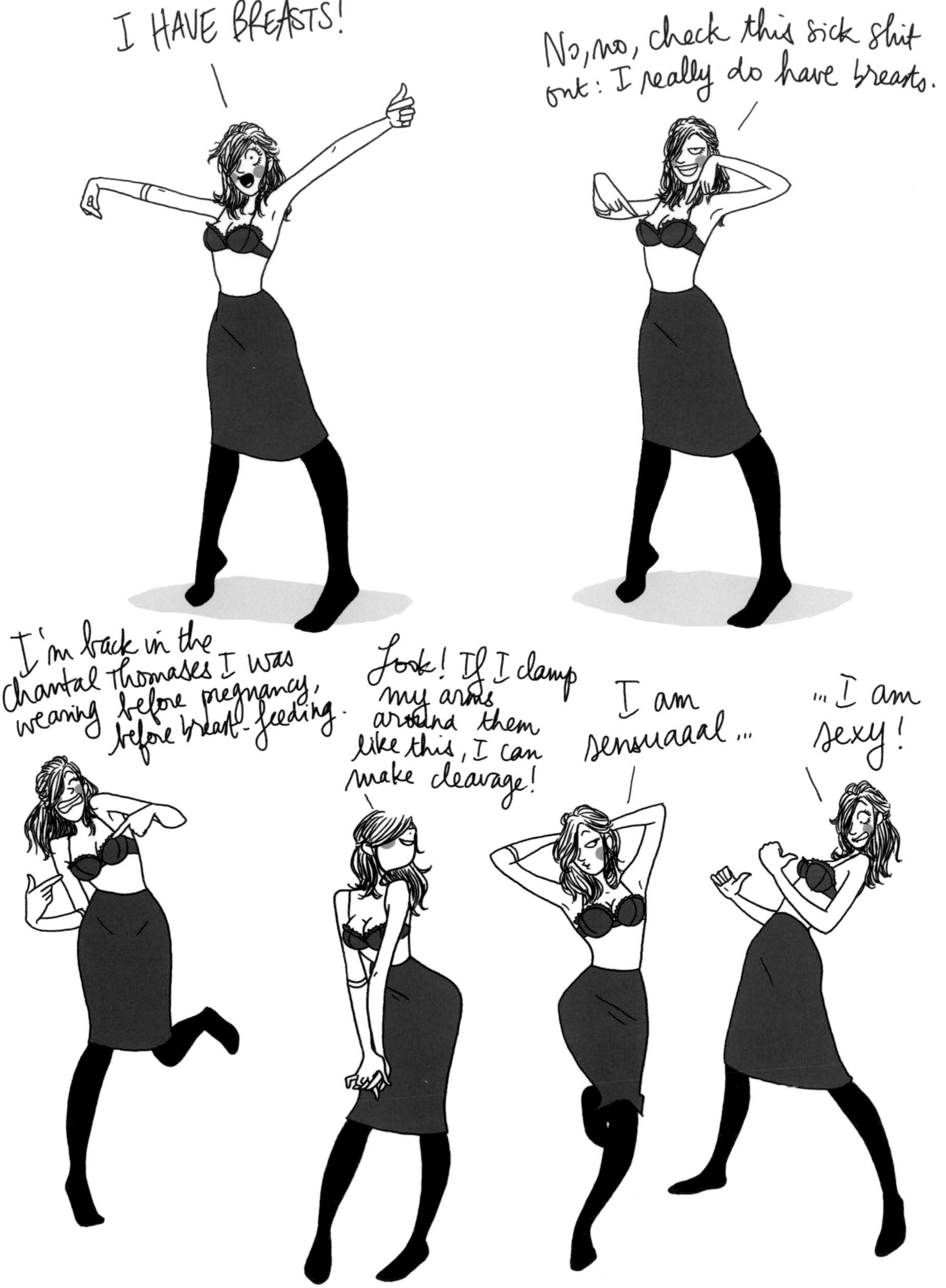
I HAVE BREASTS!
No, no, check this sick shit out: I really do have breasts.
I'm back in the Chantal Thomases I was wearing before pregnancy, before breast-feeding.
Look! If I clamp my arms around them like this, I can make cleavage!
I am sensuaaal...
... I am sexy!

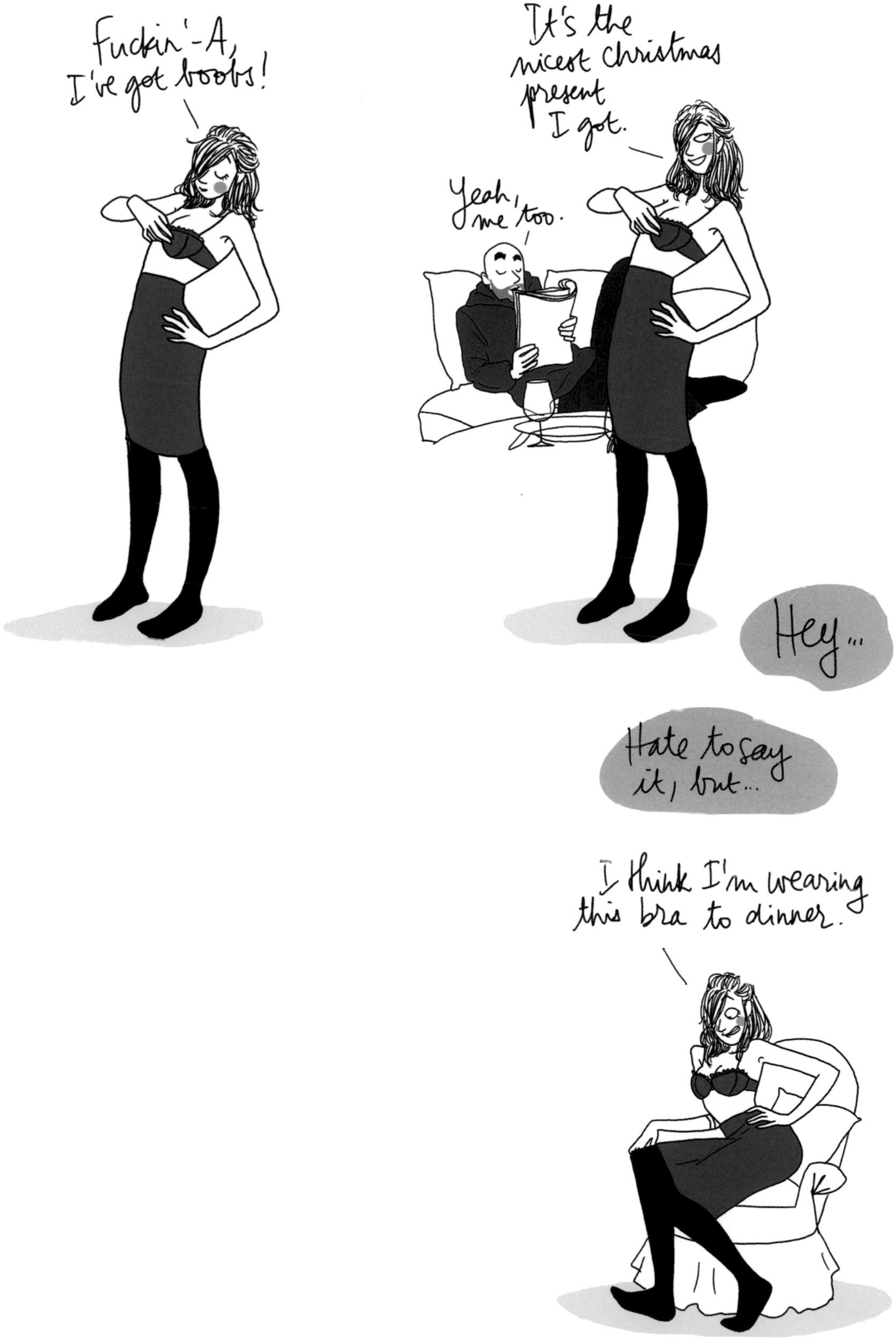

Fuckin'-A, I've got boobs!
It's the nicest christmas present I got.
Yeah, me too.
Hey...
Hate to say it, but...
I think I'm wearing this bra to dinner.

Never satisfied

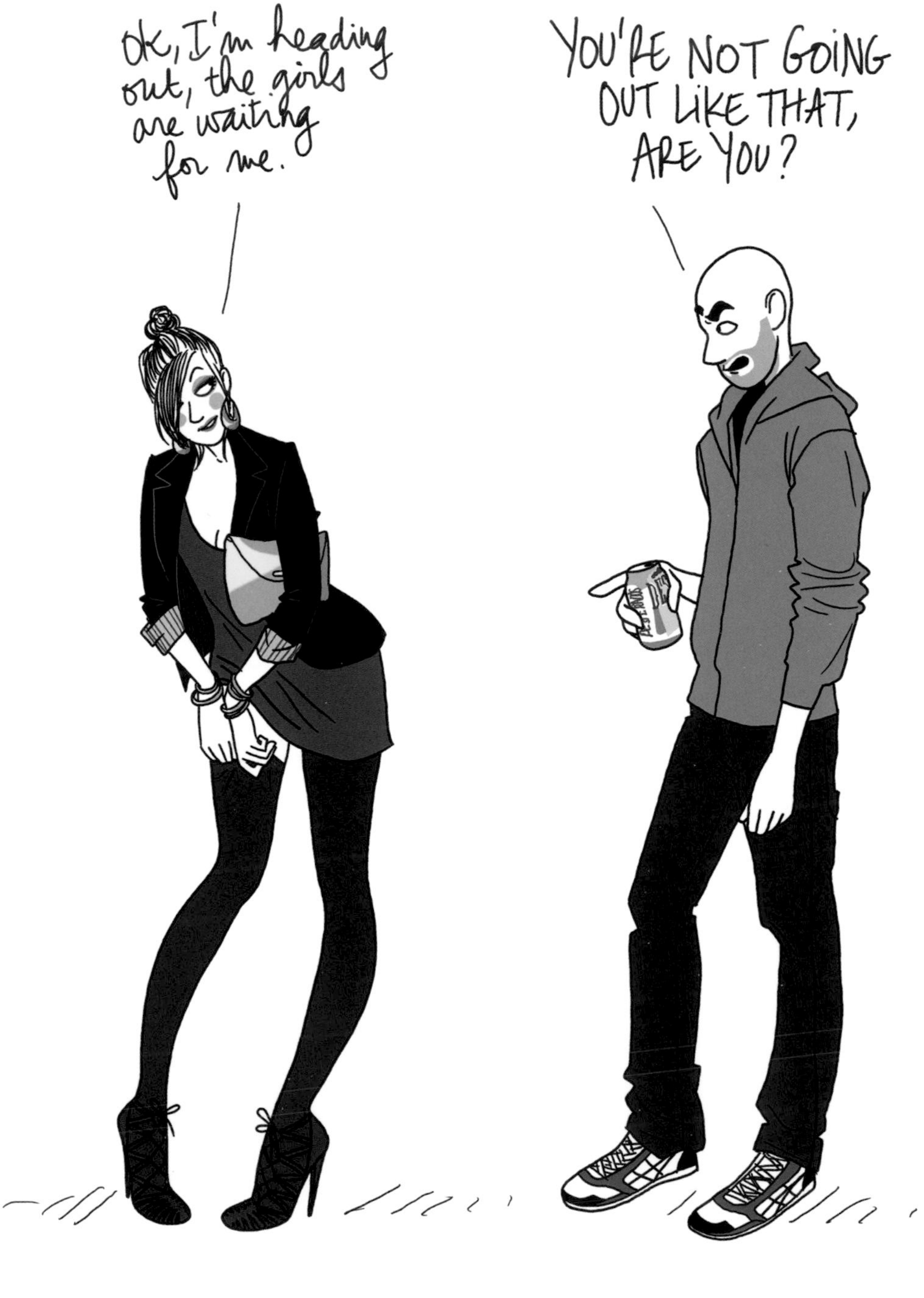
Ok, I'm heading out, the girls are waiting for me.
YOU'RE NOT GOING OUT LIKE THAT, ARE YOU?

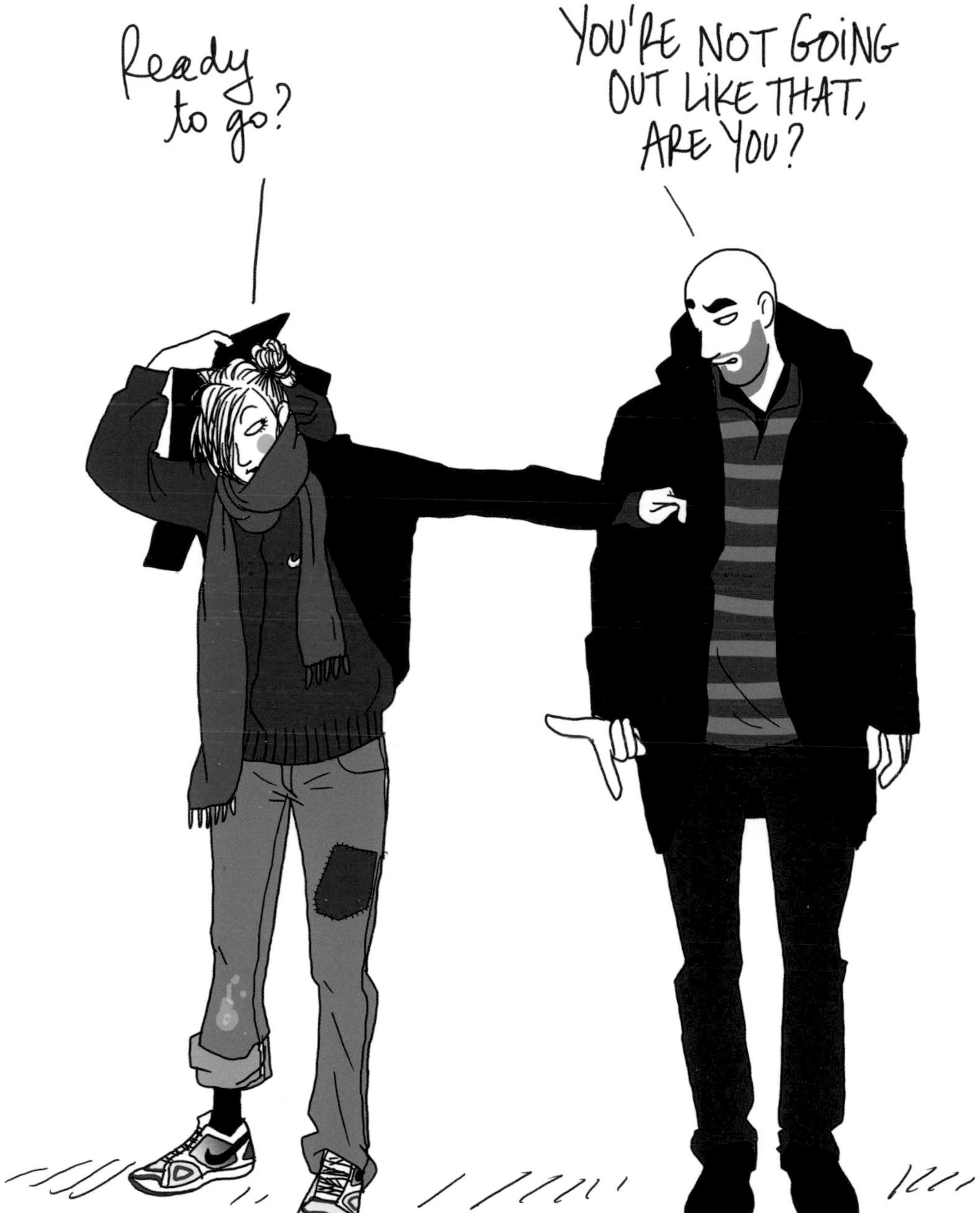
Ready to go?
YOU'RE NOT GOING OUT LIKE THAT, ARE YOU?

I'm lucky that...

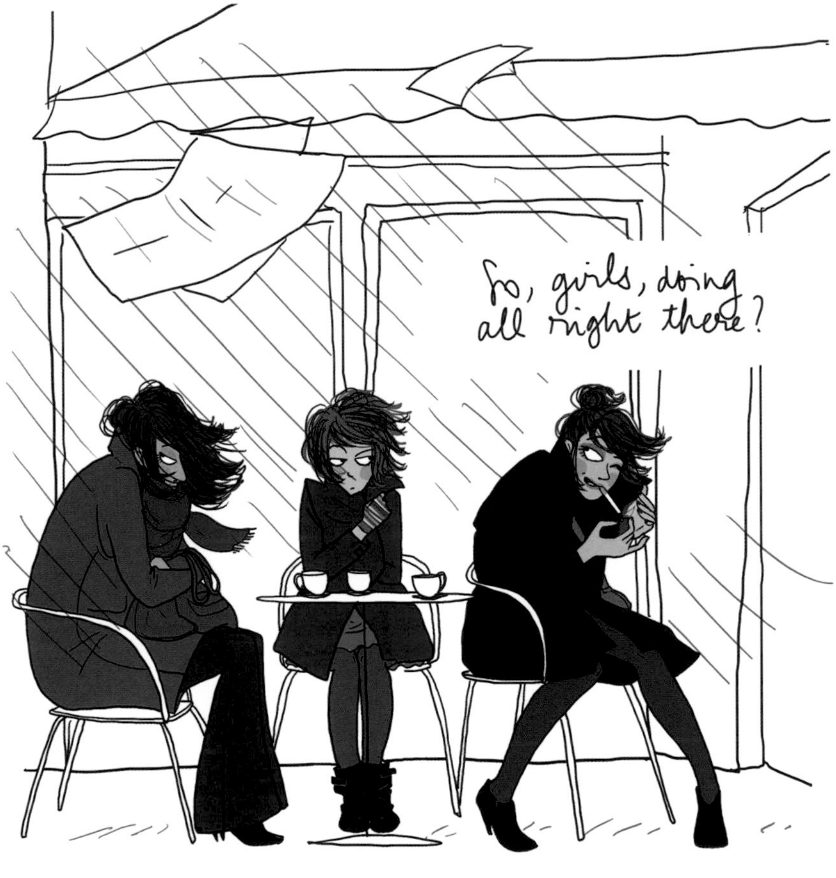

So, girls, doing all right there?

... MY NON-SMOKING FRIENDS ARE VERY SUPPORTIVE.

Friends without children suck. They're not your real friends.

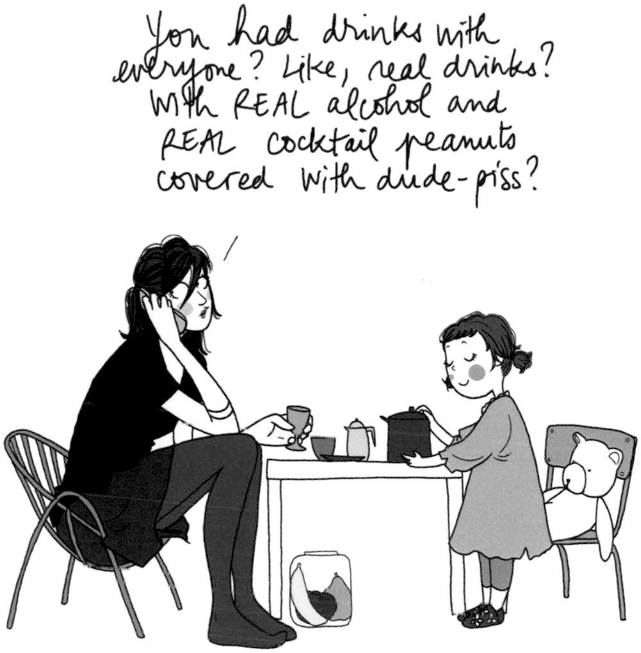
You had drinks with everyone? Like, real drinks? With REAL alcohol and REAL cocktail peanuts covered with dude-piss?

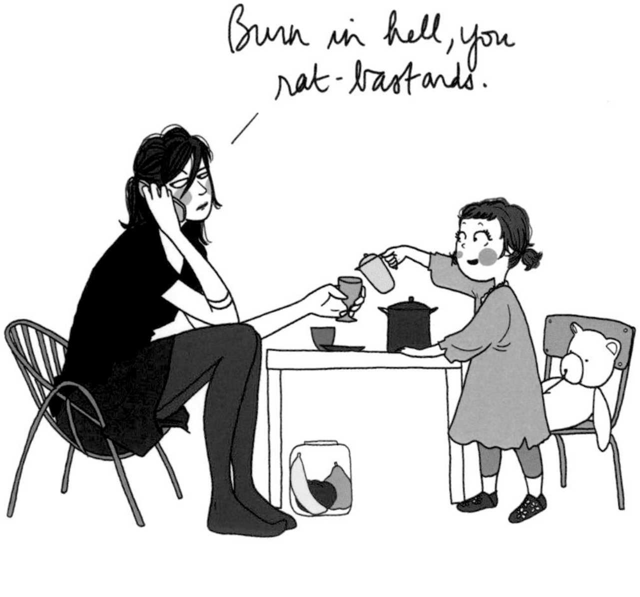
Burn in hell, you rat-bastards.

My friends and I can really hold our alcohol

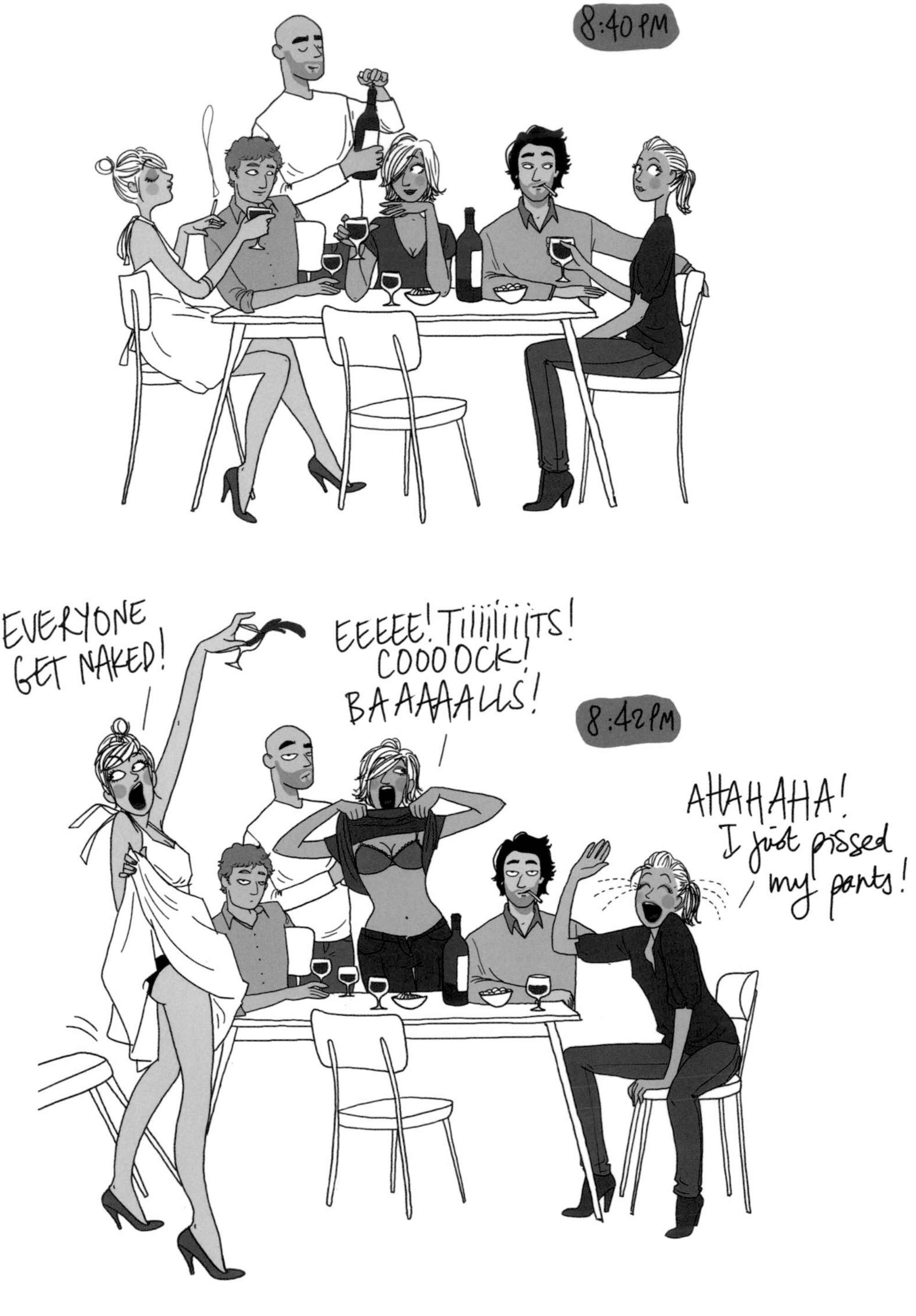
8:40 PM
EVERYONE GET NAKED!
EEEEE! TIIIIIIITS! COOOOCK! BAAAAALLS!
8:42 PM
AHAHAHA! I just pissed my pants!

My morning afters are all the same

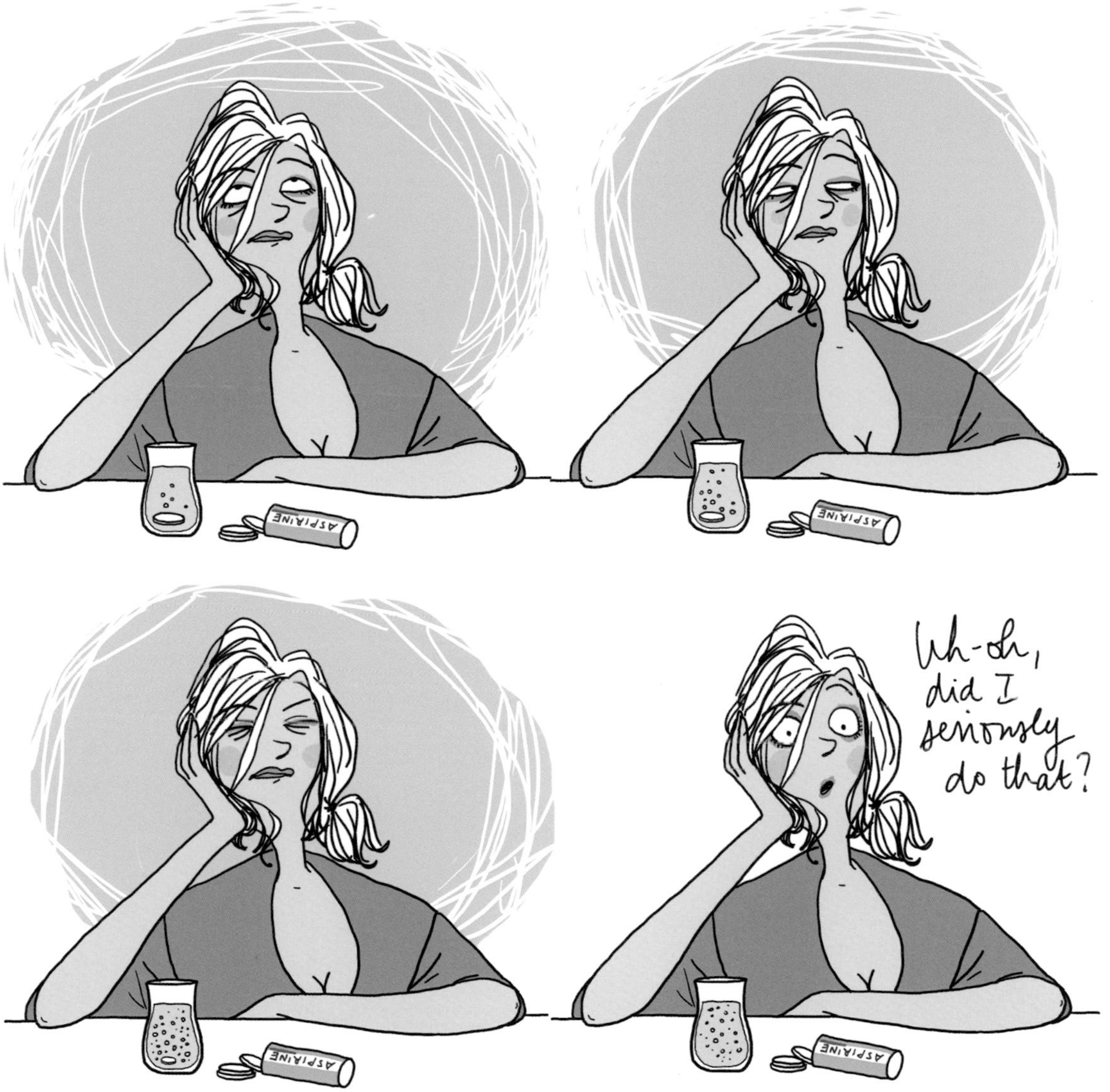
ASPIRINE
ASPIRINE
ASPIRINE
Uh-oh, did I seriously do that?
ASPIRINE

The girl, that wonderful paradox: part 1

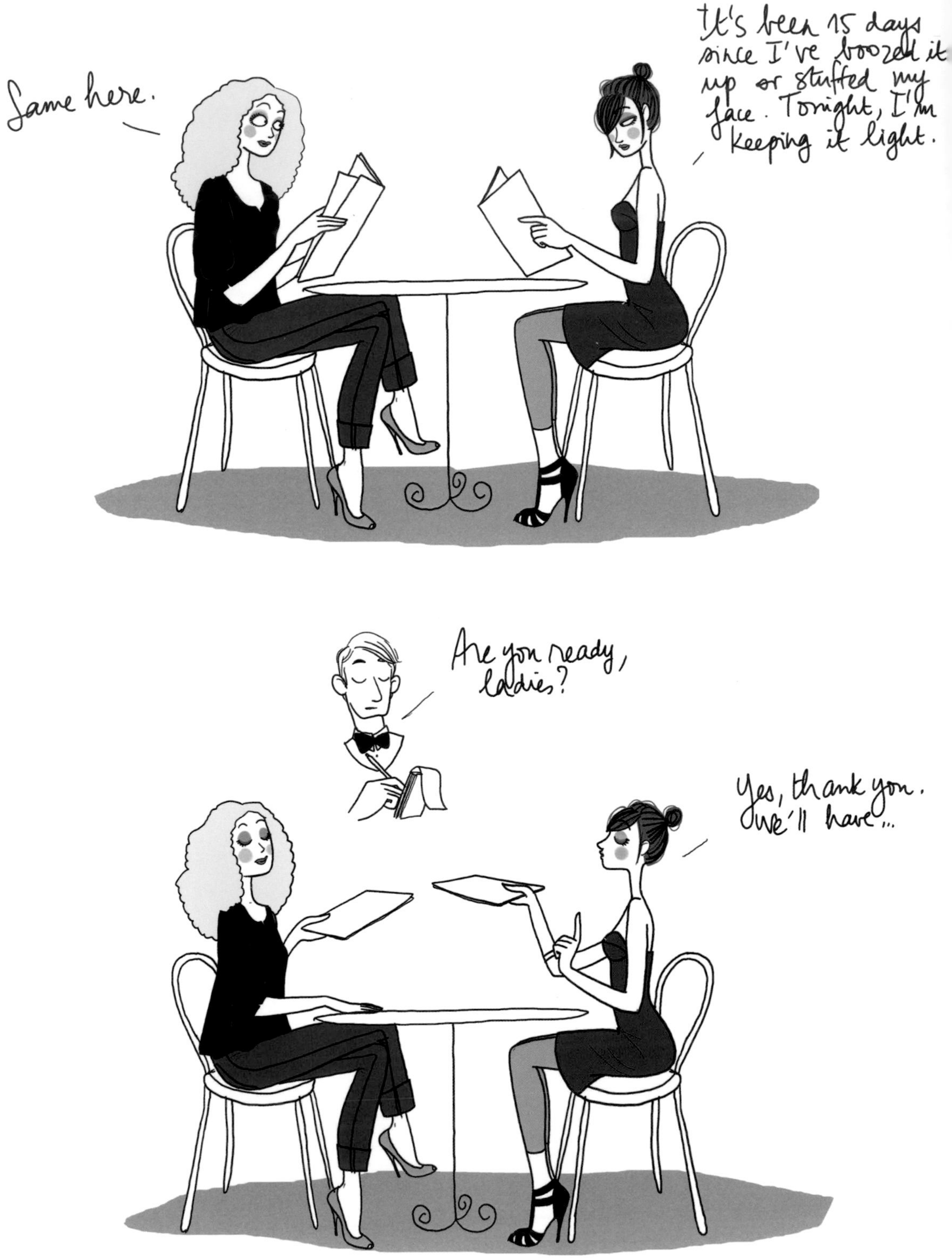
It's been 15 days since I've boozed it up or stuffed my face. Tonight, I'm keeping it light.
Same here.
Are you ready, ladies?
Yes, thank you. We'll have...

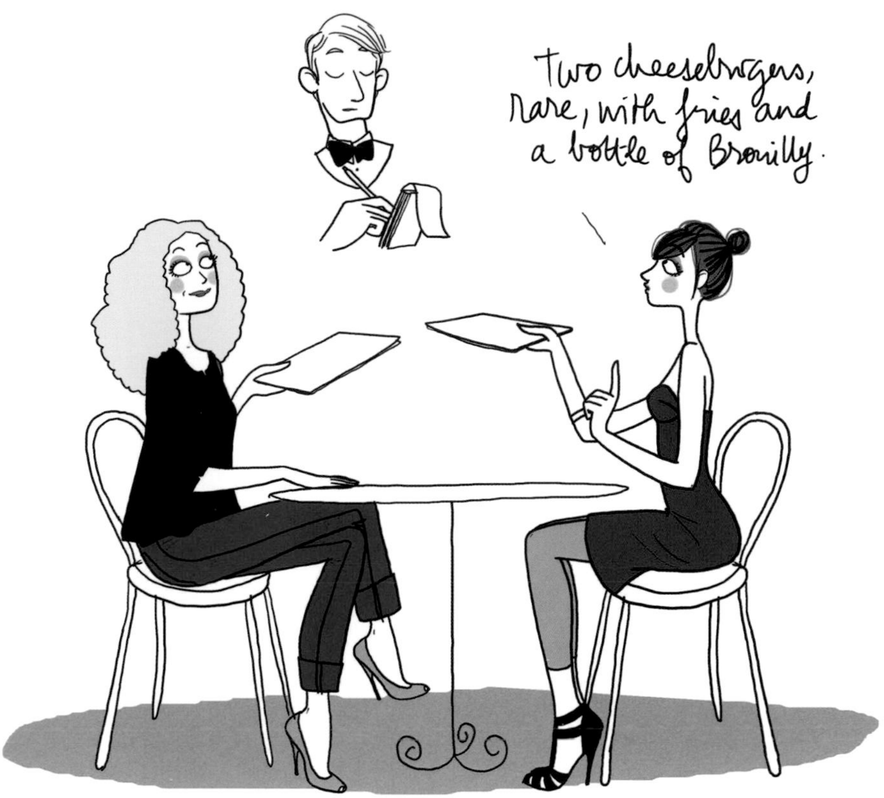
Two cheeseburgers, rare, with fries and a bottle of Brouilly.

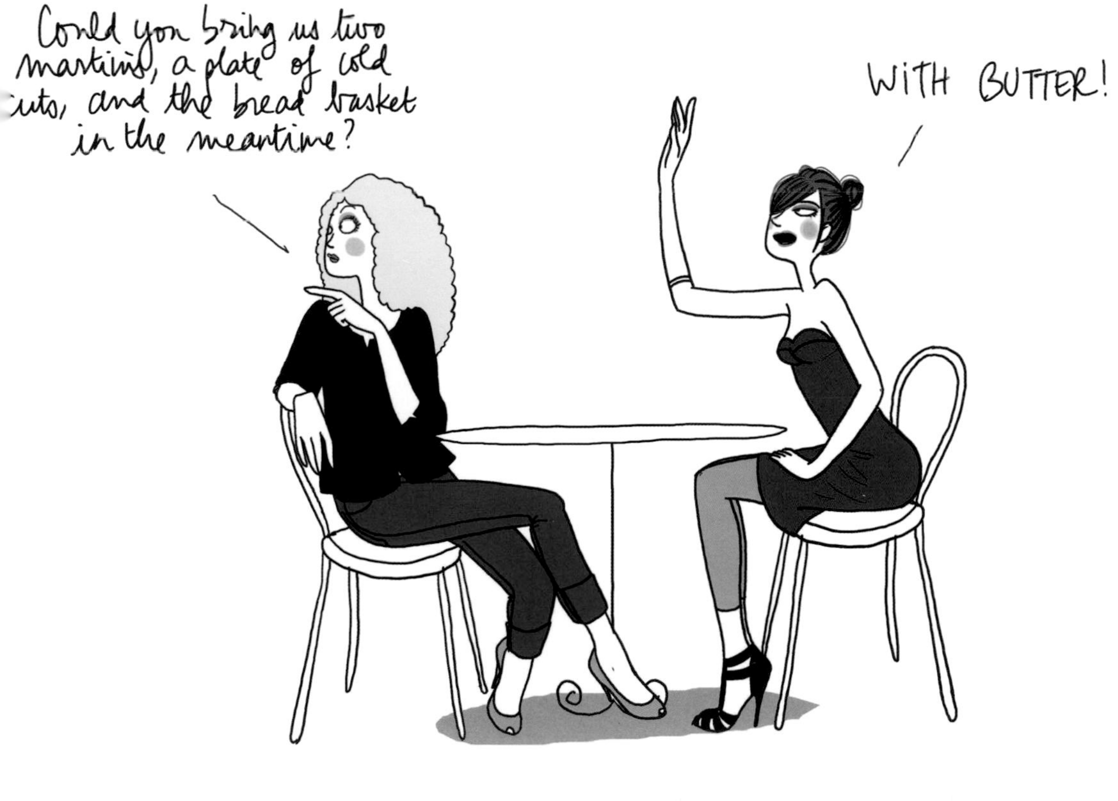
Could you bring us two martinis, a plate of cold uts, and the bread basket in the meantime?
WITH BUTTER!

Last night: a Feist concert with my friends who like girls

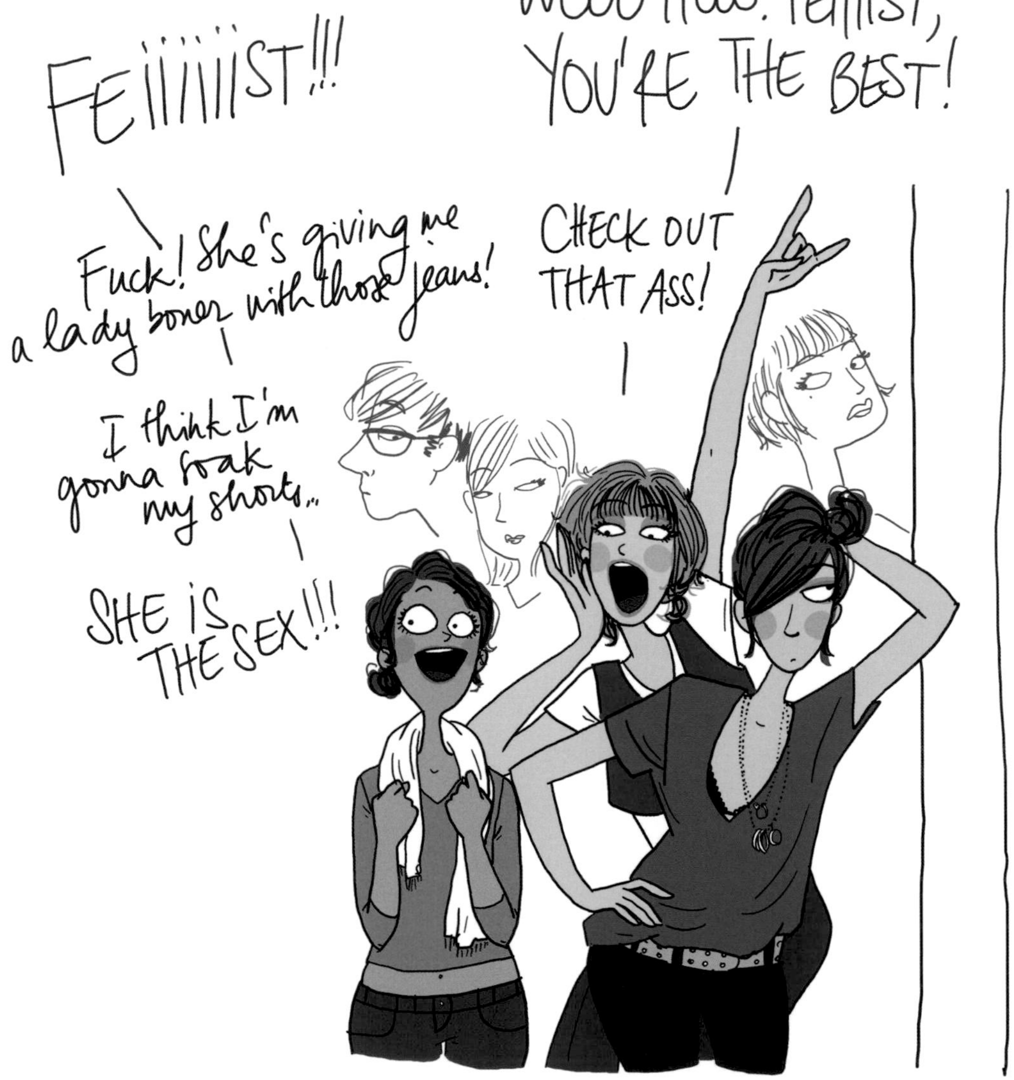
FEiiiiiiST!!!
WOOO-HOOO! FEiiiiST, YOU'RE THE BEST!
Fuck! She's giving me a lady boner with those jeans!
CHECK OUT THAT ASS!
I think I'm gonna soak my shorts...
SHE IS THE SEX!!!

-NO COMMENT-

Our friends secretly hate us

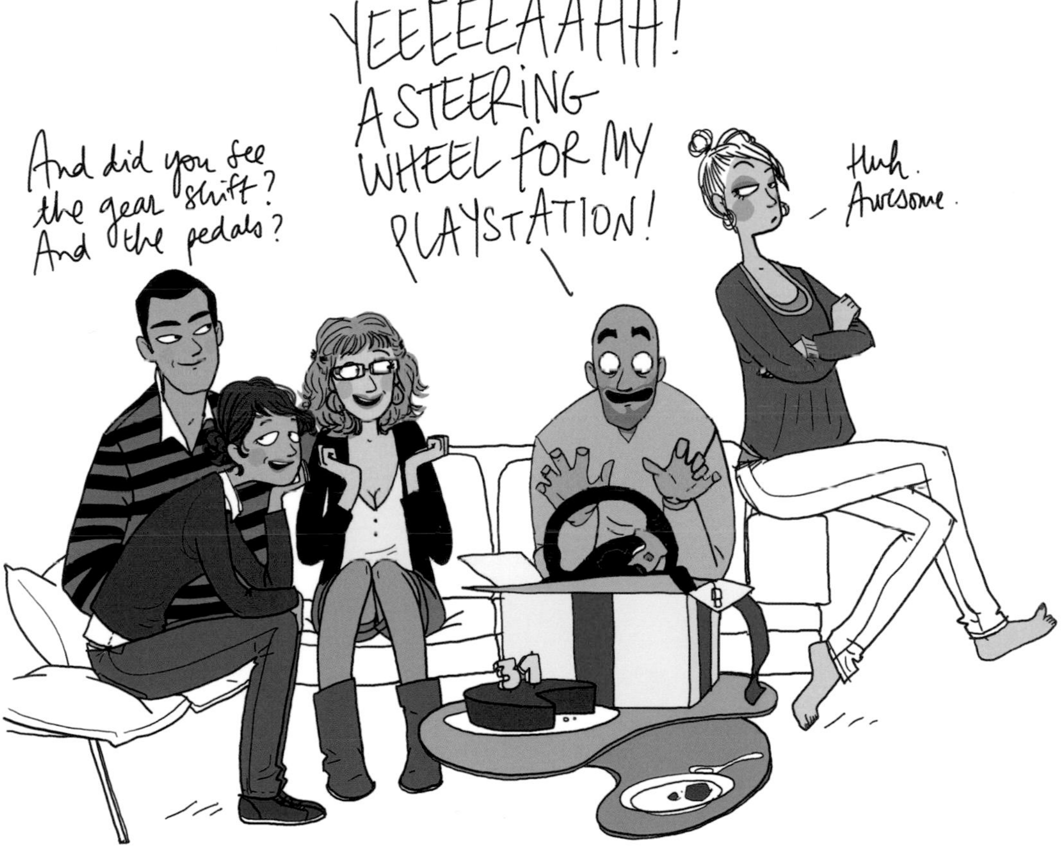
And did you see the gear shift? And the pedals?
YEEEEEAAHH! A STEERING WHEEL FOR MY PLAYSTATION!
Huh. Awesome.

My guy friends, those great romantics. Example 1:

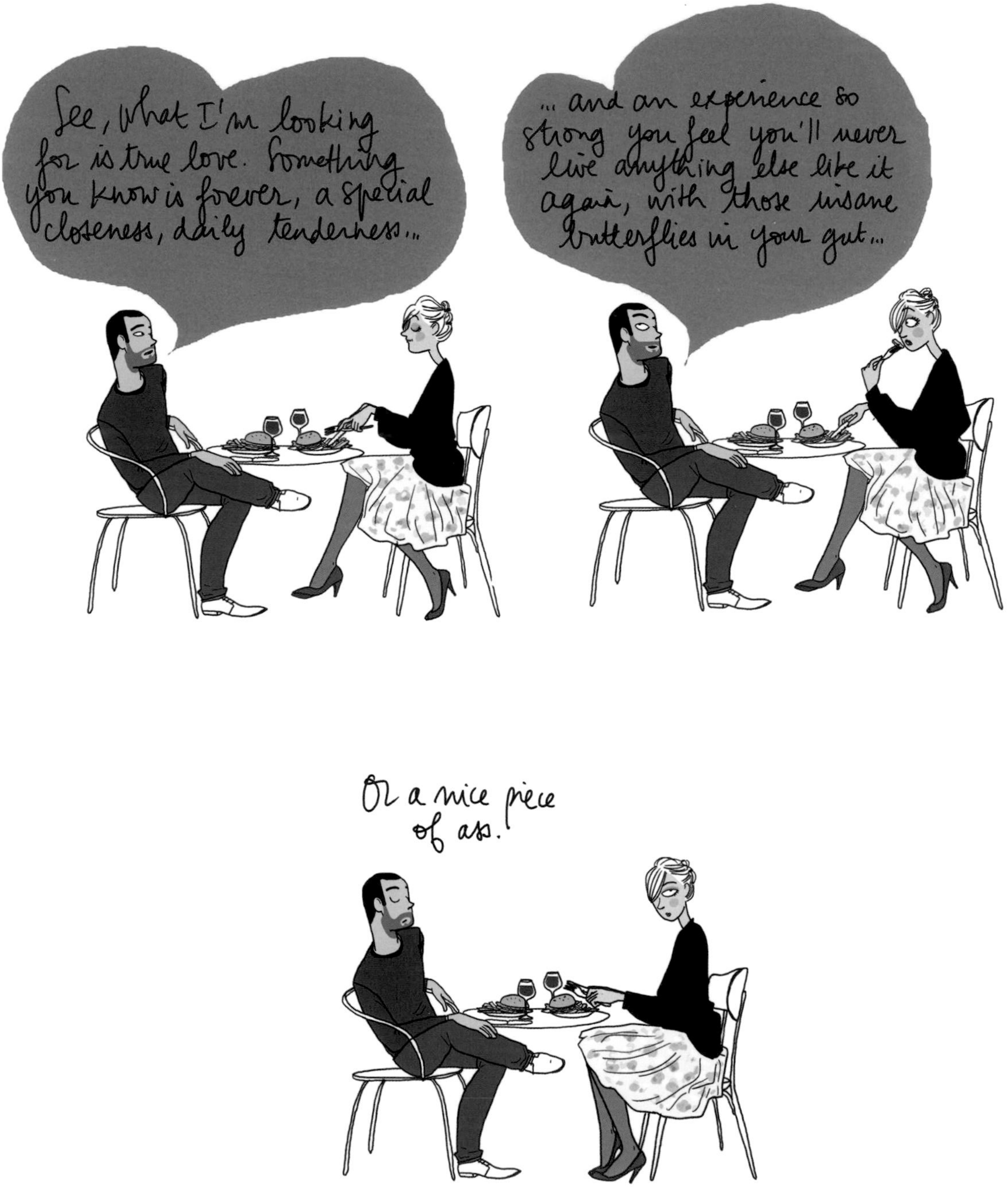
See, what I'm looking for is true love. Something you know is forever, a special closeness, daily tenderness...
... and an experience so strong you feel you'll never live anything else like it again, with those insane butterflies in your gut...
Or a nice piece of ass!

My guy friends, those great romantics. Example 2:

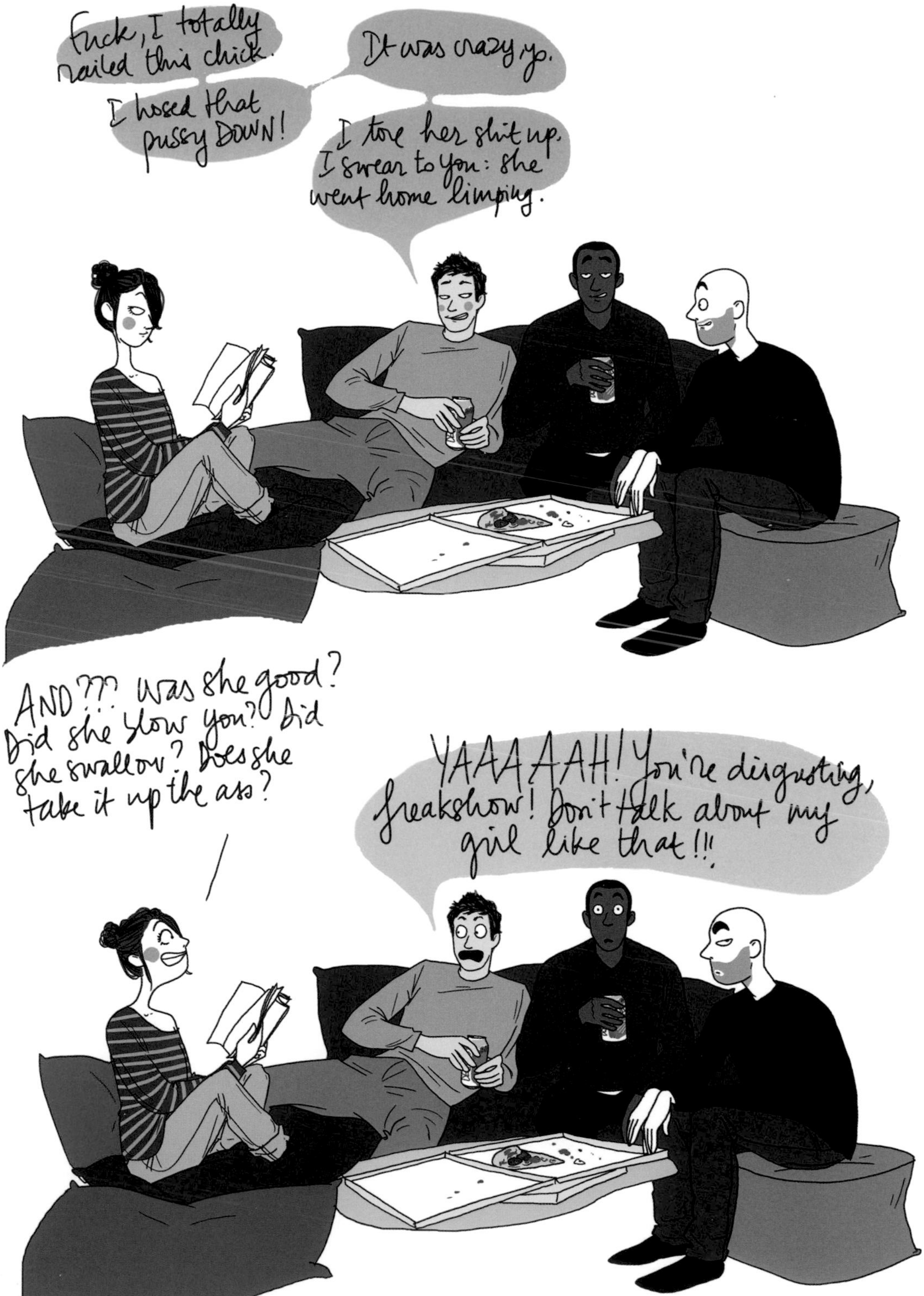
Fuck, I totally nailed this chick.
I hosed that pussy DOWN!
It was crazy, yo.
I tore her shit up. I swear to you: she went home limping.
AND??? Was she good? Did she blow you? Did she swallow? Does she take it up the ass?
YAAAAAH! You're disgusting, freakshow! Don't talk about my girl like that!!!

The girl, that wonderful paradox: part 2

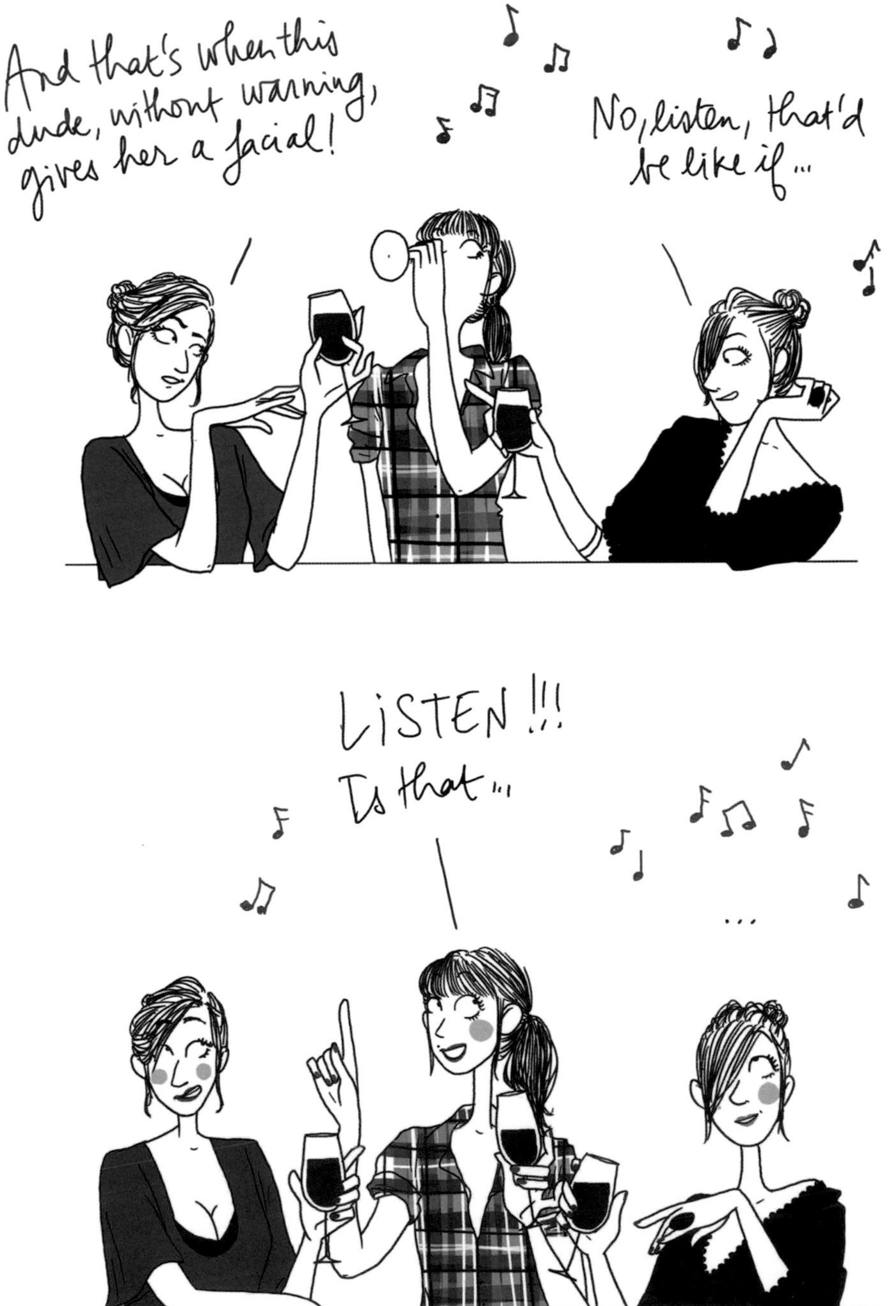

And that's when this dude, without warning, gives her a facial!
No, listen, that'd be like if...
LISTEN!!!
Is that...
...

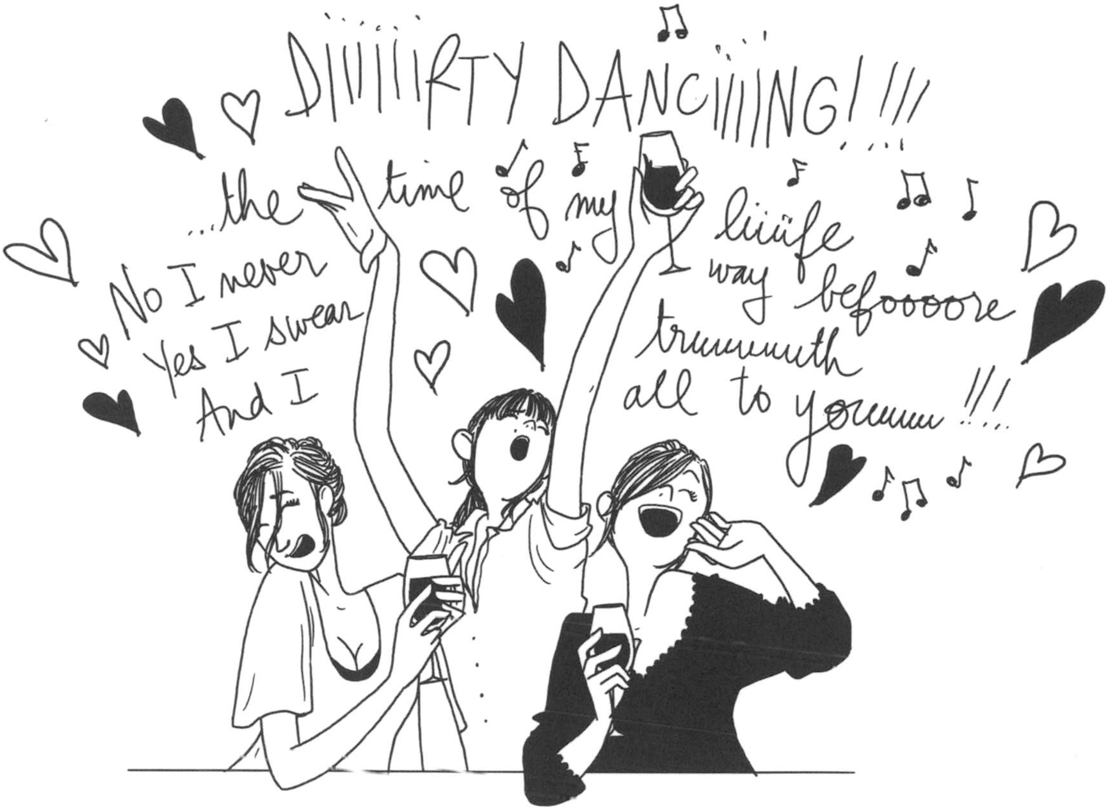
DIIIIIRTY DANCIIIING!!!!
...the time of my liiiife
No I never
Yes I swear
And I
way befoooore
truuuuuth
all to youuuuu!!!

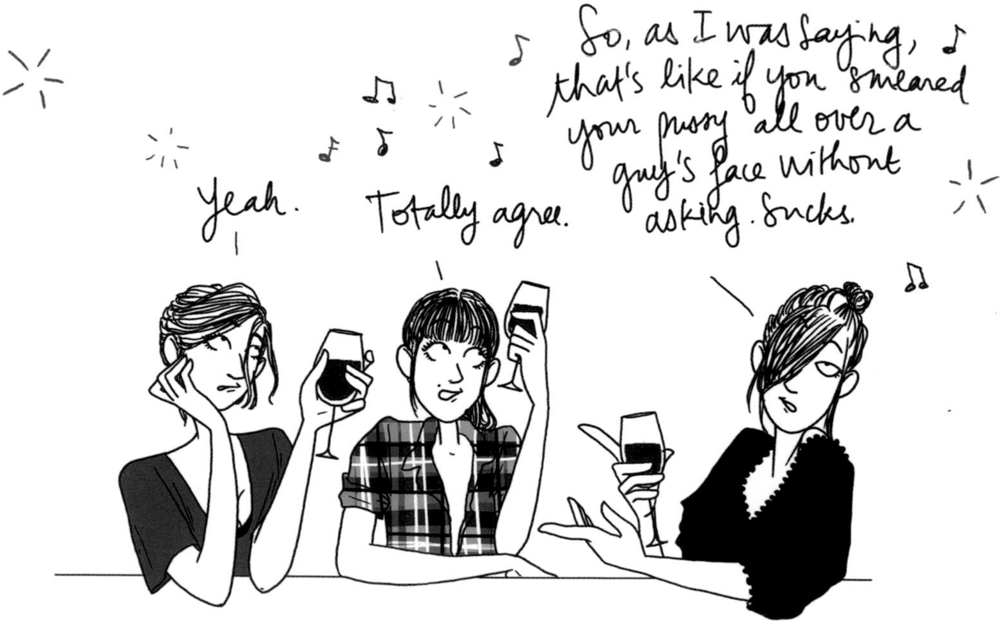
Yeah.
Totally agree.
So, as I was saying, that's like if you smeared your pussy all over a guy's face without asking. Sucks.

A junkie in need is ugly indeed

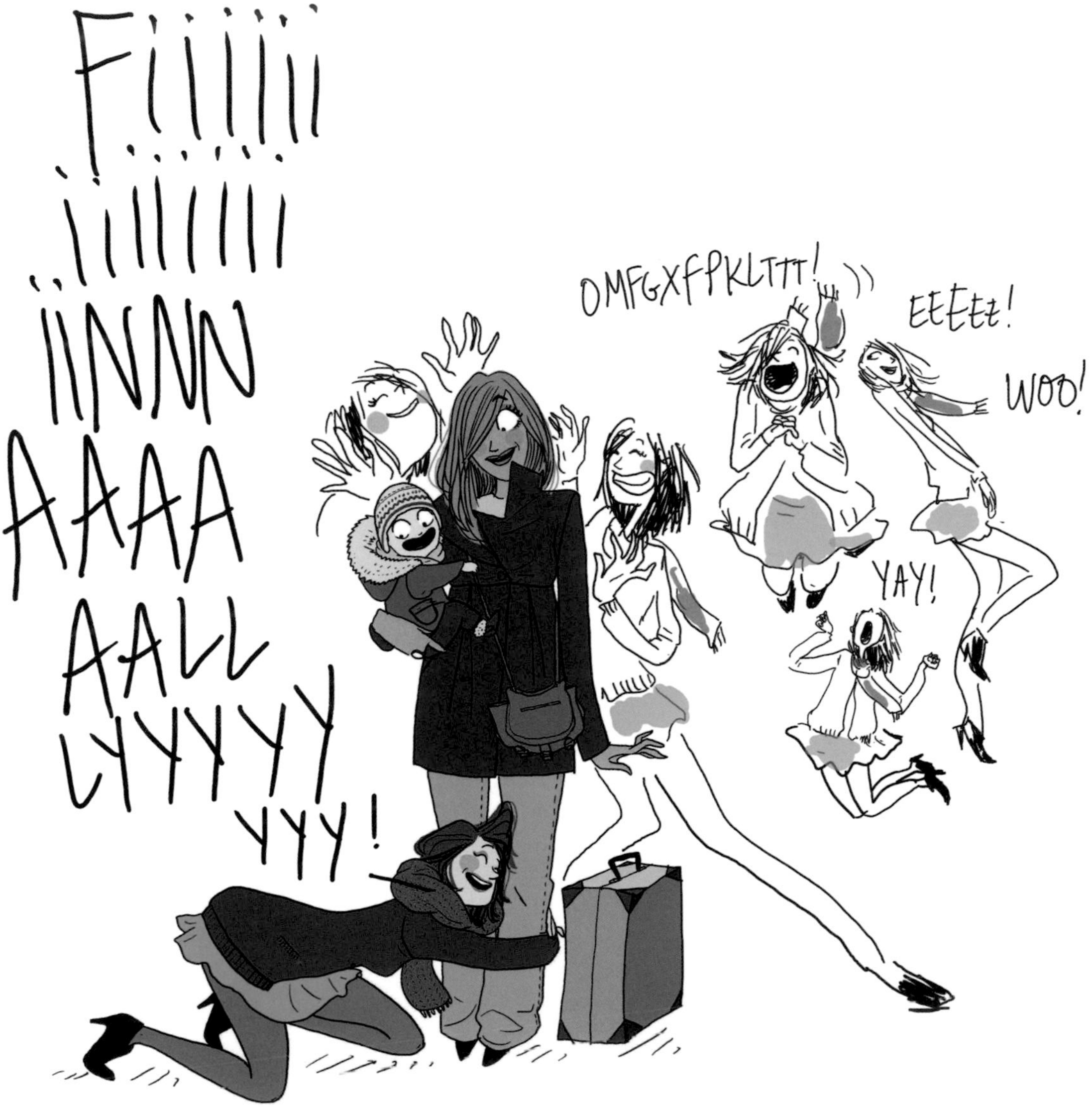
FIIIIIII
IIIIIIII
IINNN
AAAA
AALL
LYYYYY
YYY!
OMFGXFPKLTTT!
EEEEE!
WOO!
YAY!

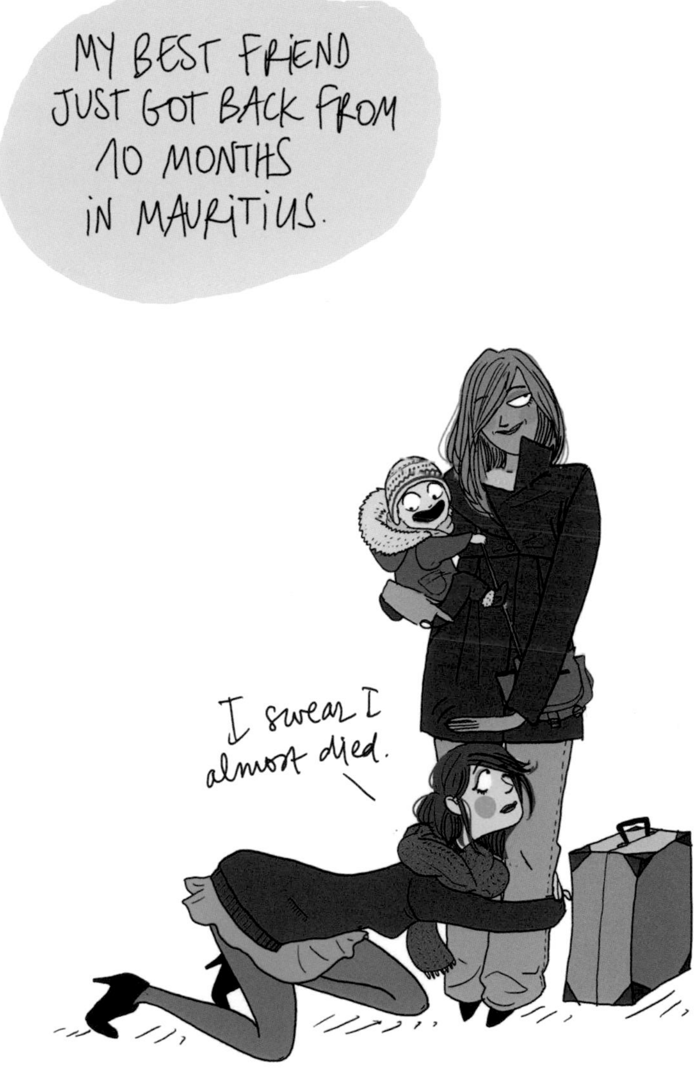
MY BEST FRIEND JUST GOT BACK FROM 10 MONTHS IN MAURITIUS.
I swear I almost died.

The magic elevator

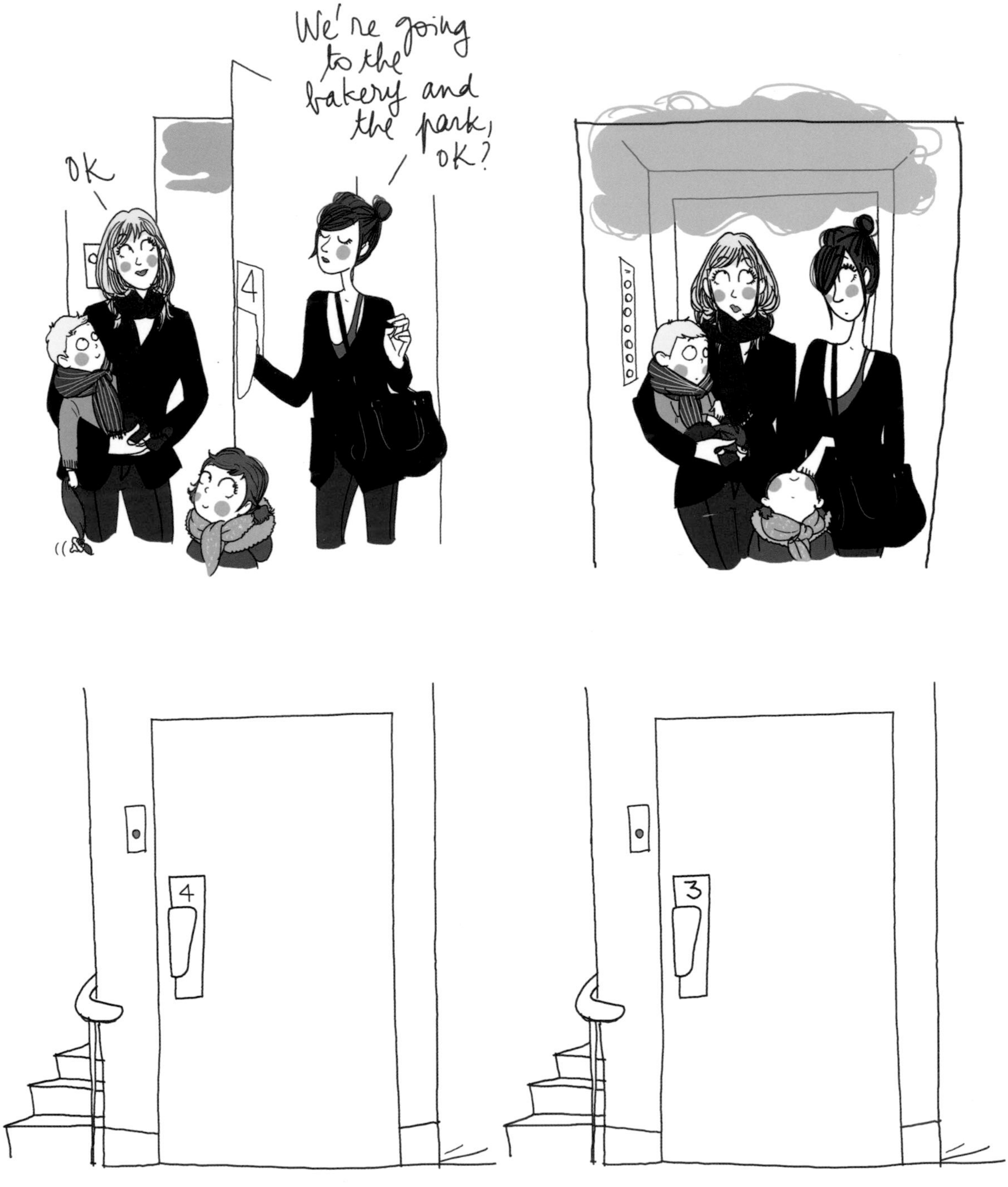
OK
We're going to the bakery and the park, OK?
4
4
3

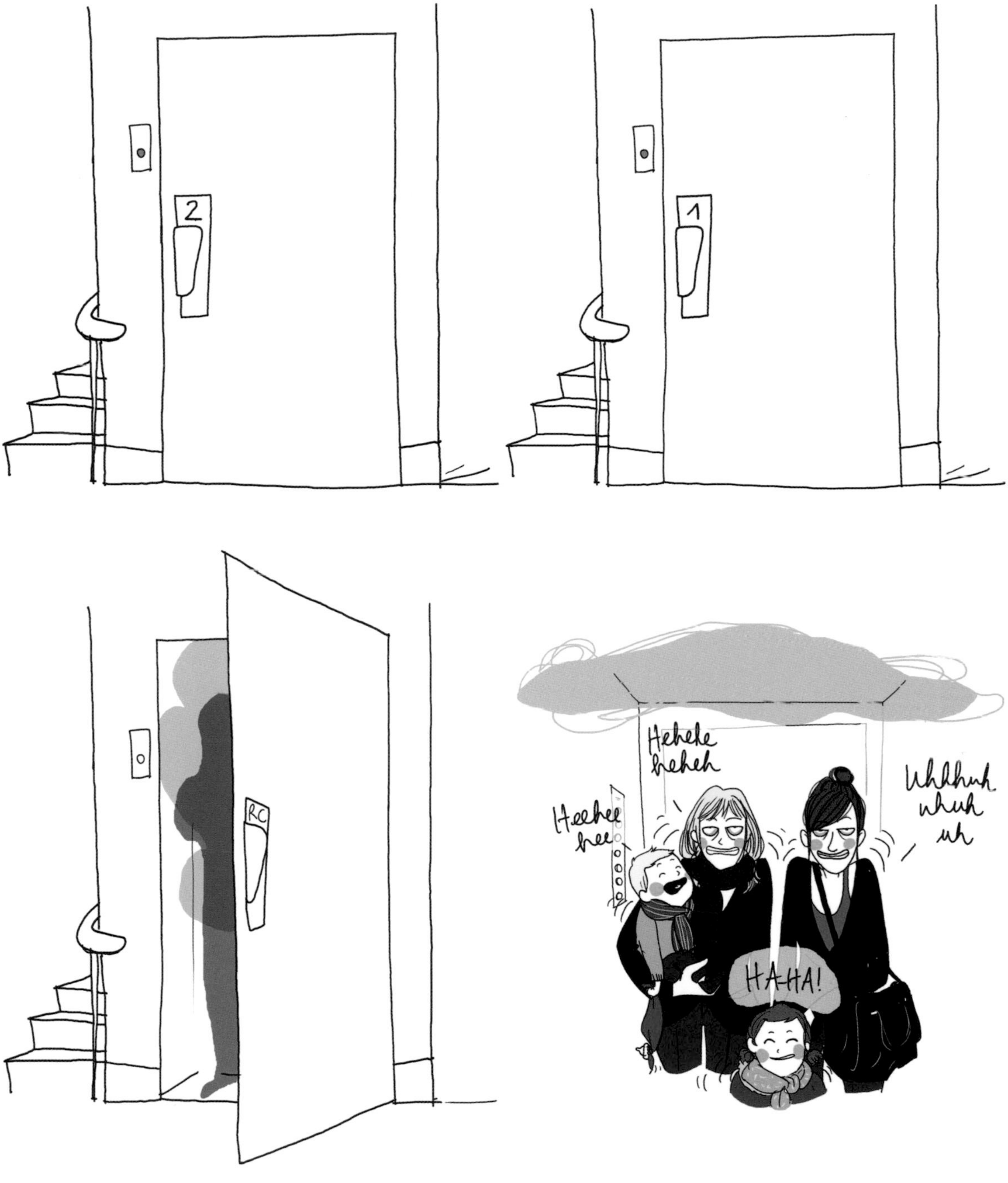
2
1
RC
Heehee hee
Hehehe heheh
Uhhhuh uhuh uh
HA-HA!

I'M PRETTY SURE I HAVE A NEIGHBOR WHO SMOKES POT.

There are tragedies in a girl's life

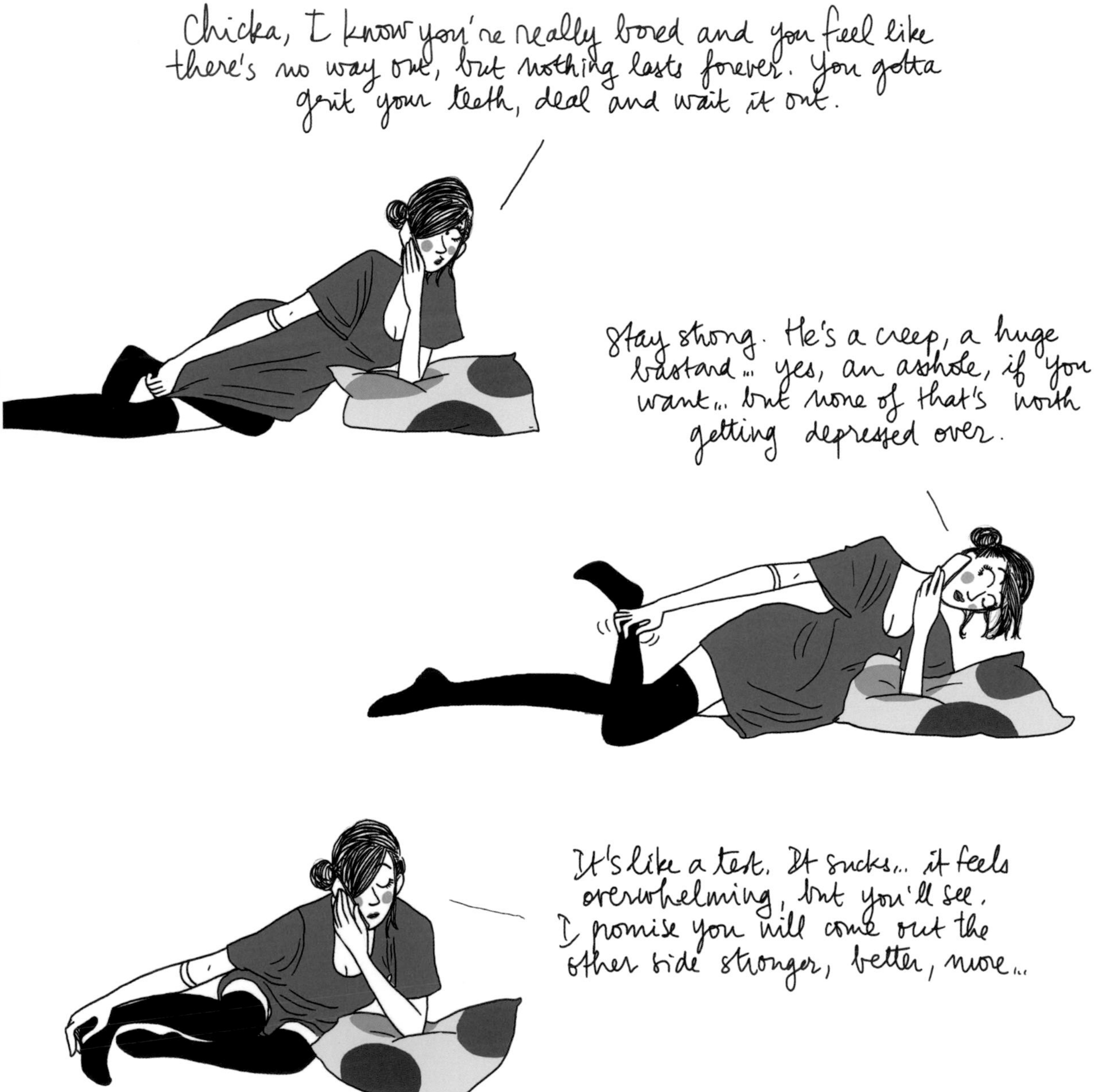
Chicka, I know you're really bored and you feel like there's no way out, but nothing lasts forever. You gotta grit your teeth, deal and wait it out.
Stay strong. He's a creep, a huge bastard... yes, an asshole, if you want... but none of that's worth getting depressed over.
It's like a test. It sucks... it feels overwhelming, but you'll see. I promise you will come out the other side stronger, better, more...

"...wait, when you said "that
asshole botched my highlights",
what kind did you have?
Blondish streaks or full-on platinum?

I'm a modern woman, I don't need anyone

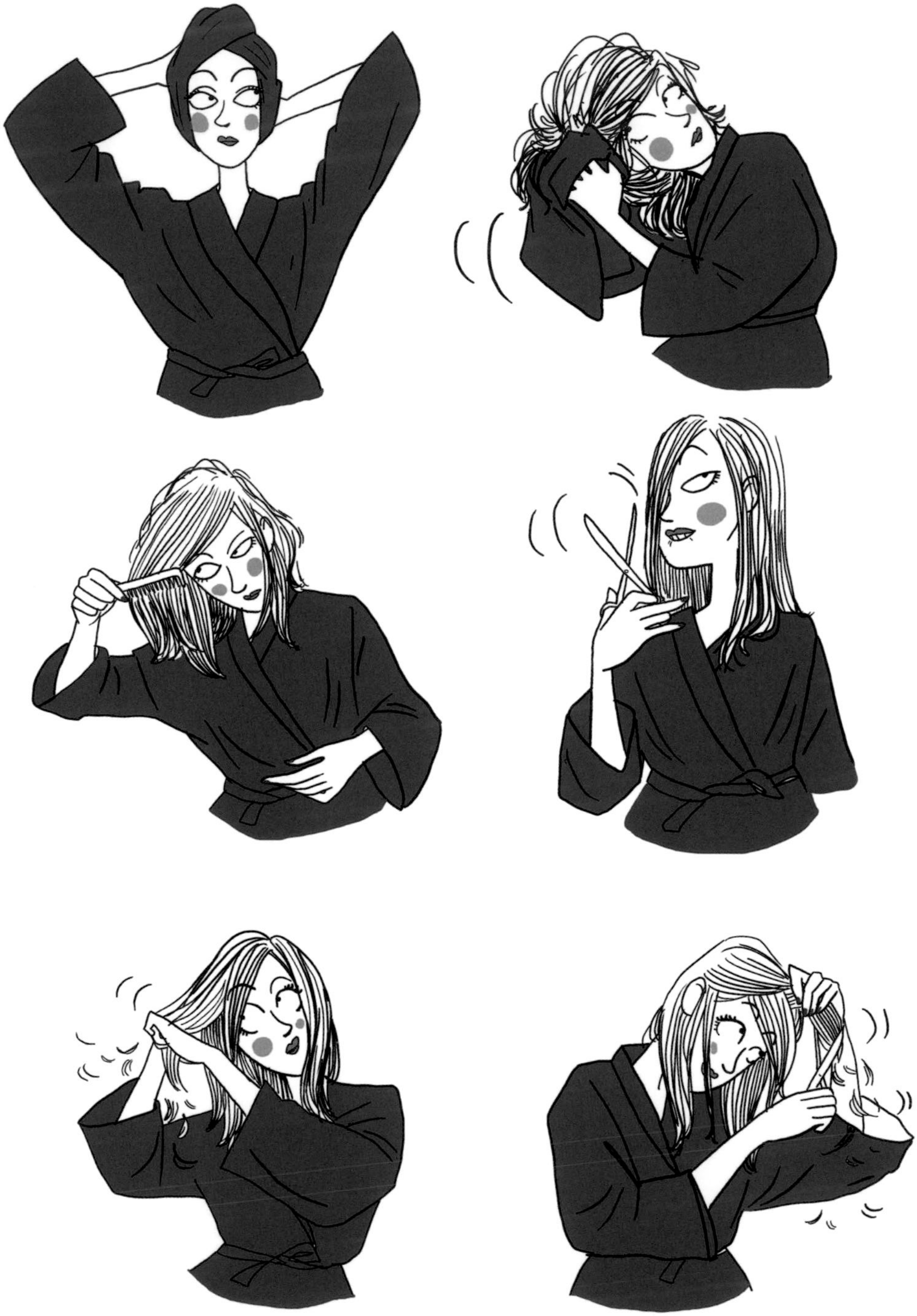

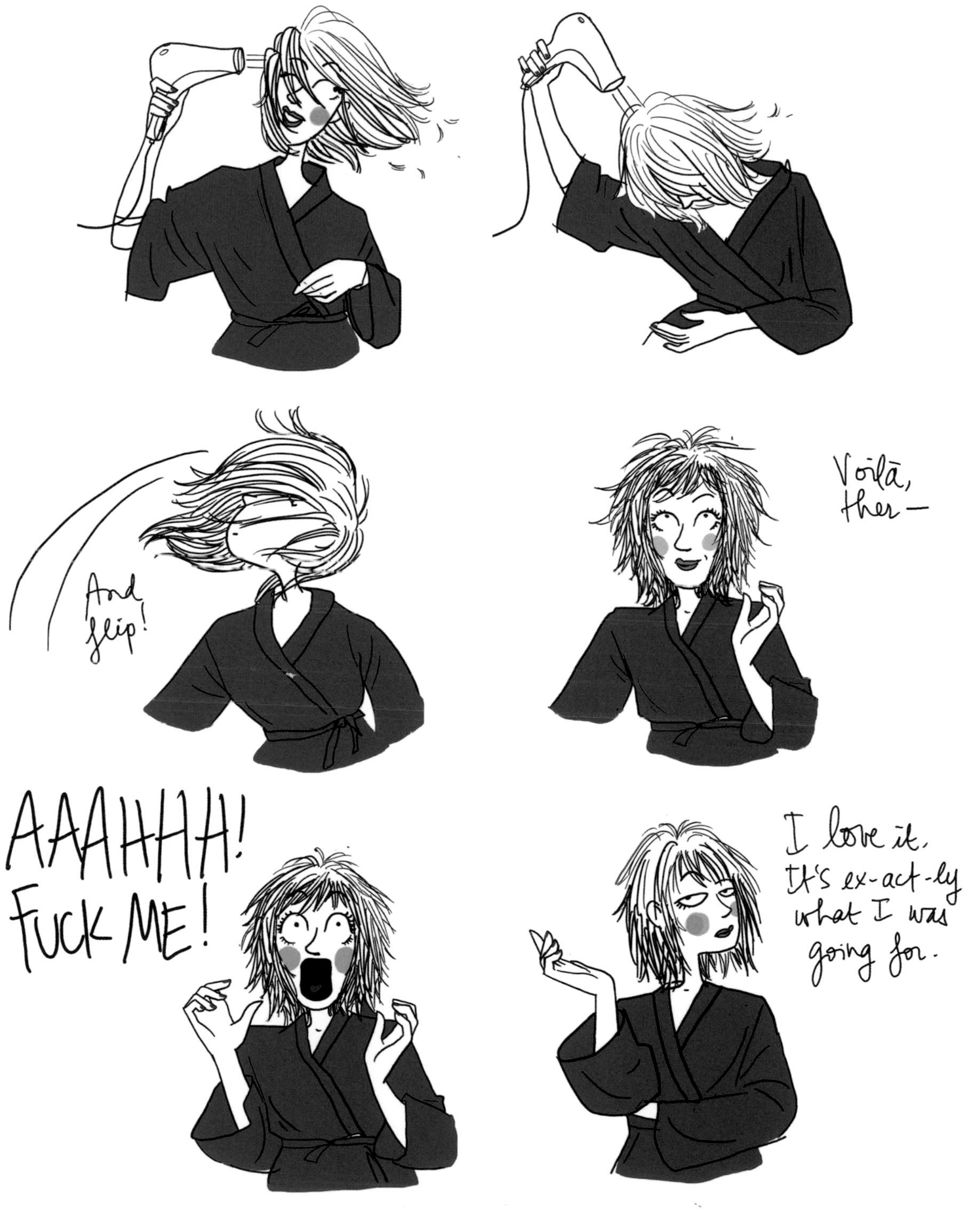
And flip!
Voilà, ther—
AAAHHH! FUCK ME!
I love it. It's ex-act-ly what I was going for.

Life is a struggle

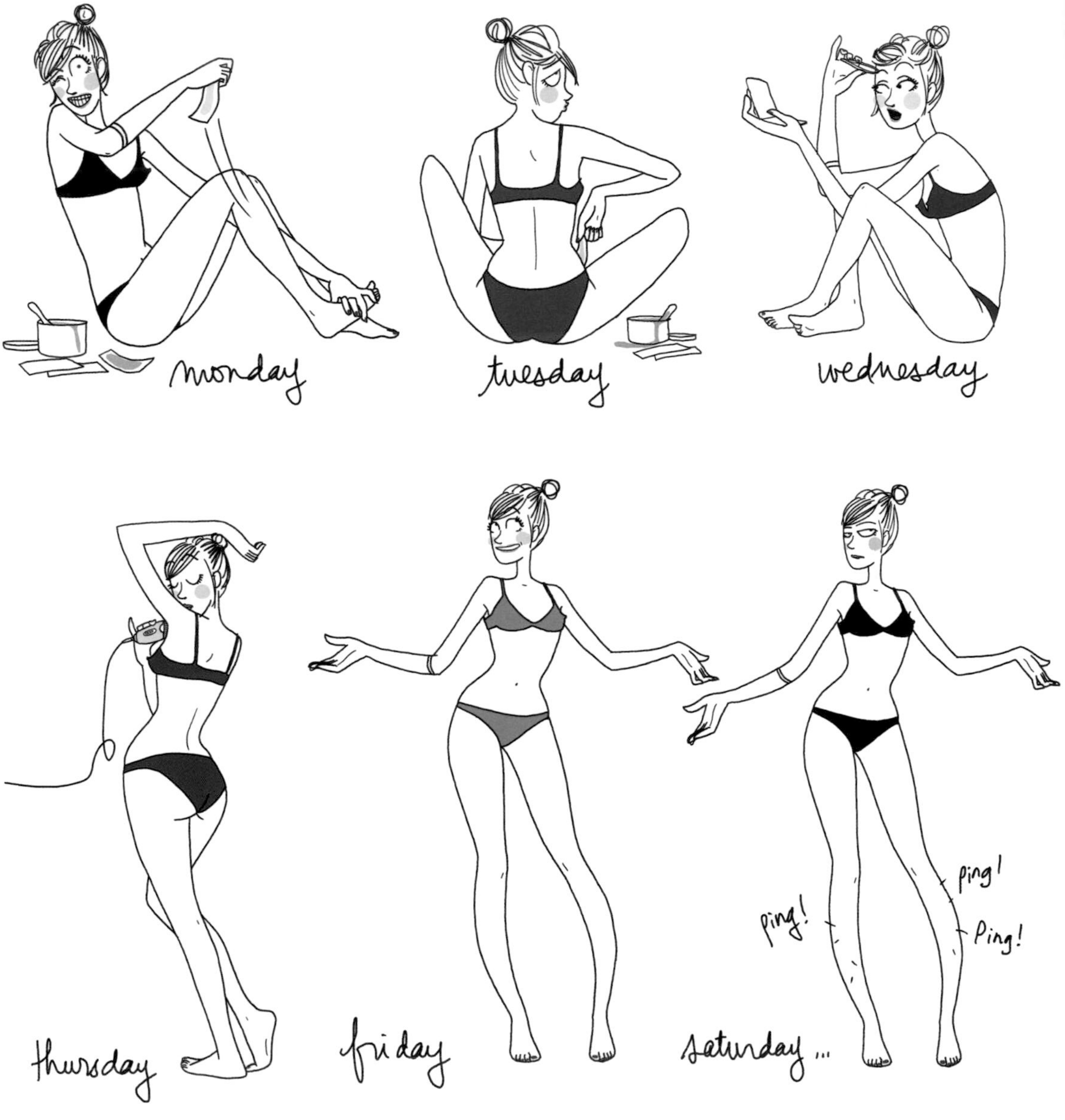
monday
tuesday
wednesday
thursday
friday
saturday...
ping!
ping!
Ping!

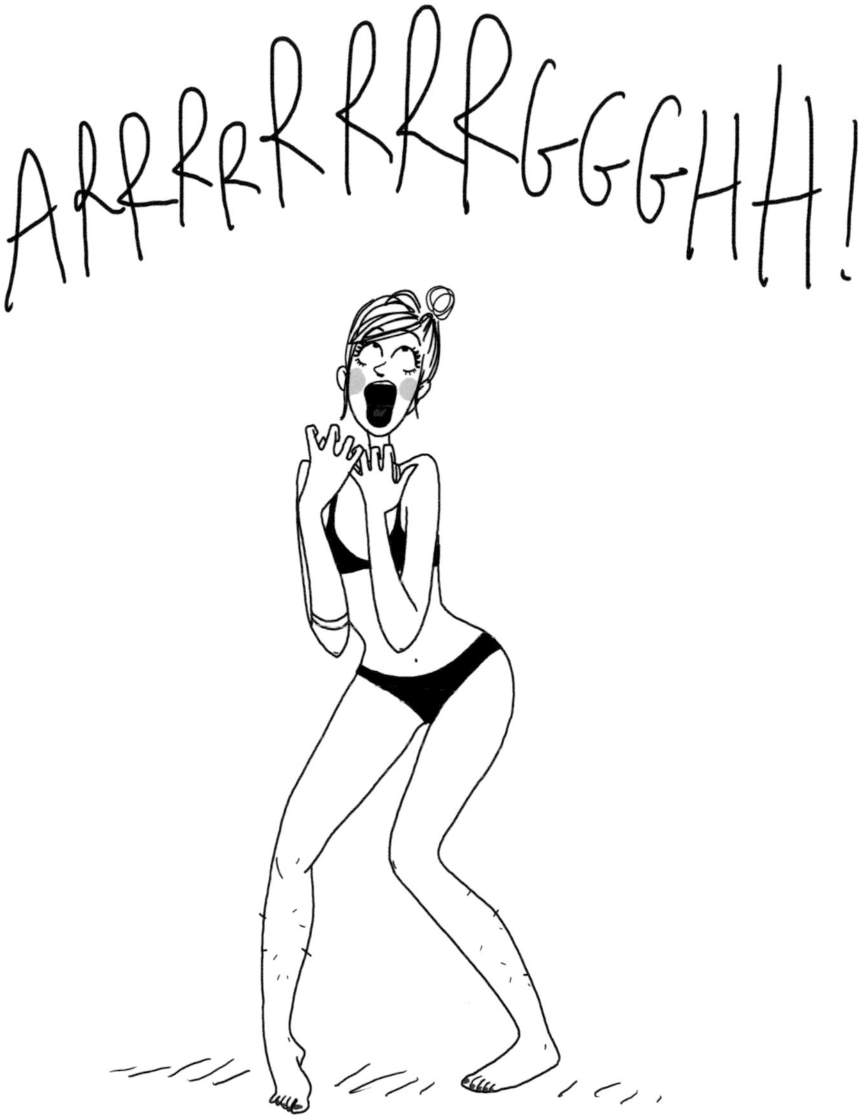
ARRRRRRRRGGGHH!

The monster

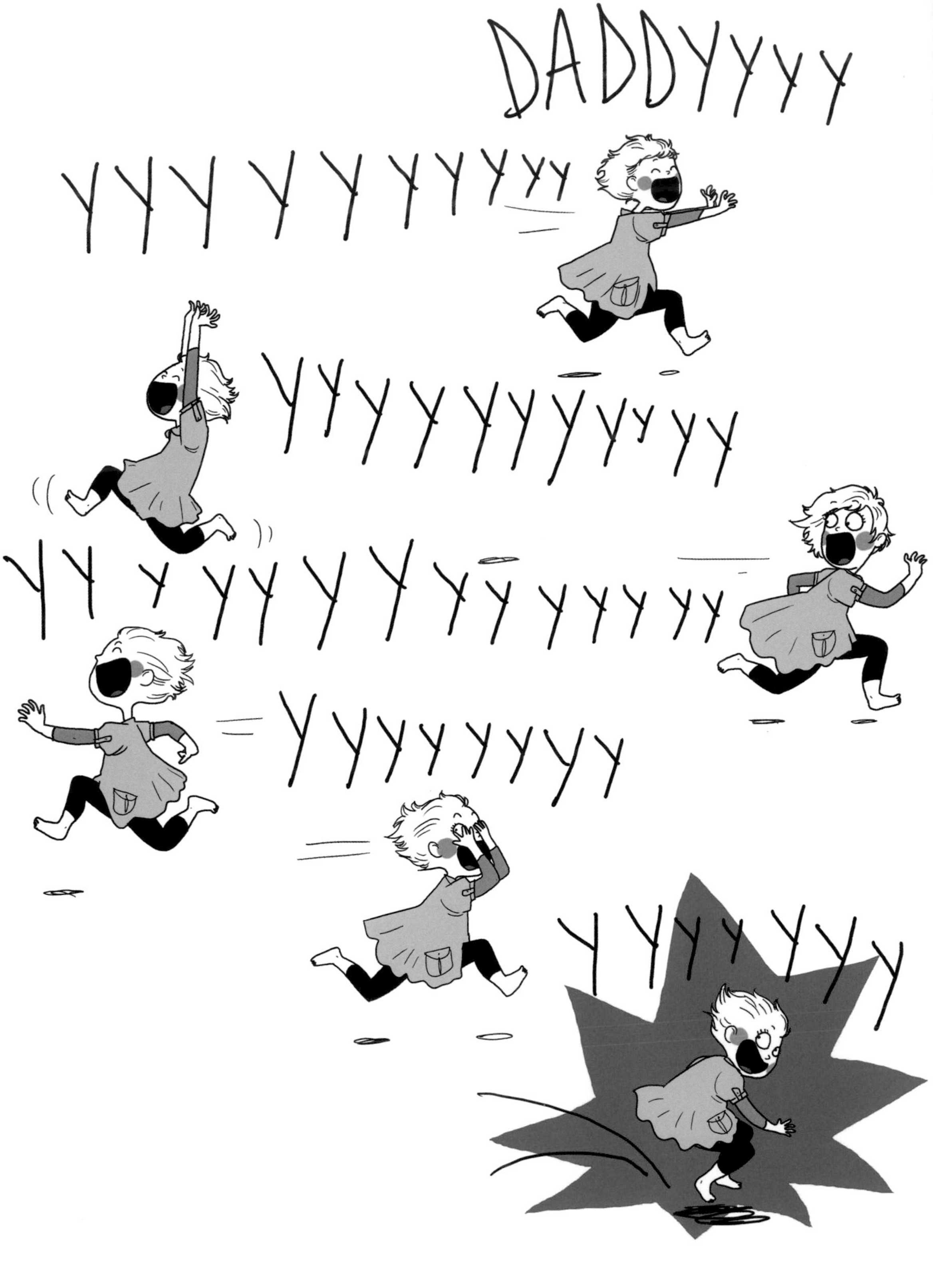

DADDYYYY
YYYYYYYYYY
YYYYYYYYYYY
YYYYYYYYYYYYYY
YYYYYYYY
YYYYYYY

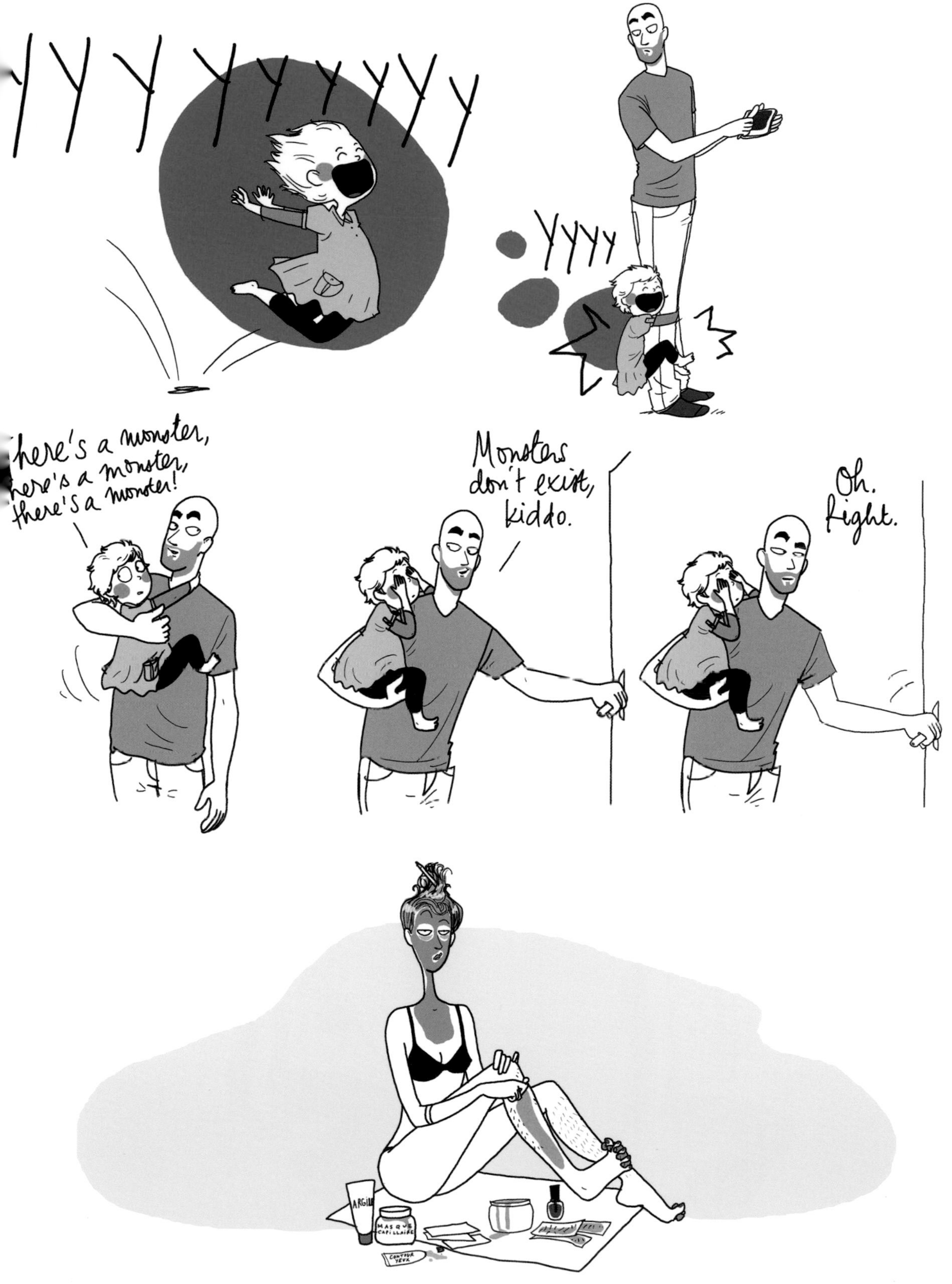
YYYYYYYYYY
YYYY
here's a monster, here's a monster, there's a monster!
Monsters don't exist, kiddo.
Oh. Right.
ARGILE
MASQUE CAPILLAIRE
CONTOUR YEUX

Chronic fatigue

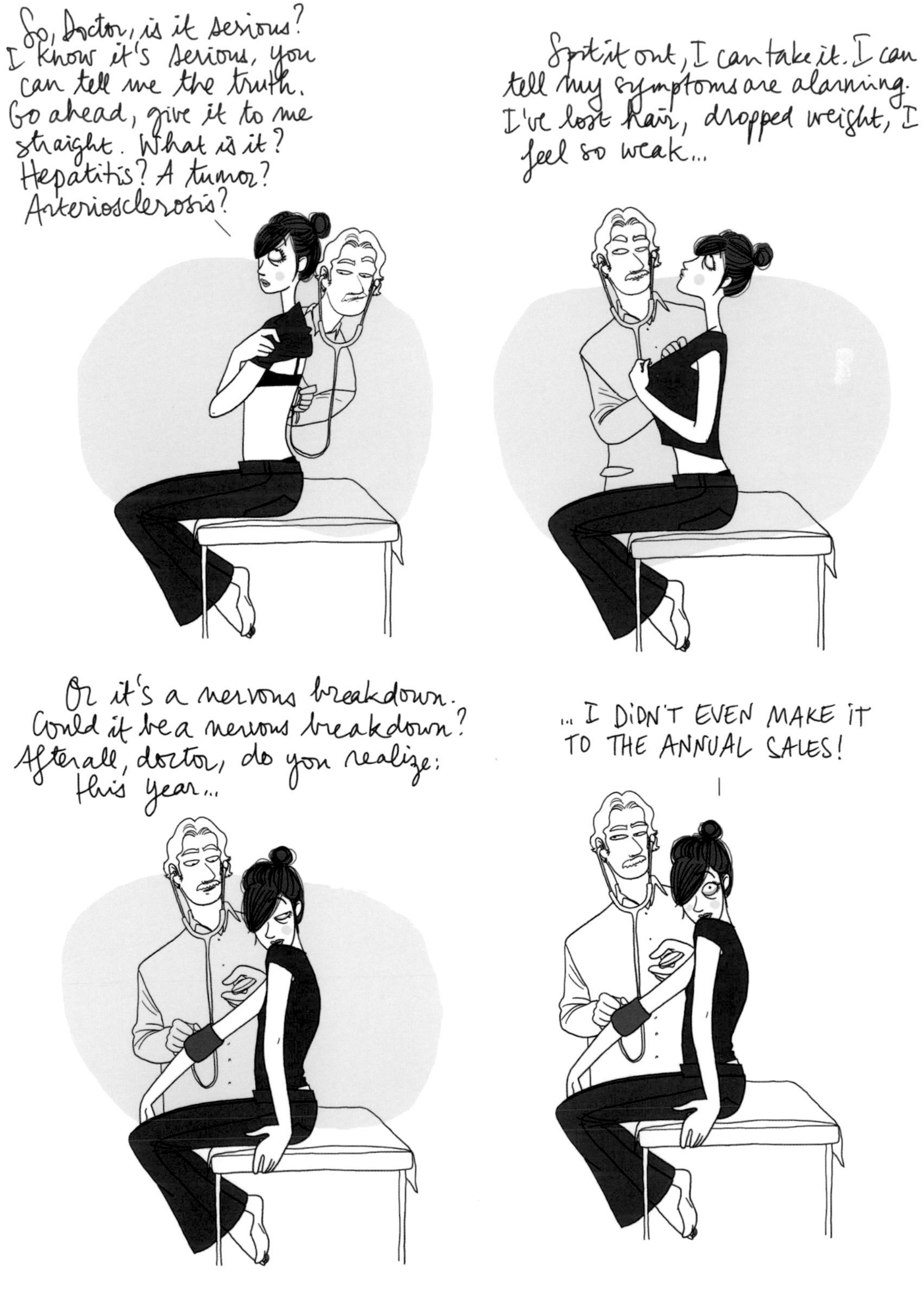
So, Doctor, is it serious? I know it's serious, you can tell me the truth. Go ahead, give it to me straight. What is it? Hepatitis? A tumor? Arteriosclerosis?
Spit it out, I can take it. I can tell my symptoms are alarming. I've lost hair, dropped weight, I feel so weak...
Or it's a nervous breakdown. Could it be a nervous breakdown? After all, doctor, do you realize: this year...
... I DIDN'T EVEN MAKE IT TO THE ANNUAL SALES!

My phaaaaaaarmacist!

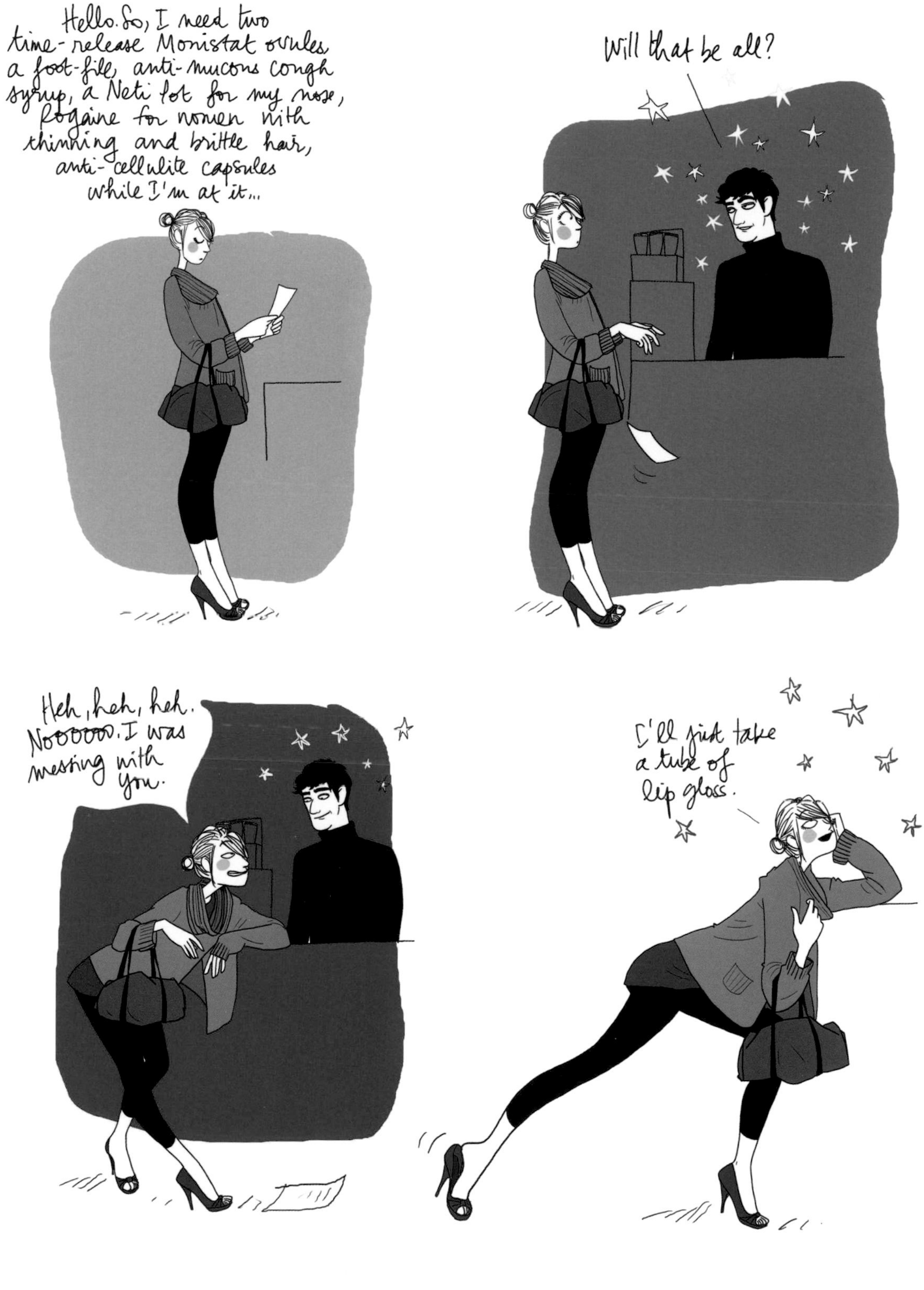
Hello. So, I need two time-release Monistat ovules, a foot-file, anti-mucous cough syrup, a Neti Pot for my nose, Rogaine for women with thinning and brittle hair, anti-cellulite capsules while I'm at it...
Will that be all?
Heh, heh, heh. Noooooo. I was messing with you.
I'll just take a tube of lip gloss.

Long live the sun!

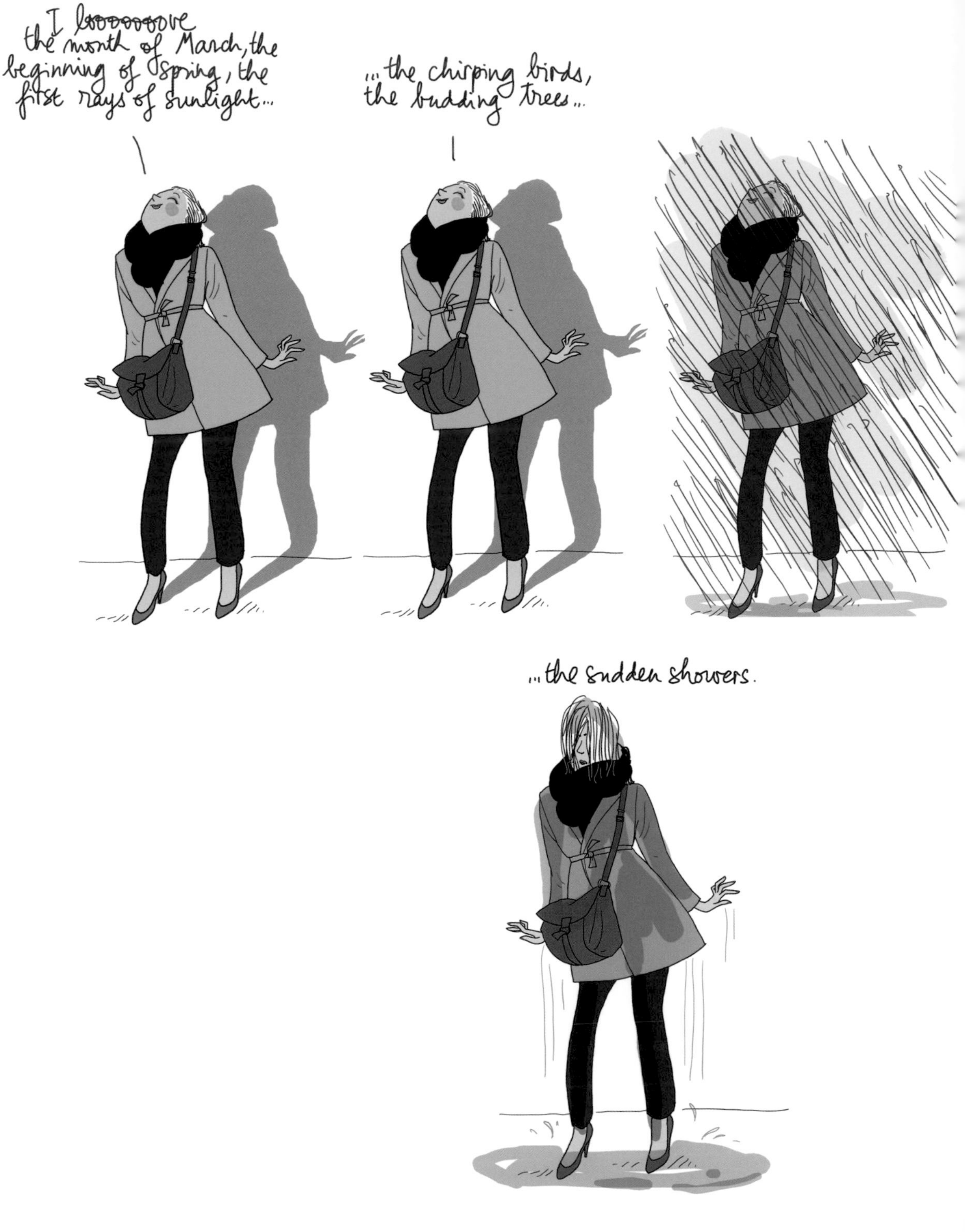

I looooooove the month of March, the beginning of spring, the first rays of sunlight...
... the chirping birds, the budding trees...
... the sudden showers.

Girl vacations

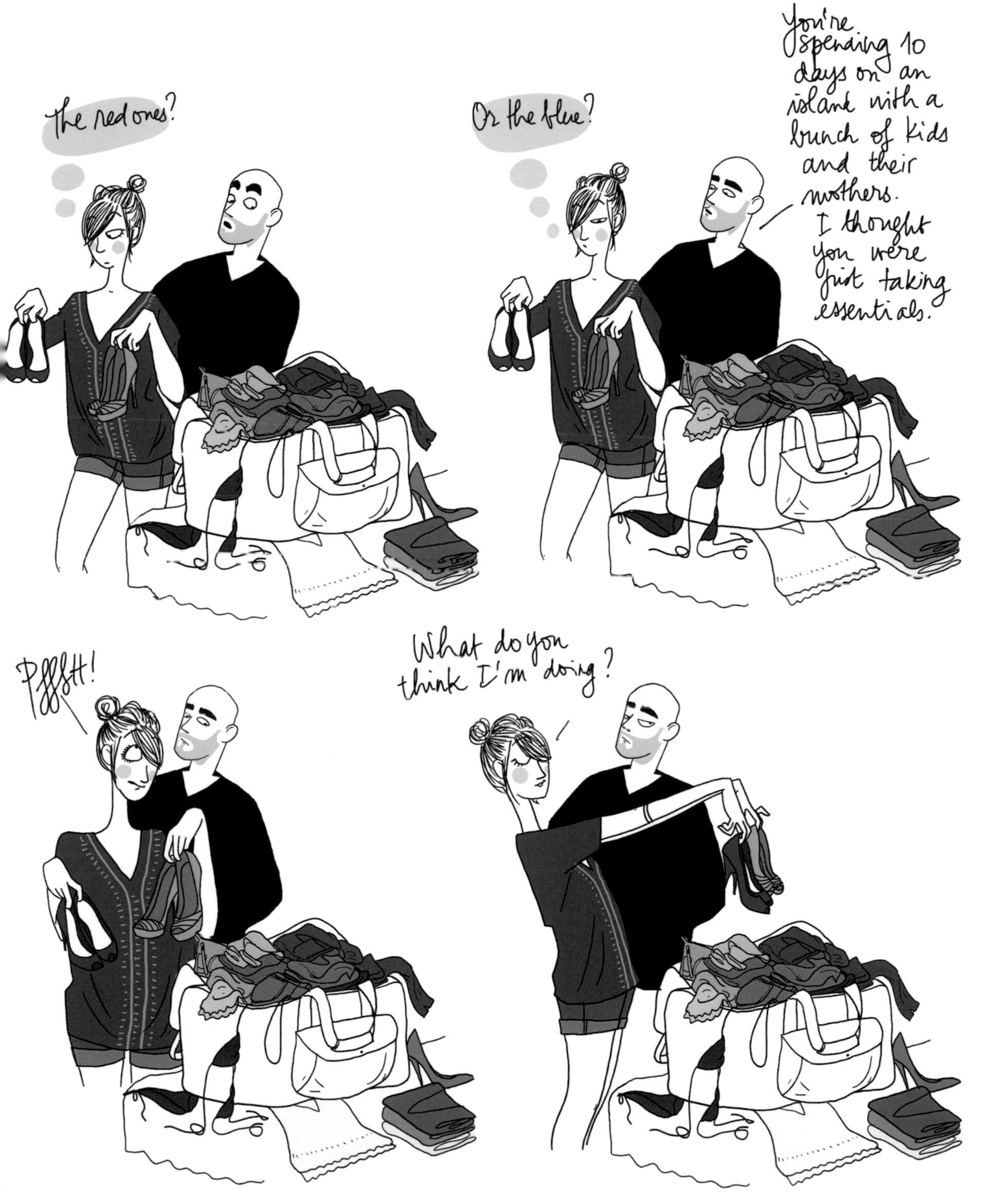
The red ones?
Or the blue?
You're spending 10 days on an island with a bunch of kids and their mothers. I thought you were just taking essentials.
PFFSH!
What do you think I'm doing?

A Corsican dream

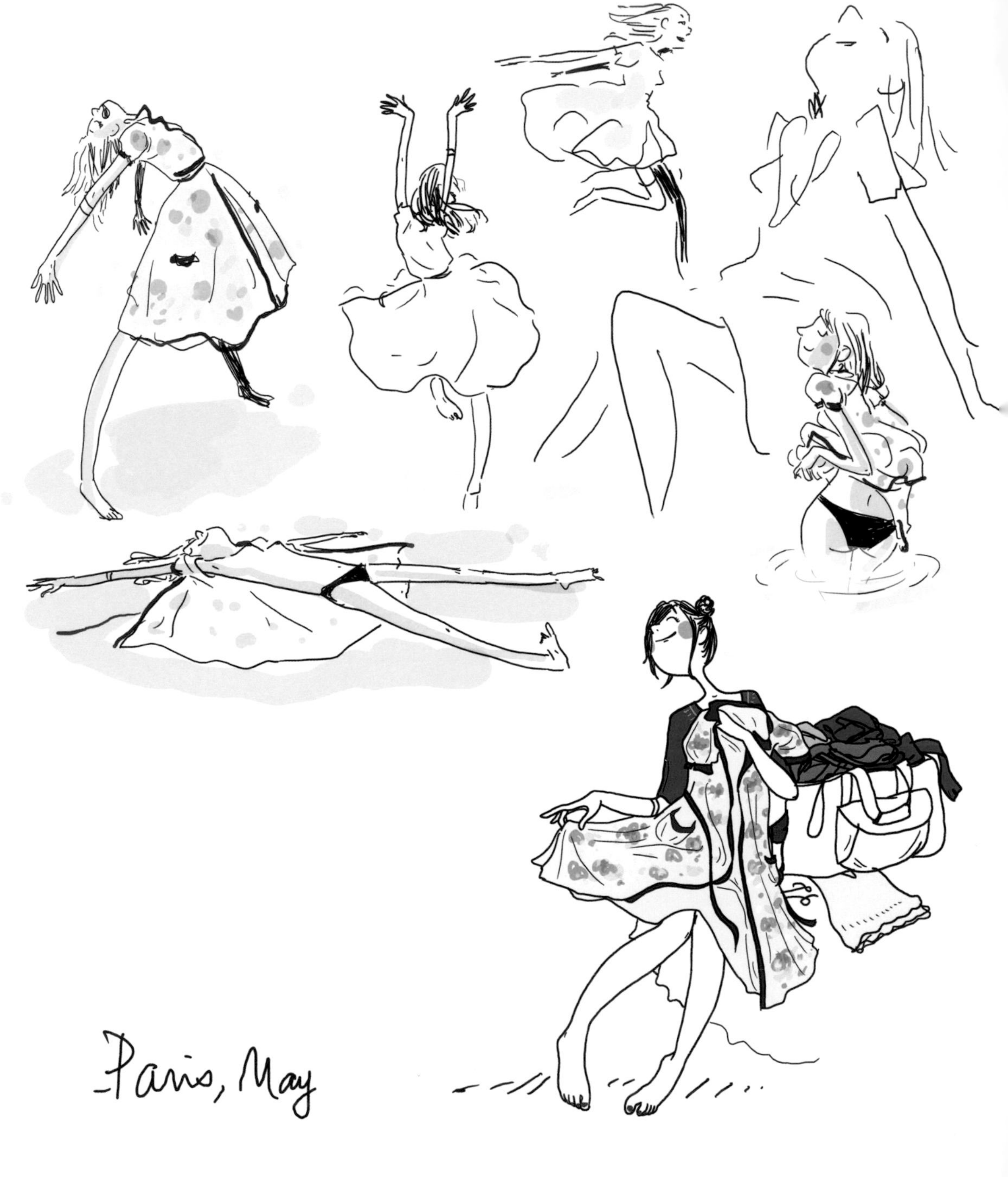

Paris, May

A Corsican double-cross

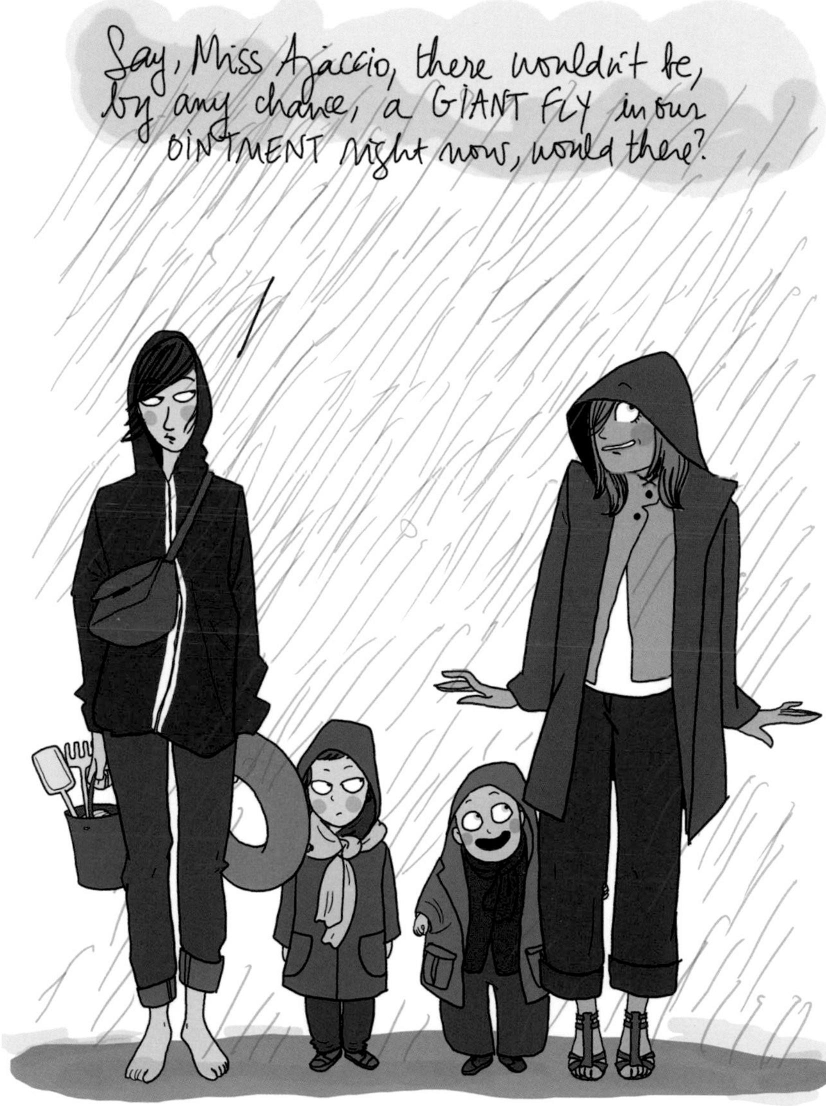

Say, Miss Ajaccio, there wouldn't be, by any chance, a GIANT FLY in our OINTMENT right now, would there?
!

- Ajaccio, May

I would make a terrible Robinson Crusoe

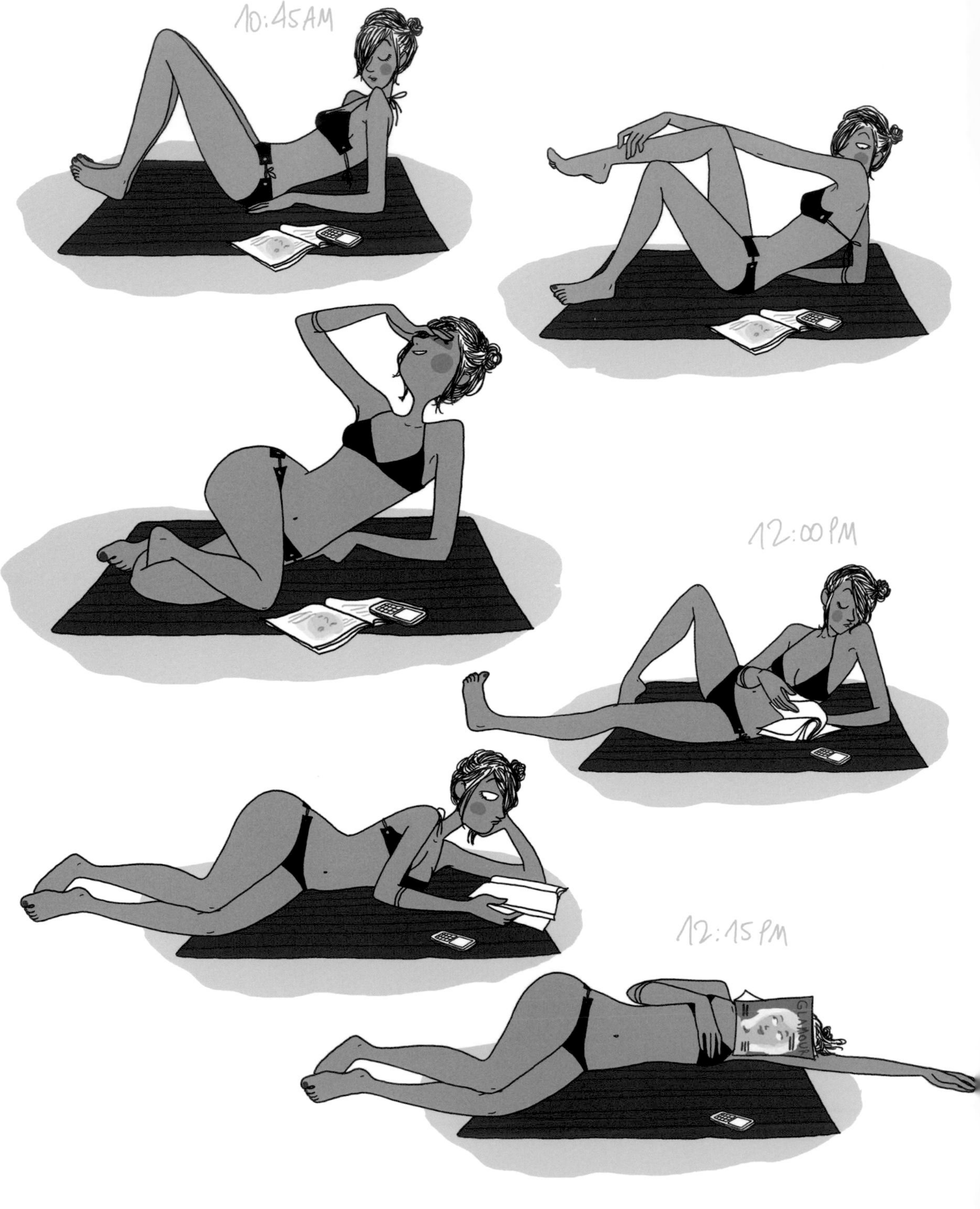
10:45AM
12:00PM
12:15PM
GLAMOUR

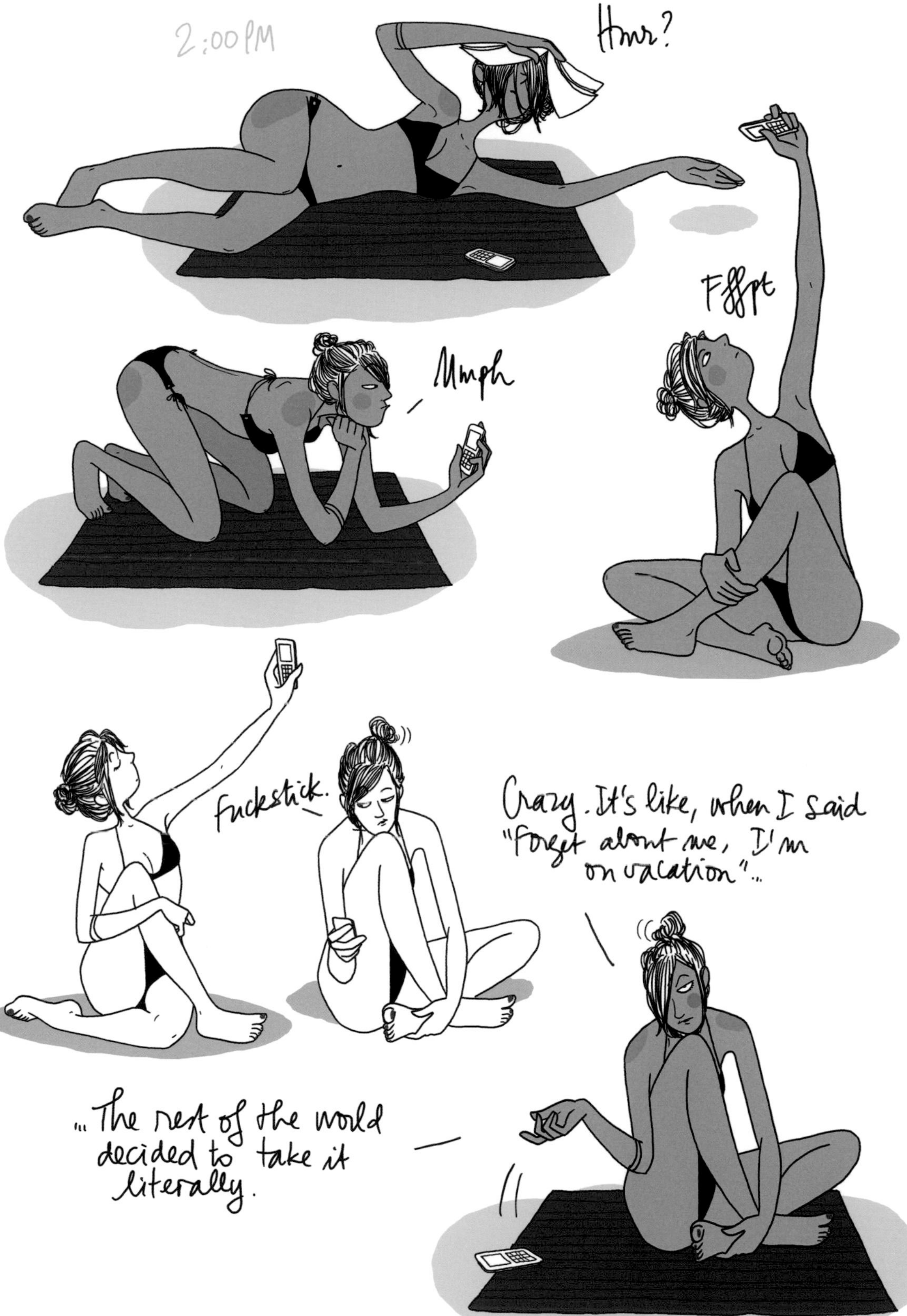
2:00PM
Hmr?
Mmph
Fffpt
Fuckstick.
Crazy. It's like, when I said "Forget about me, I'm on vacation"...
... The rest of the world decided to take it literally.

That's quite a gust, my good lady!

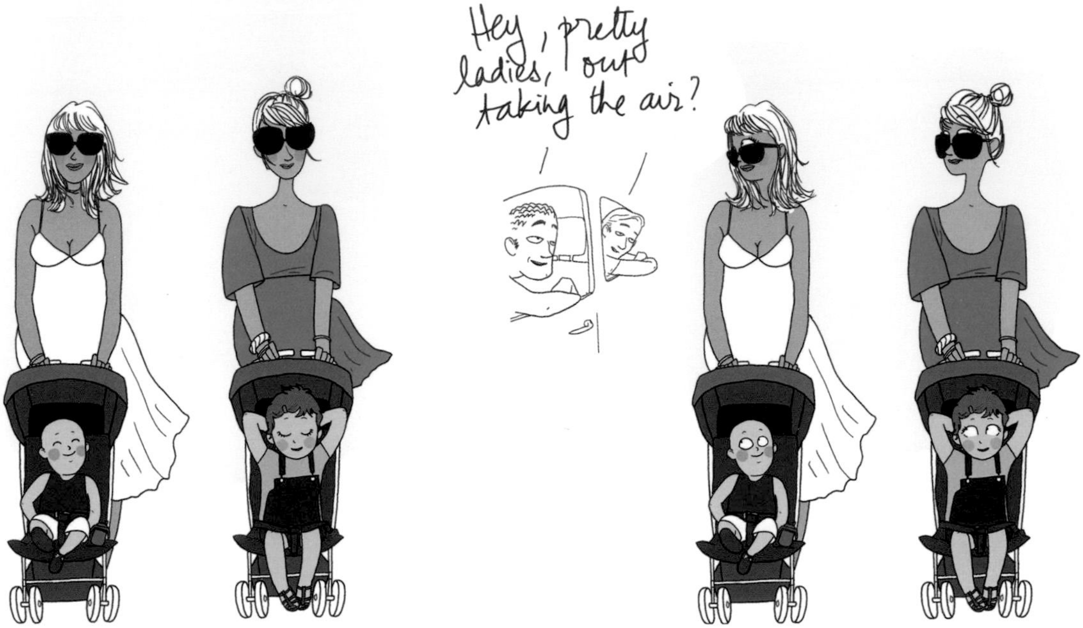
Hey, pretty ladies, out taking the air?

Yeah, kidlets, isn't it great to have super-hot mums full of grace and sophistication?

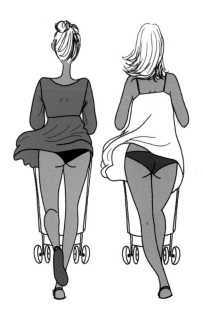

Ten man-free days is really great!

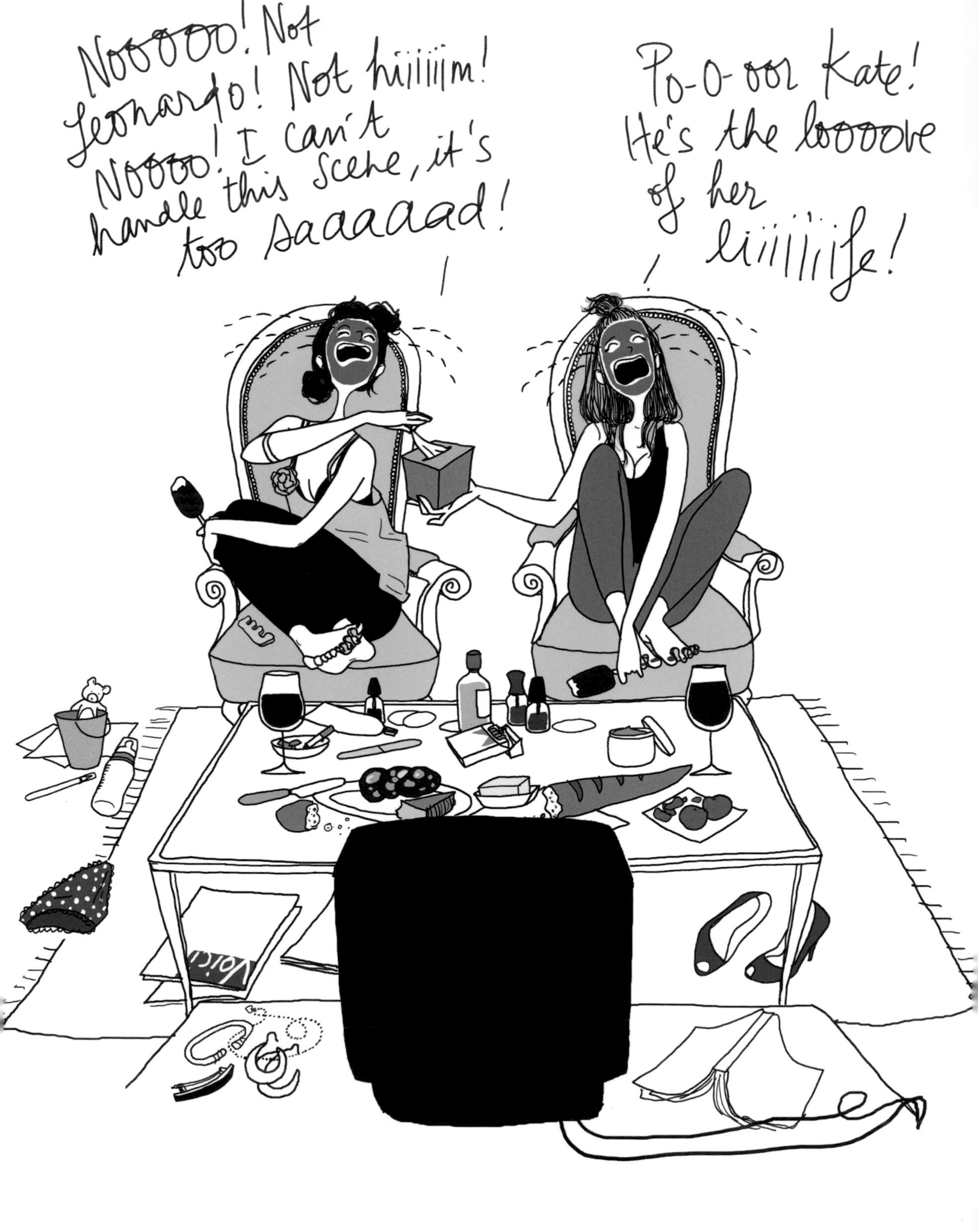
Nooooo! Not Leonardo! Not hiiiiiim! Noooo! I can't handle this scene, it's too saaaaad!
Po-o-oor Kate! He's the looooove of her liiiiiife!

Ten man-free days is really too long

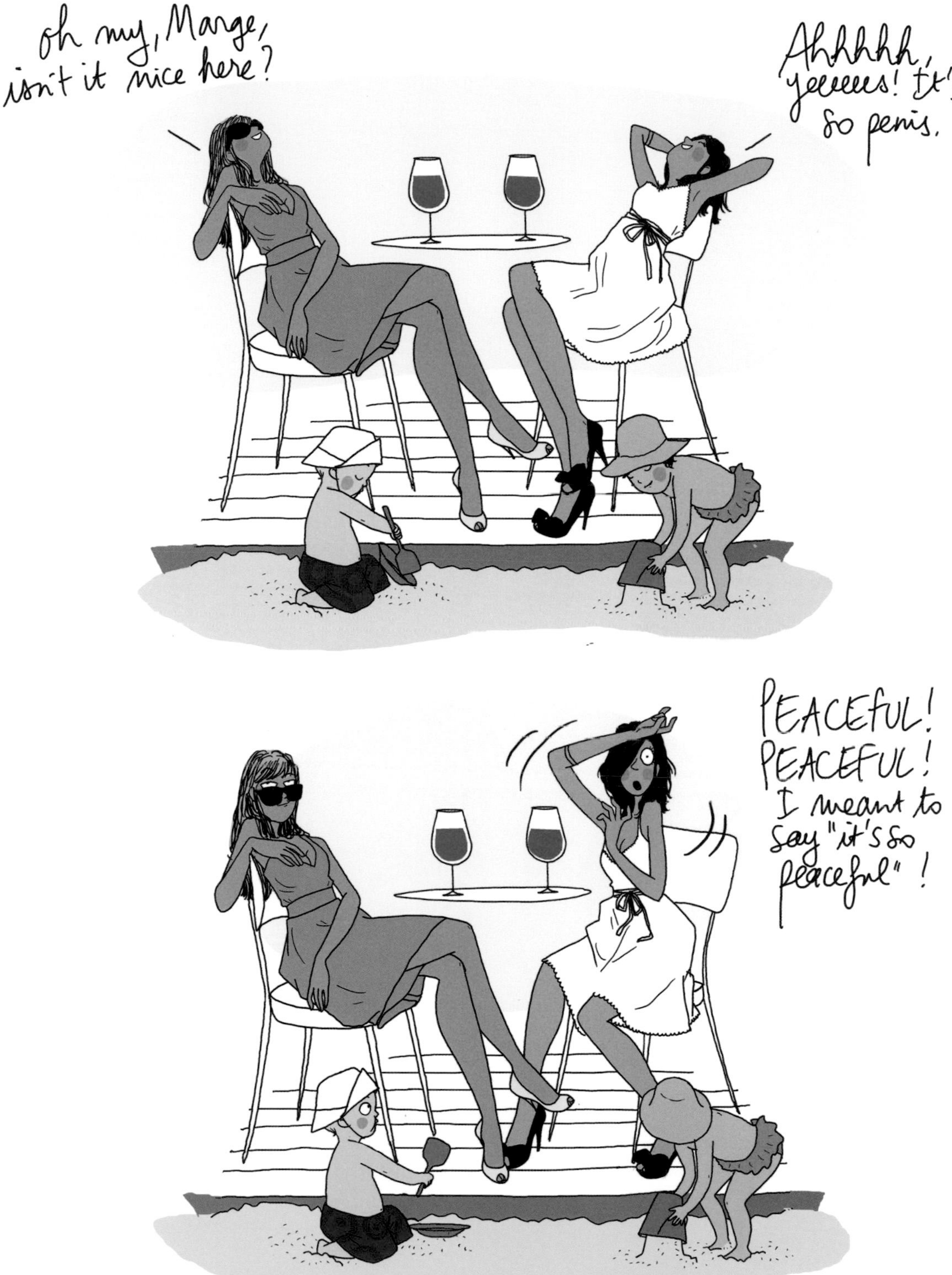

Oh my, Marge, isn't it nice here?
Ahhhhh, yeeeees! It's so penis.
PEACEFUL! PEACEFUL! I meant to say "it's so peaceful"!

By the end of a vacation, fashion victims often
let themselves go a little...

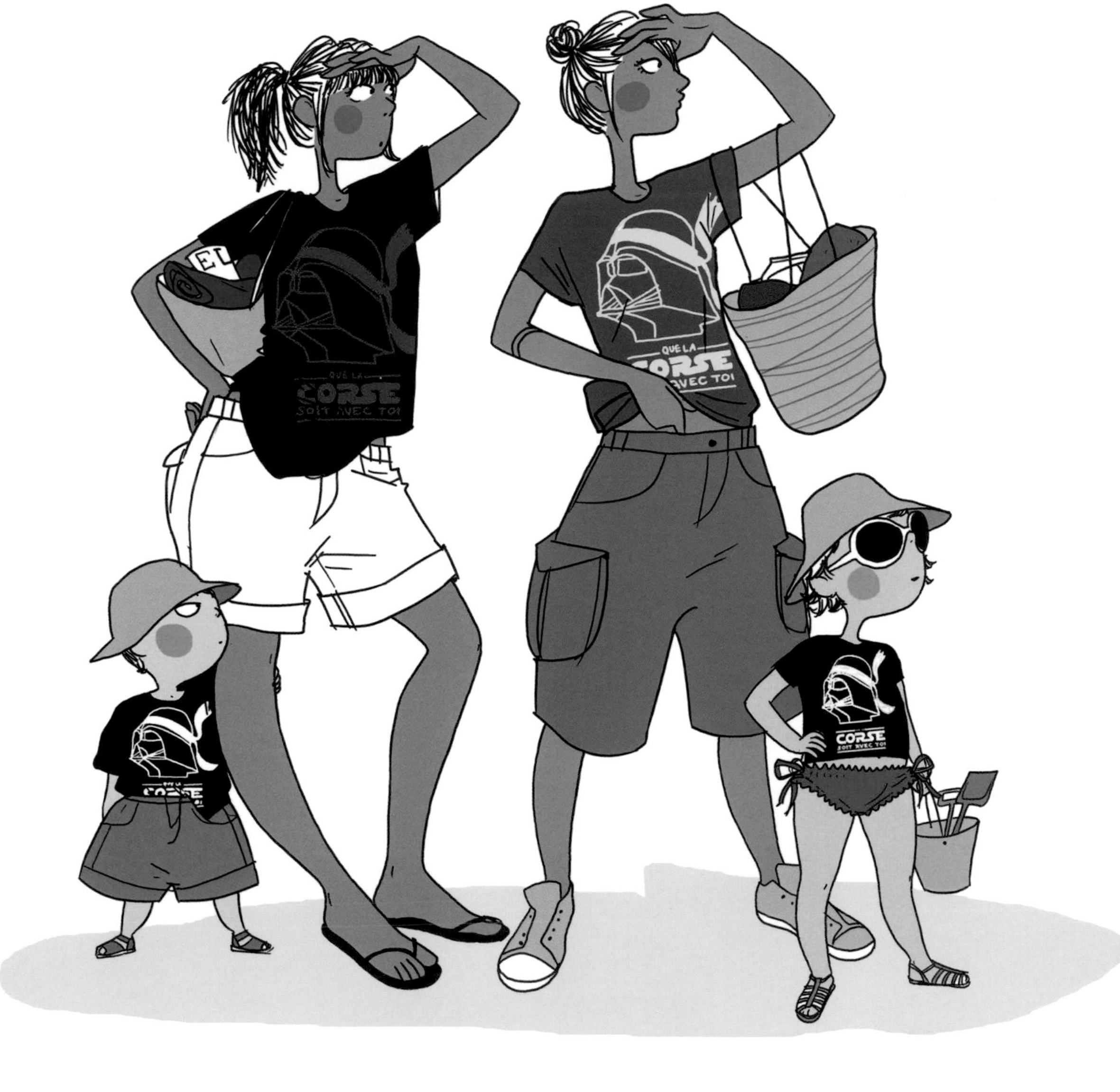
QUE LA
CORSE
SOIT AVEC TOI

I really do hate coming back from vacation

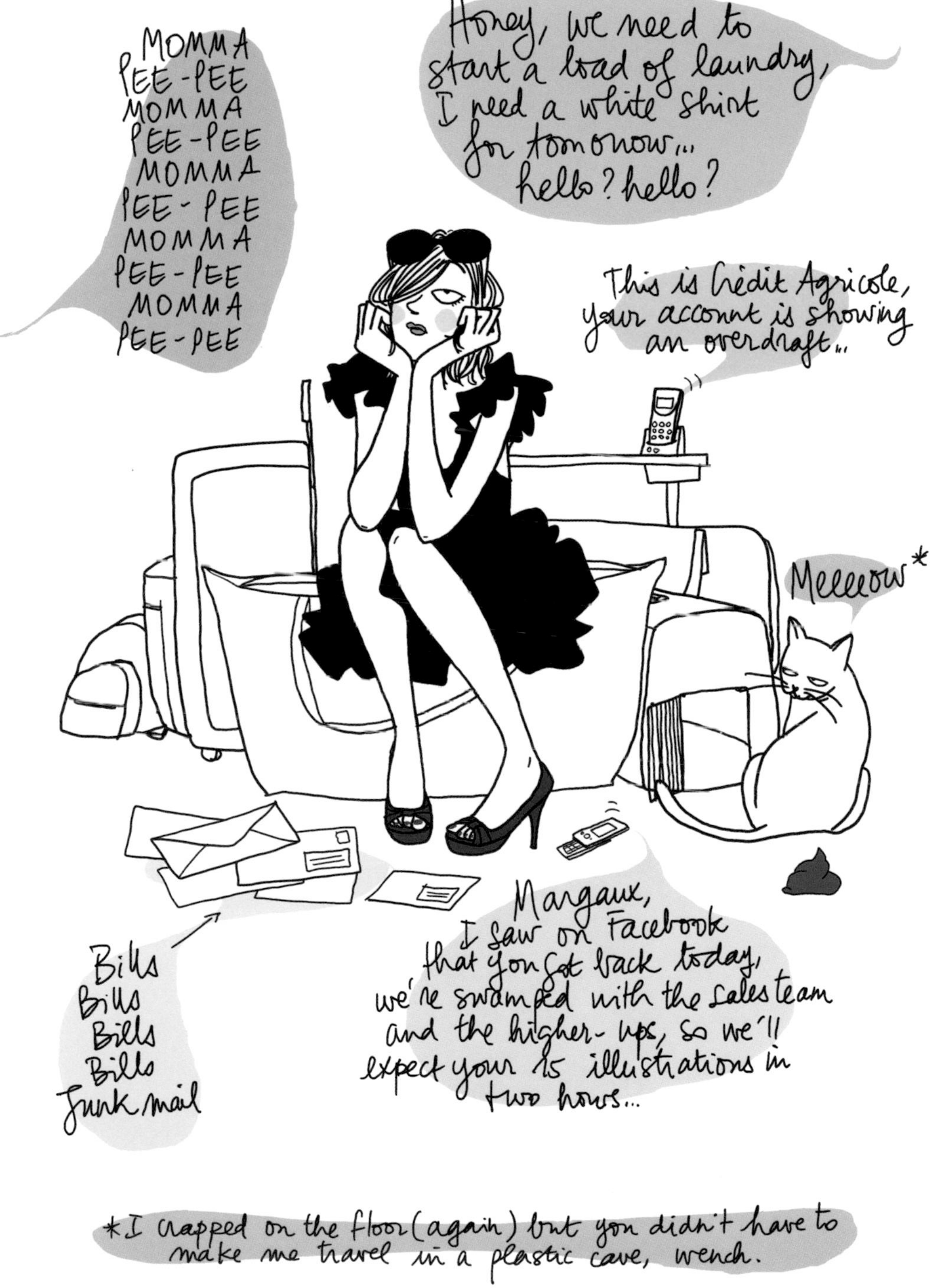
MOMMA PEE-PEE MOMMA PEE-PEE MOMMA PEE-PEE MOMMA PEE-PEE MOMMA PEE-PEE
Honey, we need to start a load of laundry, I need a white shirt for tomorrow... hello? hello?
This is Crédit Agricole, your account is showing an overdraft...
Meeeeow*
Bills Bills Bills Bills Junk mail
Margaux, I saw on Facebook that you got back today, we're swamped with the sales team and the higher-ups, so we'll expect your 15 illustrations in two hours...
*I crapped on the floor (again) but you didn't have to make me travel in a plastic cave, wench.

This guy served in the military? Noob

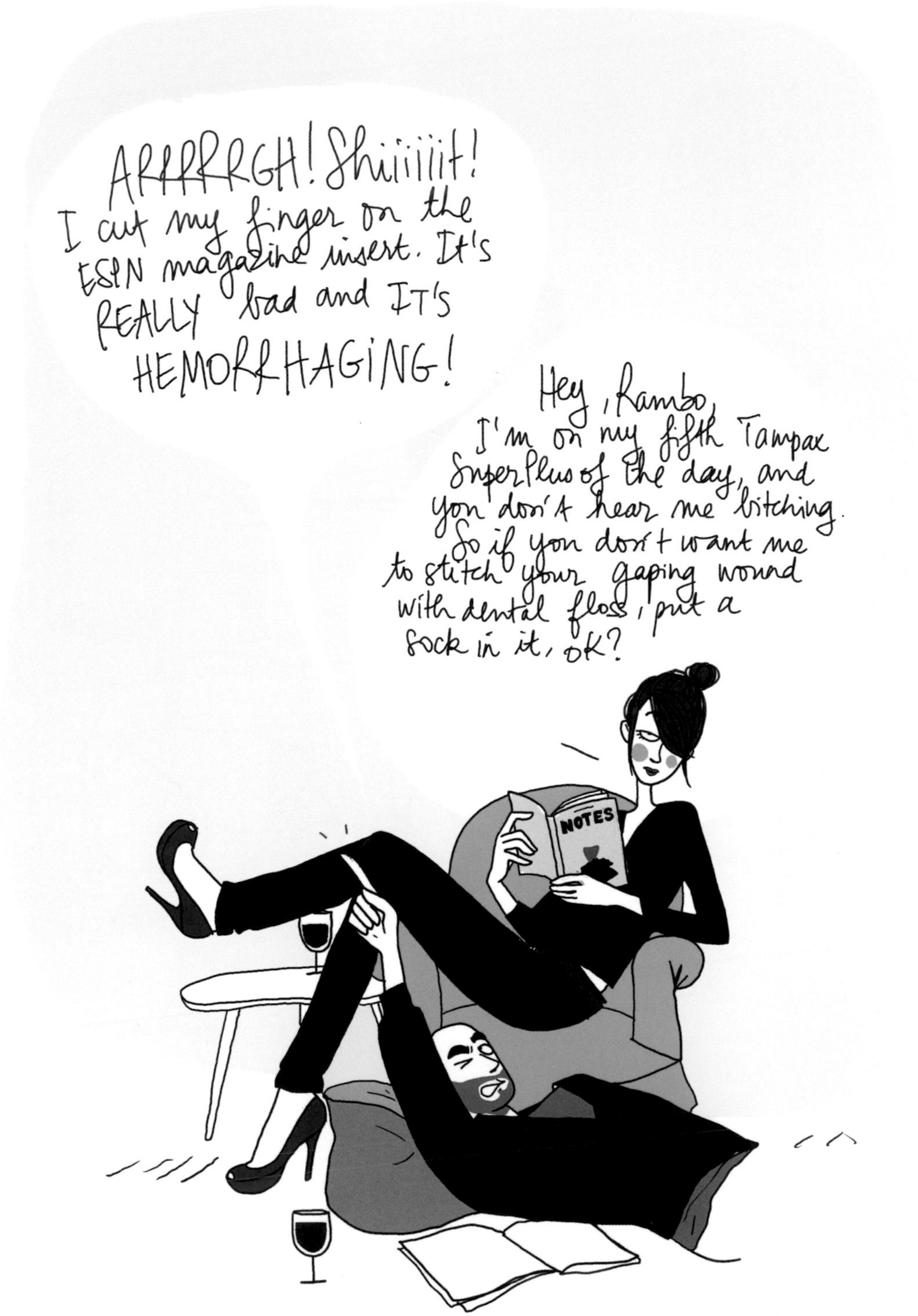
ARRRRRGH! Shiiiiiit!
I cut my finger on the ESPN magazine insert. It's REALLY bad and IT'S HEMORRHAGING!
Hey, Rambo, I'm on my fifth Tampax SuperPlus of the day, and you don't hear me bitching. So if you don't want me to stitch your gaping wound with dental floss, put a sock in it, ok?
NOTES

Ahhh… hormones

Everything's cool, I'm just on my period.

Hair in repose

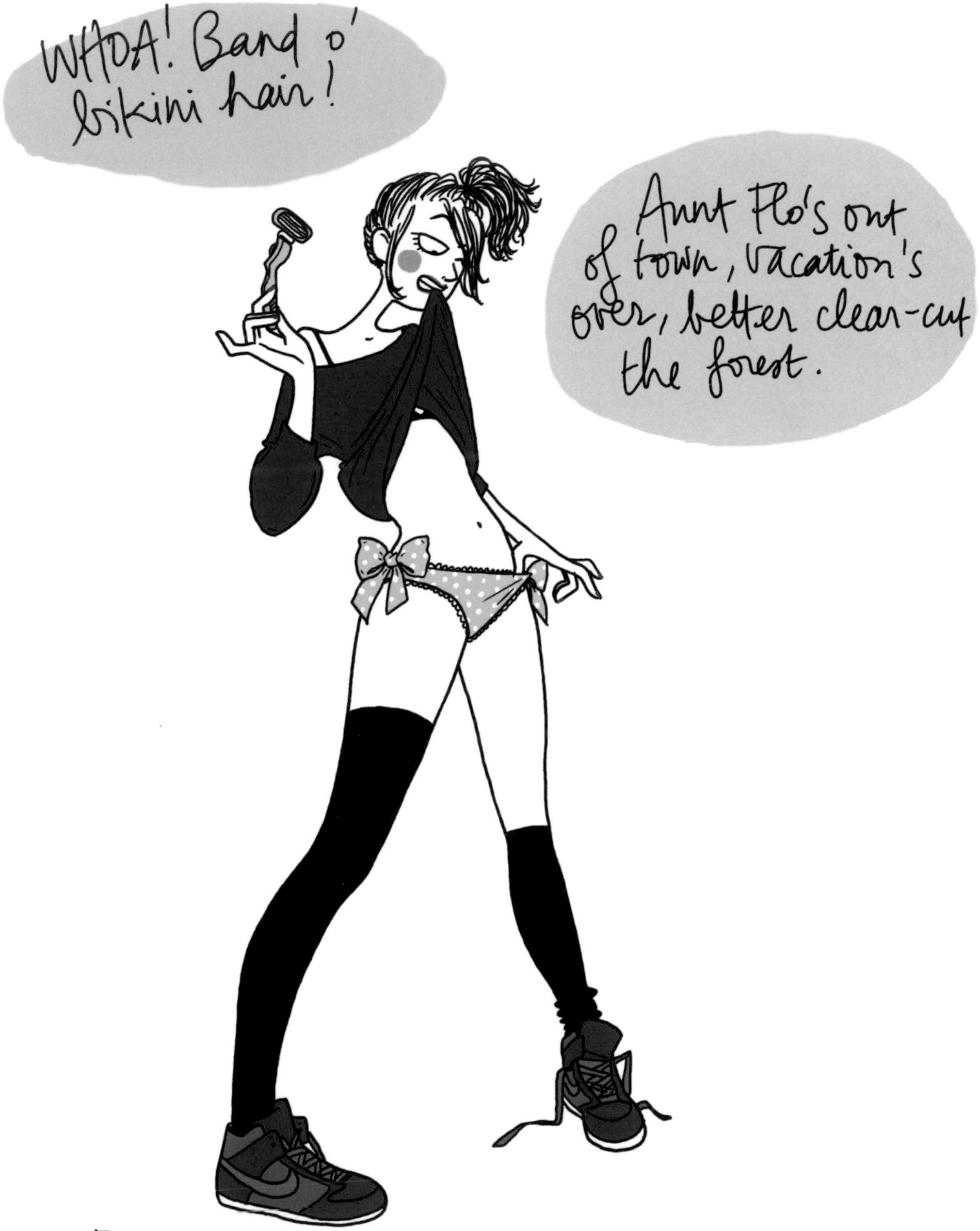
WHOA! Band o' bikini hair!
Aunt Flo's out of town, vacation's over, better clear-cut the forest.

I LIKE TO LET MY PUBIC HAIR HAVE A BREAK DURING MY PERIOD WEEK.

A moment of frankness

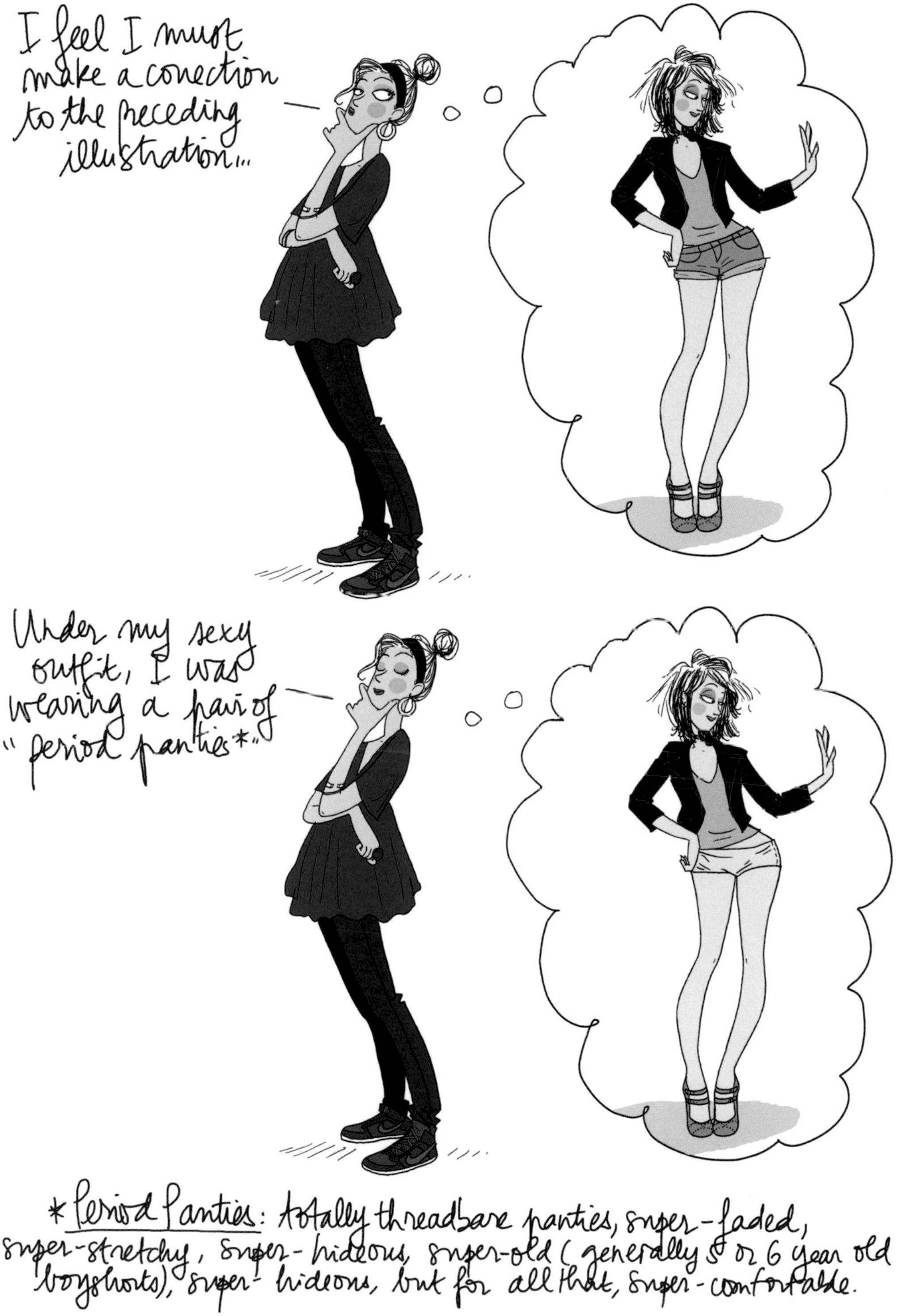
I feel I must make a conection to the preceding illustration...
Under my sexy outfit, I was wearing a pair of "period panties*."

*Period Panties: totally threadbare panties, super-faded, super-stretchy, super-hideous, super-old (generally 5 or 6 year old boyshorts), super-hideous, but for all that, super-comfortable.

A good soul

I AM GENERALLY FULL OF LOVE AND COMPASSION FOR MOST LIVING ORGANISMS.

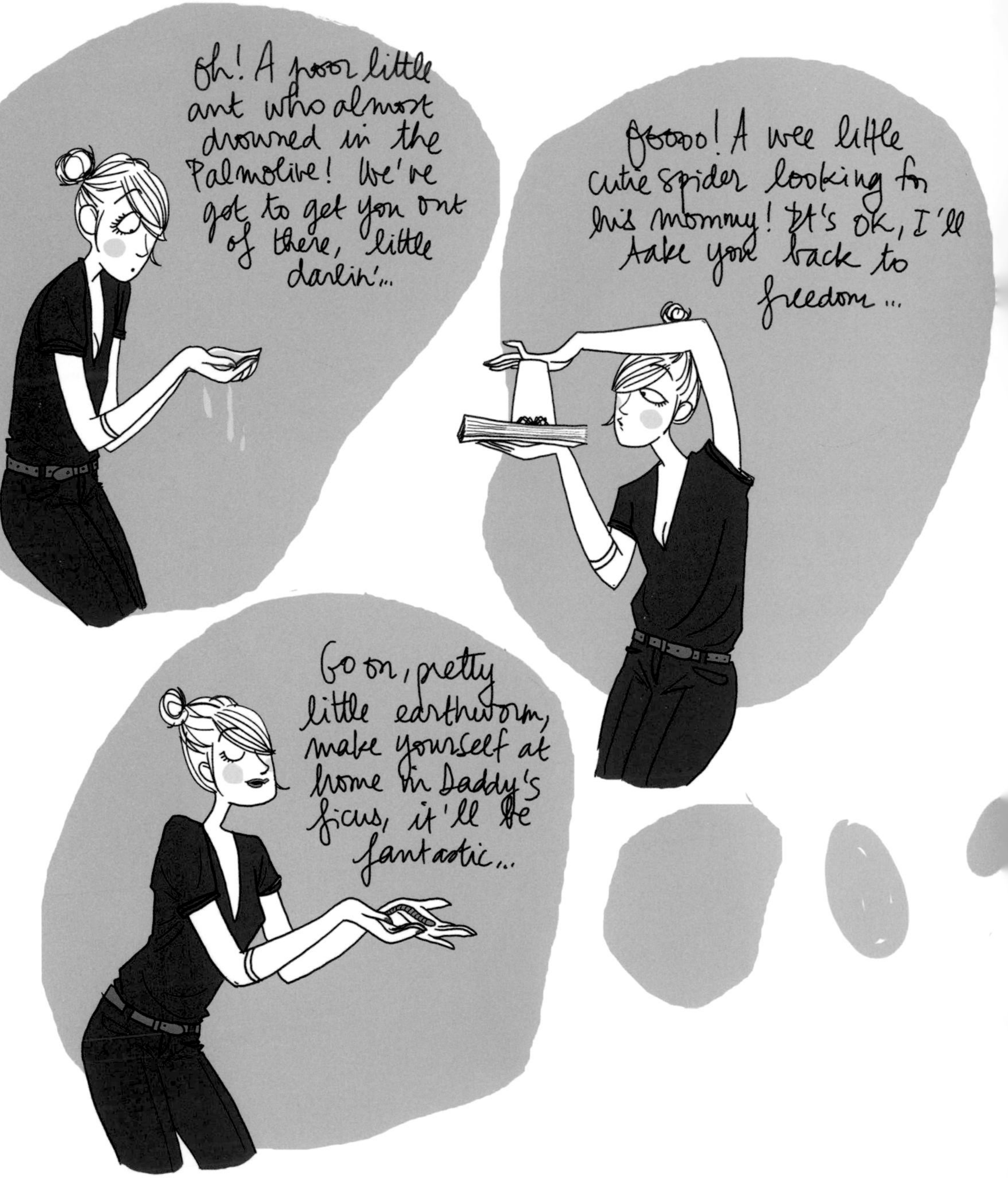
Oh! A poor little ant who almost drowned in the Palmolive! We've got to get you out of there, little darlin'...
Ooooo! A wee little cutie spider looking for his mommy! It's OK, I'll take you back to freedom...
Go on, pretty little earthworm, make yourself at home in Daddy's ficus, it'll be fantastic...

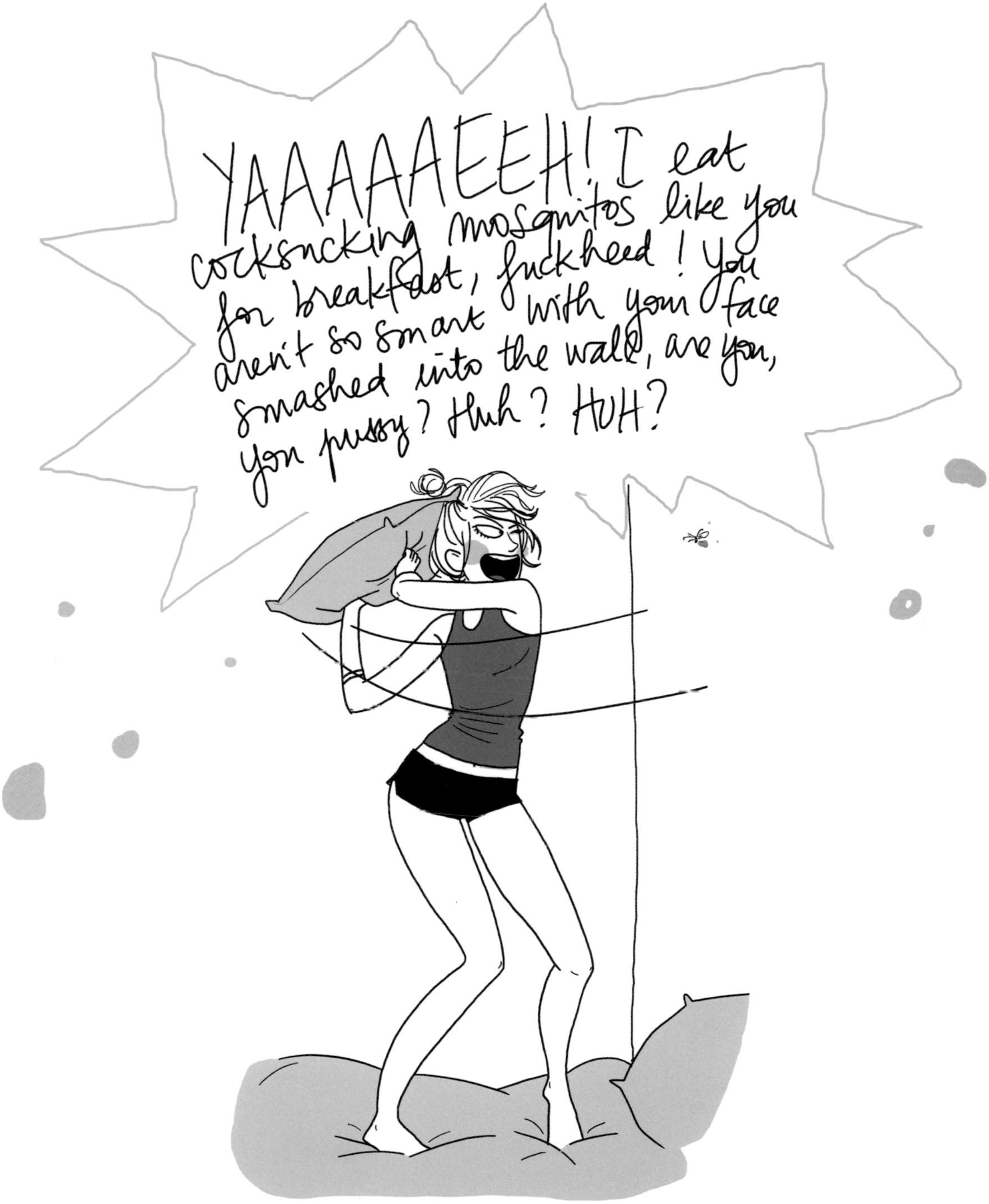
YAAAAAEEH! I eat cocksucking mosquitos like you for breakfast, fuckhead! You aren't so smart with your face smashed into the wall, are you, you pussy? Huh? HUH?

I SAID "GENERALLY" and "MOST".

My Mediterranean heritage

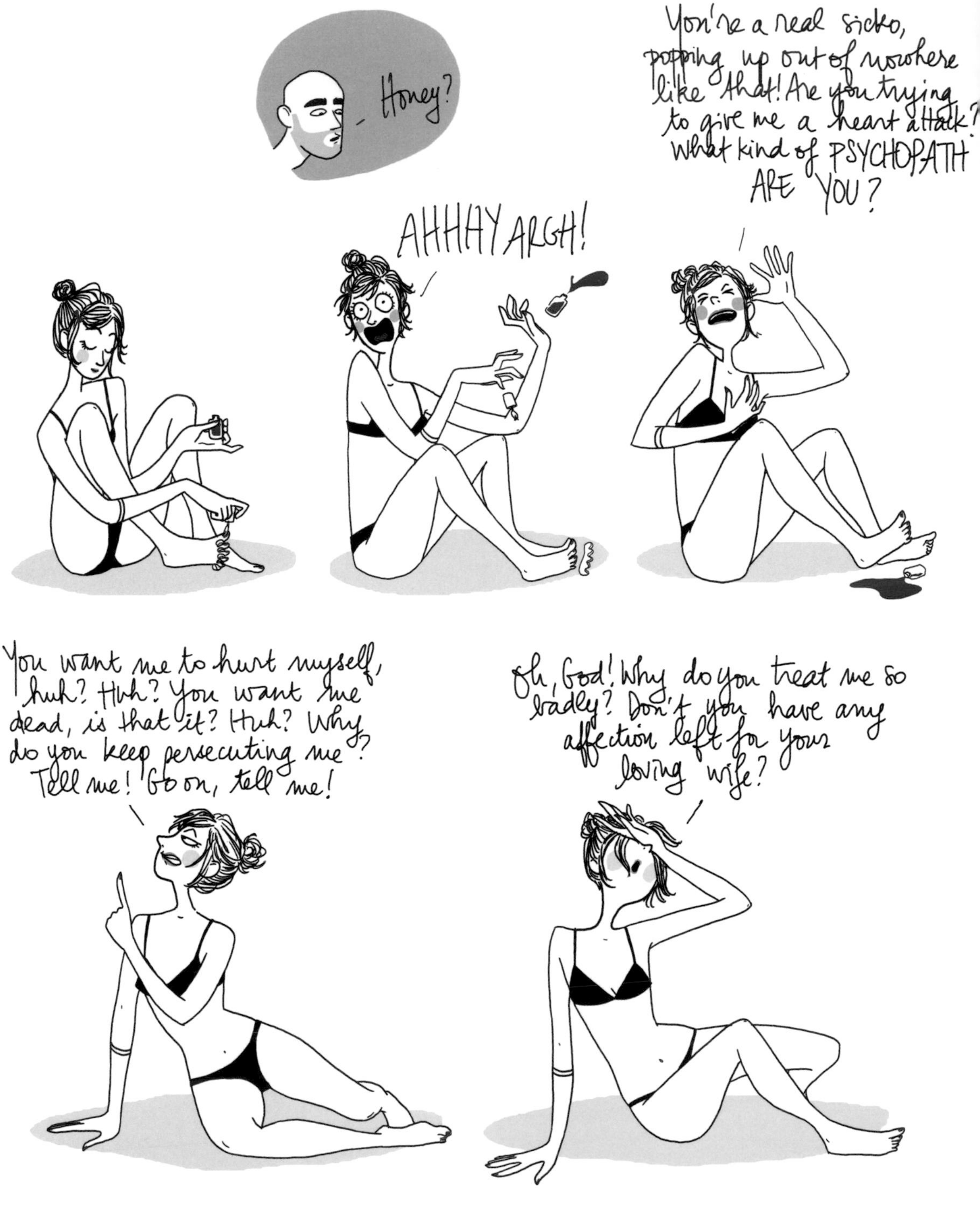

Honey?
AHHHYARGH!
You're a real sicko, popping up out of nowhere like that! Are you trying to give me a heart attack? What kind of PSYCHOPATH ARE YOU?
You want me to hurt myself, huh? Huh? You want me dead, is that it? Huh? Why do you keep persecuting me? Tell me! Go on, tell me!
Oh, God! Why do you treat me so badly? Don't you have any affection left for your loving wife?

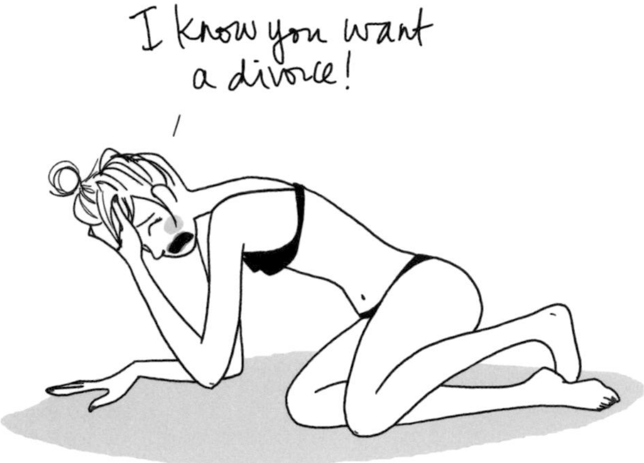
I know you want a divorce!

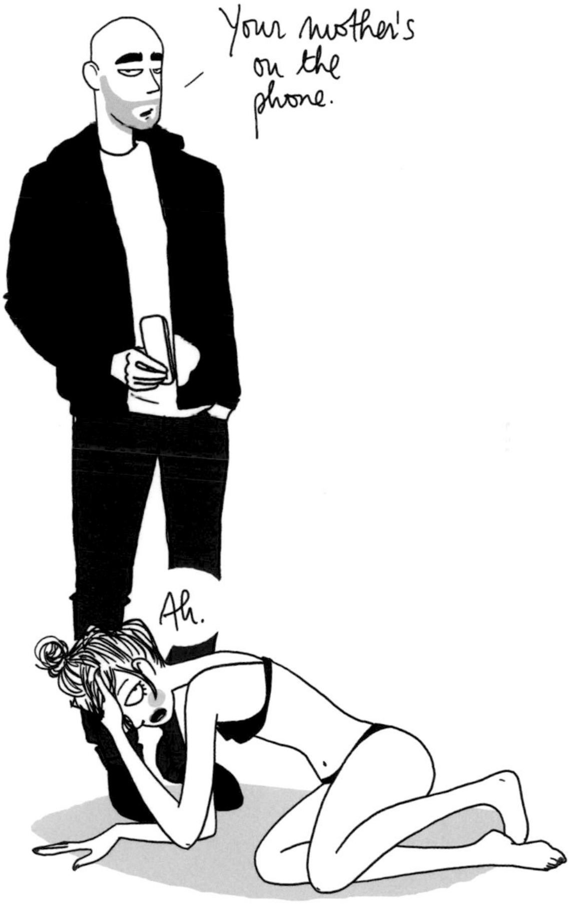
Your mother's on the phone.
Ah.

IT'S POSSIBLE THAT WAS JUST A TAD OTT.

They grow up so fast

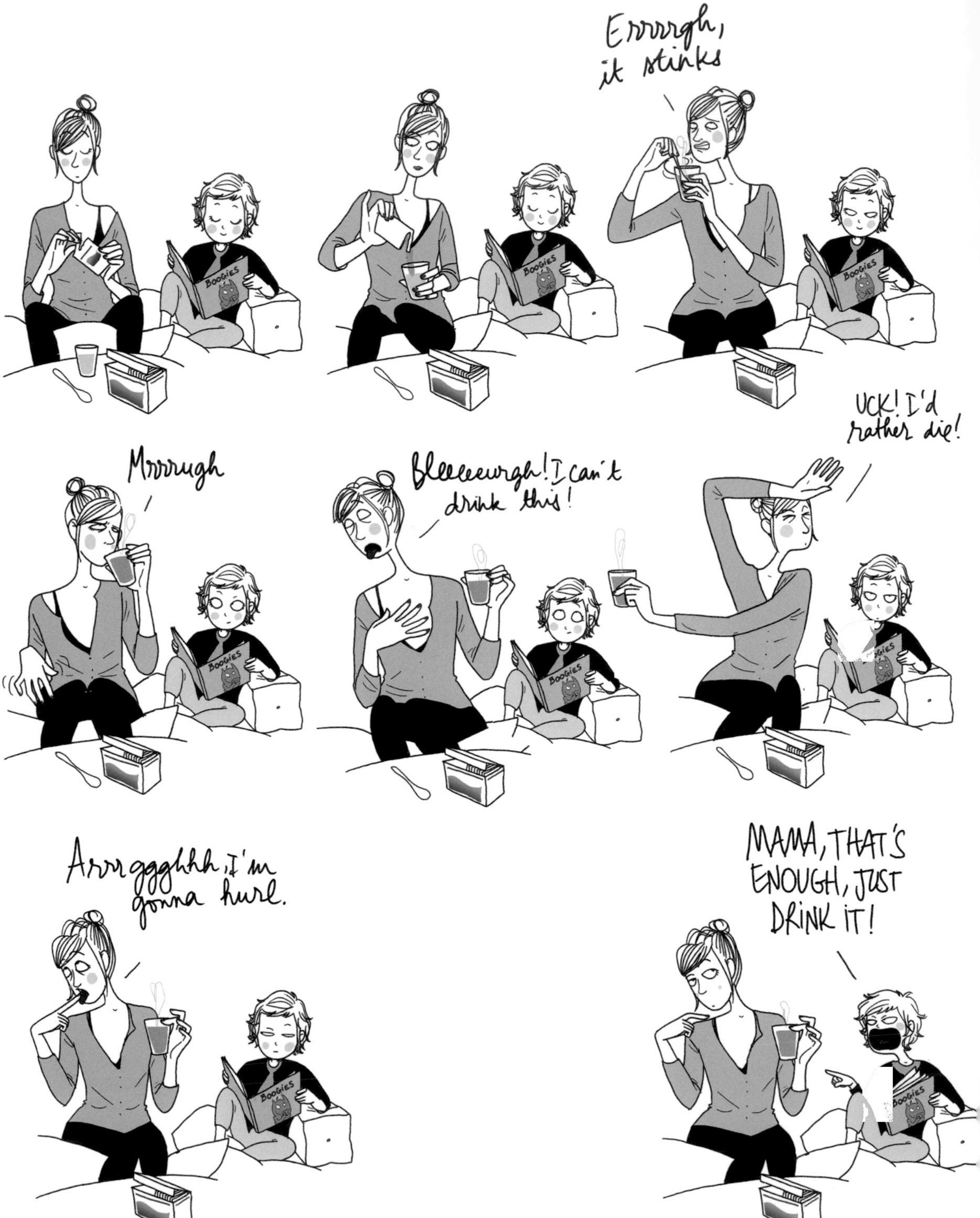
Errrrgh, it stinks
Mrrrugh
Bleeeeurgh! I can't drink this!
UCK! I'd rather die!
Arrrggghhh, I'm gonna hurl.
MAMA, THAT'S ENOUGH, JUST DRINK IT!

Obviously

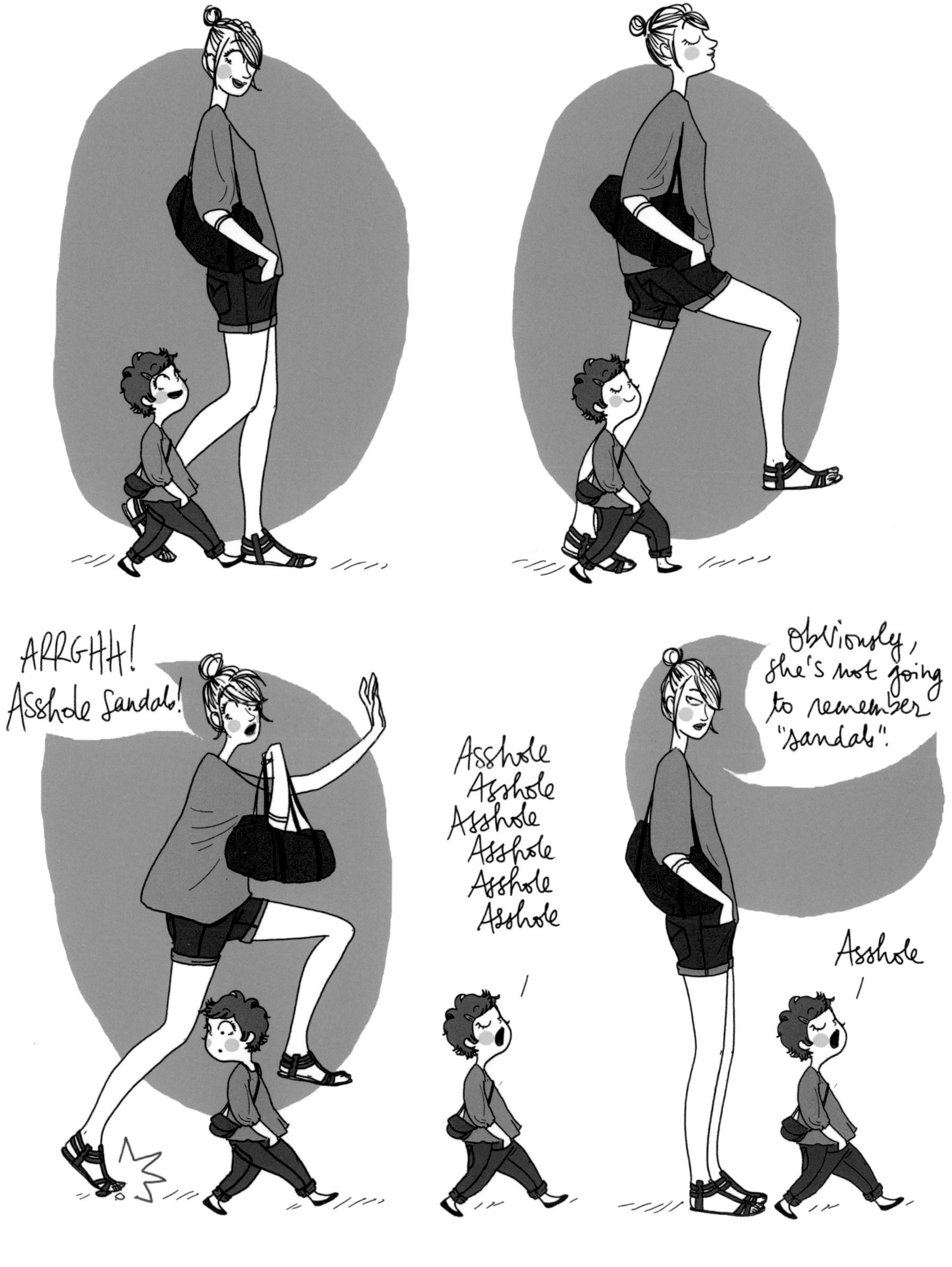
ARRGHH! Asshole sandals!
Asshole
Asshole
Asshole
Asshole
Asshole
Asshole
Obviously, she's not going to remember "sandals".
Asshole

Parrot repartee

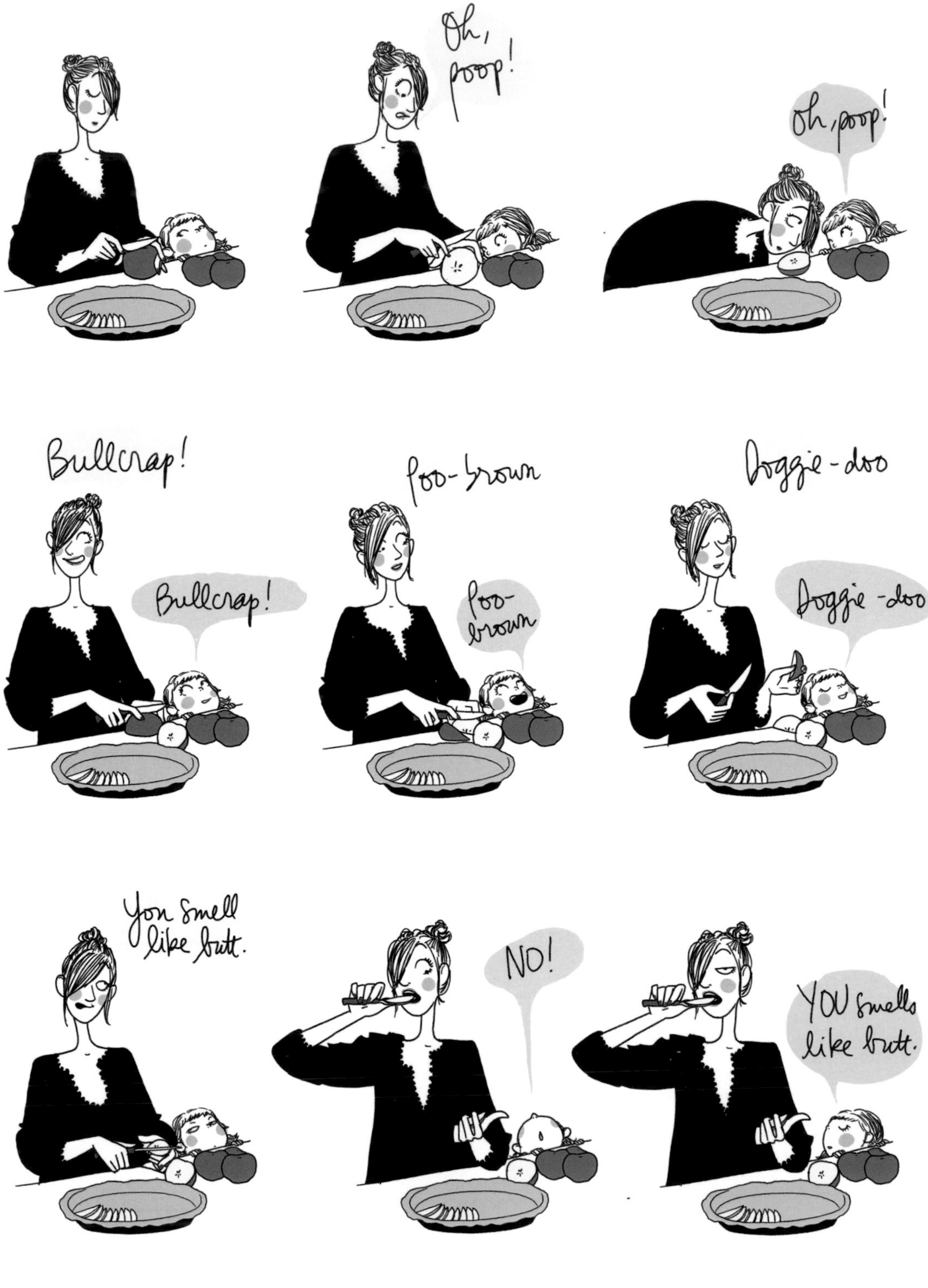
Oh, poop!
Oh, poop!
Bullcrap!
Bullcrap!
Poo-brown
Poo-brown
Doggie-doo
Doggie-doo
You smell like butt.
NO!
YOU smells like butt.

She's right: gotta nip it in the bud

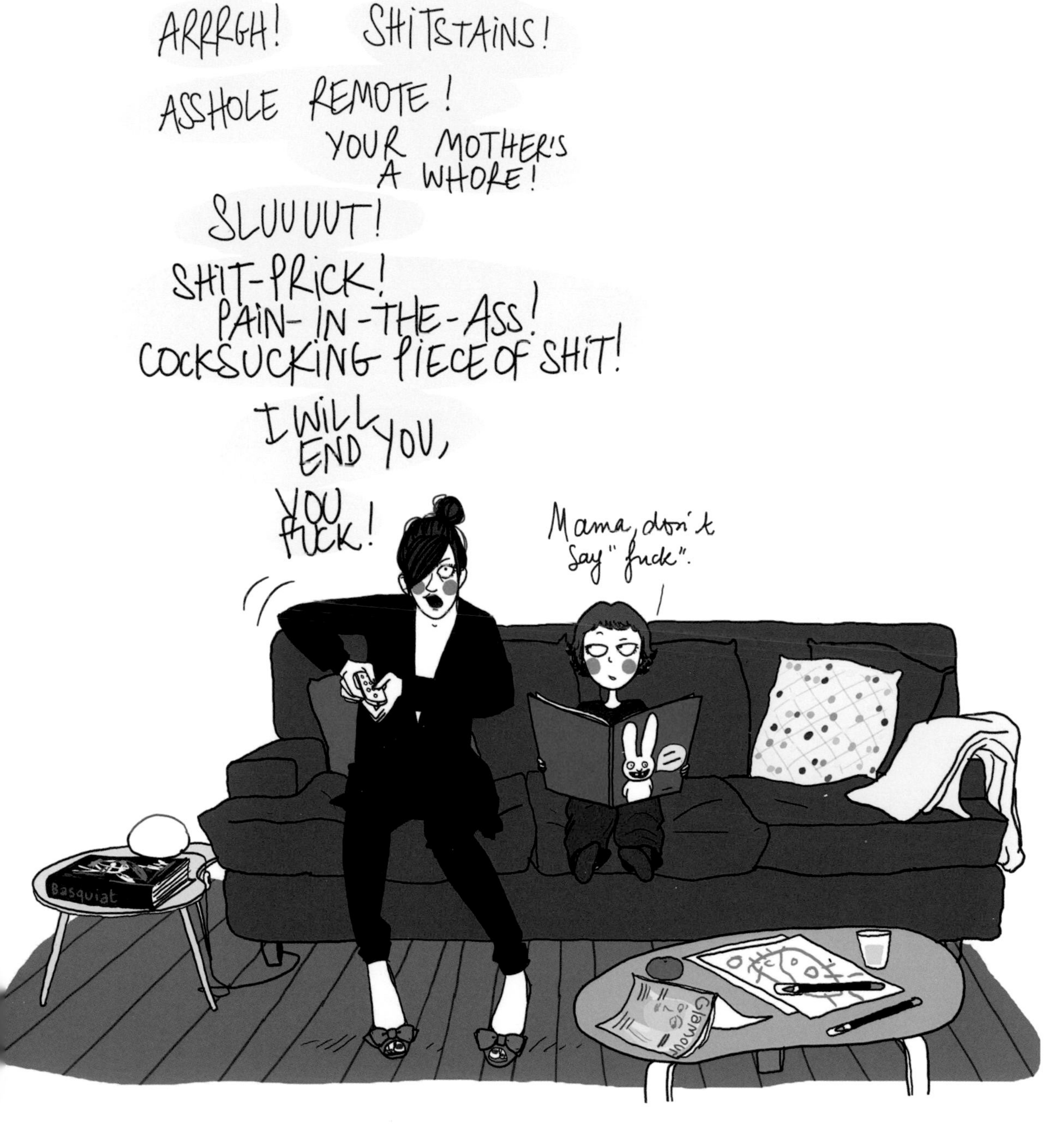
ARRRGH! SHITSTAINS!
ASSHOLE REMOTE!
YOUR MOTHER'S A WHORE!
SLUUUUT!
SHIT-PRICK!
PAIN-IN-THE-ASS!
COCKSUCKING PIECE OF SHIT!
I WILL END YOU,
YOU FUCK!
Mama, don't say "fuck".
Basquiat
Glamour

Can I get the number of a good speech therapist?

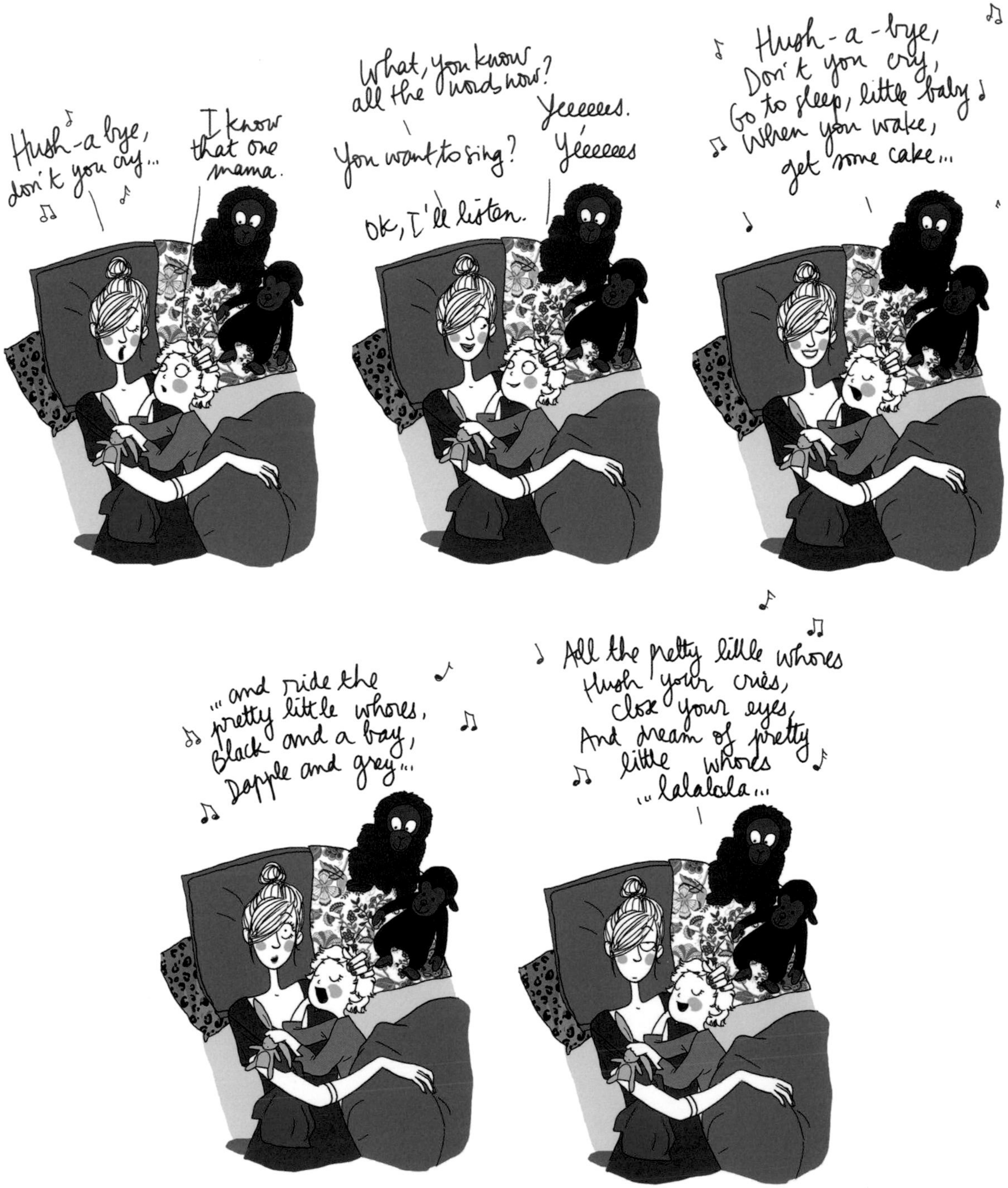
Hush-a-bye, don't you cry...
I know that one mama.
What, you know all the words now?
You want to sing?
Yeeeees.
Yéeeees
OK, I'll listen.
Hush-a-bye, Don't you cry, Go to sleep, little baby When you wake, get some cake...
...and ride the pretty little whores, Black and a bay, Dapple and grey...
All the pretty little whores Hush your cries, Close your eyes, And dream of pretty little whores ...lalalala...

The BEEEEEEEAST

06:45. The juvenile female apex predator emerges from her lair in search of game.

She sniffs the sweet perfume of a pair of sleeping prey, defenseless in their den...

On the tips of her savage paws, she heads silently towards her victims...

... ever alert to her surroundings, ready to hurdle any obstacle...

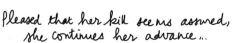

Pleased that her kill seems assured, she continues her advance...

Hiding in the shadows, she is primed for her attack...

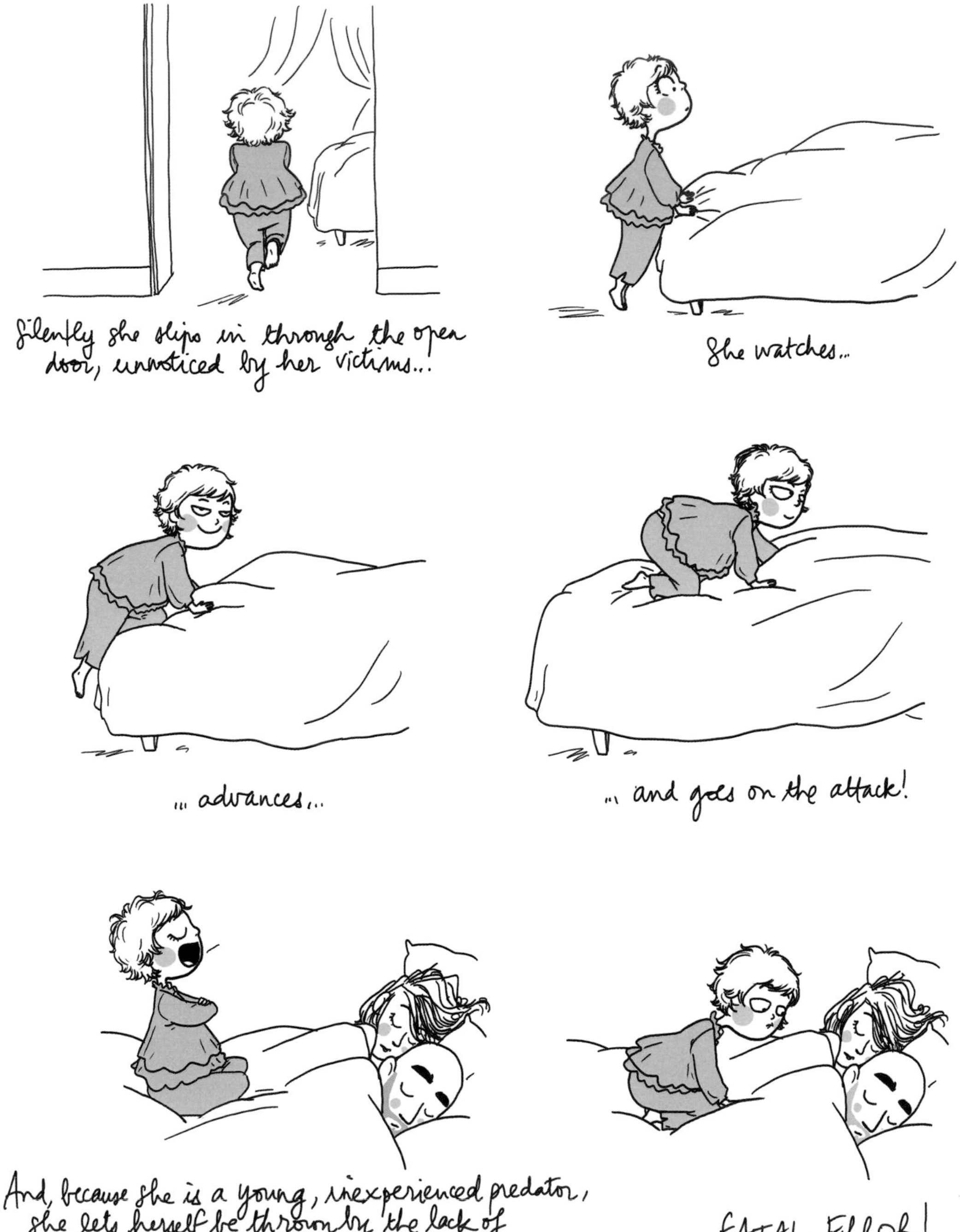
Silently she slips in through the open door, unnoticed by her victims...
She watches...
... advances...
... and goes on the attack!
And, because she is a young, inexperienced predator, she lets herself be thrown by the lack of reaction on the part of her sleeping prey and draws closer...
FATAL ERROR!

For that is when the prey, who have genetically mutated over the years and developed bio-chemical defenses based on a melange of booze, cigarettes and Sunday night's onion pizza, deal the predator a killing blow...

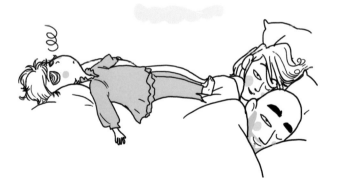

...totally laying her out cold.

Being a parent is hard on the ego

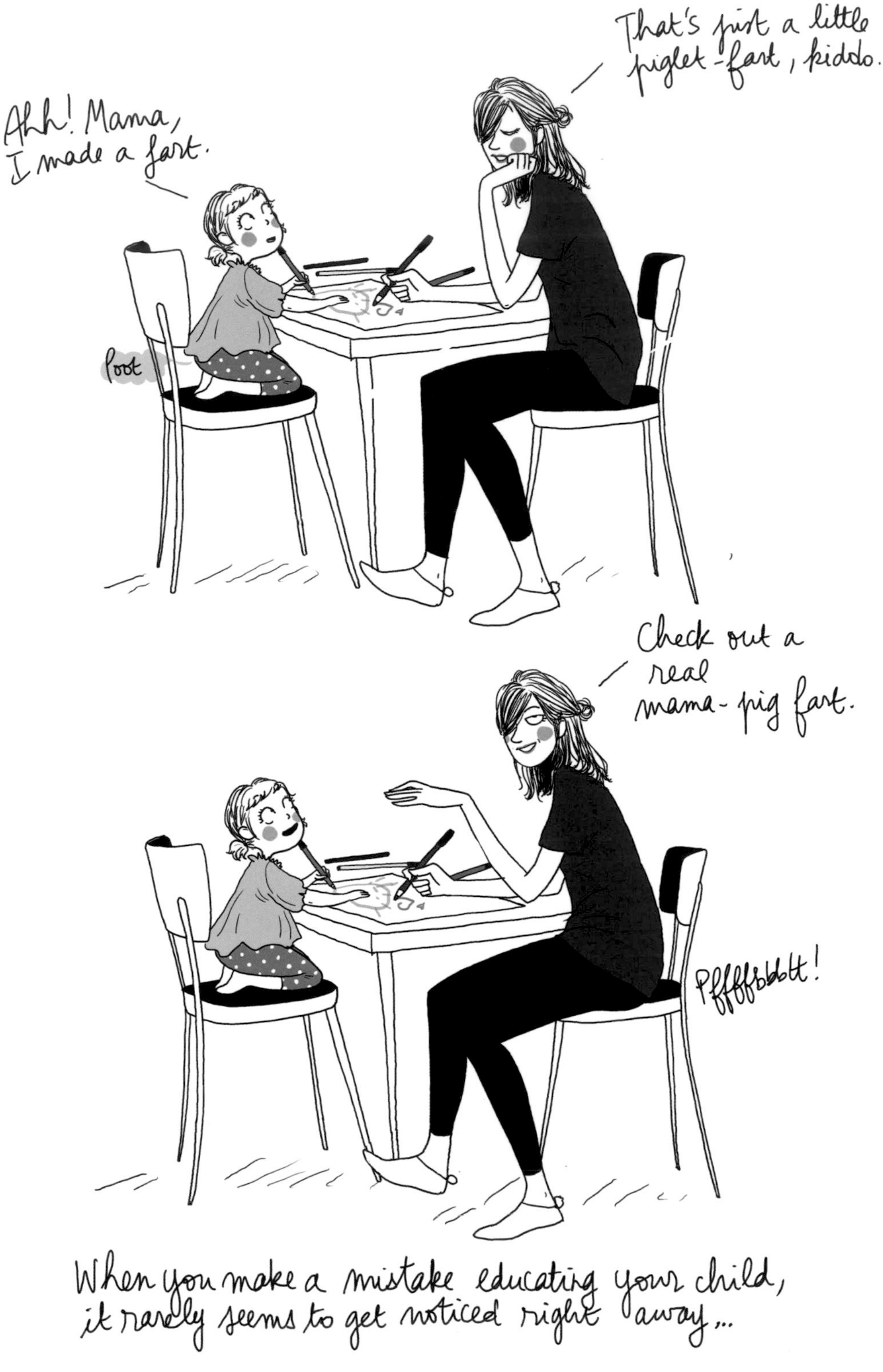
Ahh! Mama, I made a fart.
Poot
That's just a little piglet-fart, kiddo.
Check out a real mama-pig fart.
Pfffbbbtt!
When you make a mistake educating your child, it rarely seems to get noticed right away...

But sooner or later...

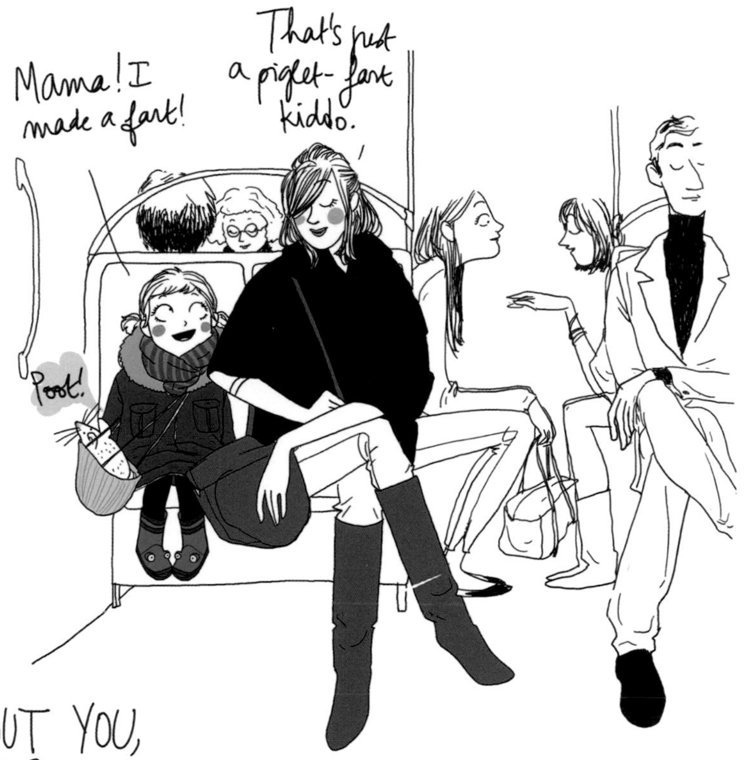

Mama! I made a fart!
That's just a piglet-fart kiddo.
Poot!

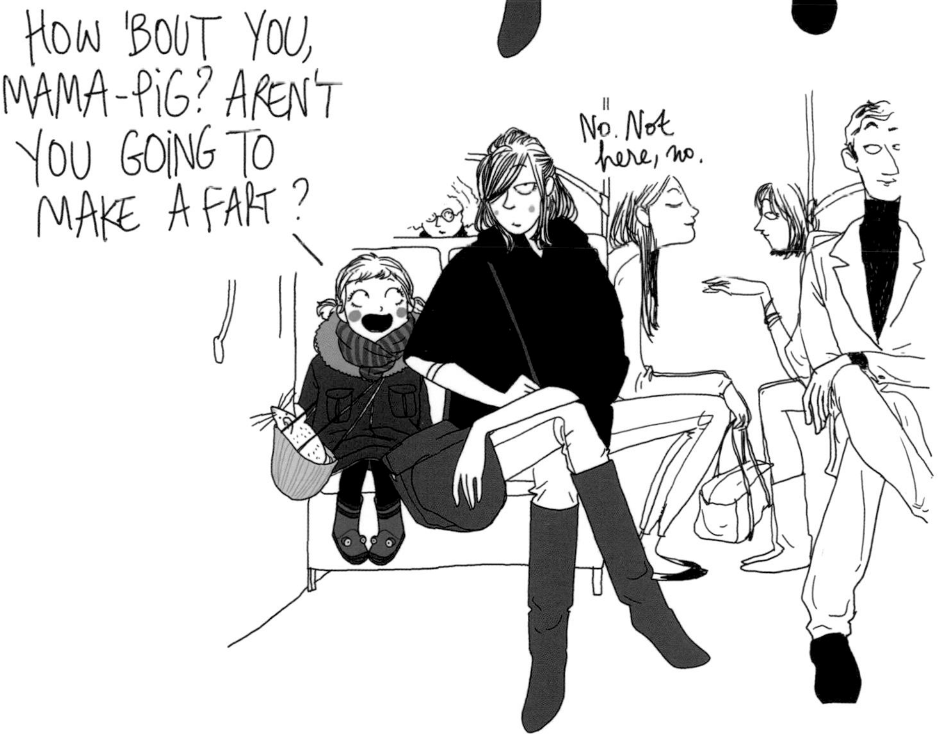

HOW 'BOUT YOU, MAMA-PIG? AREN'T YOU GOING TO MAKE A FART?
No. Not here, no.

... it catches up with you.

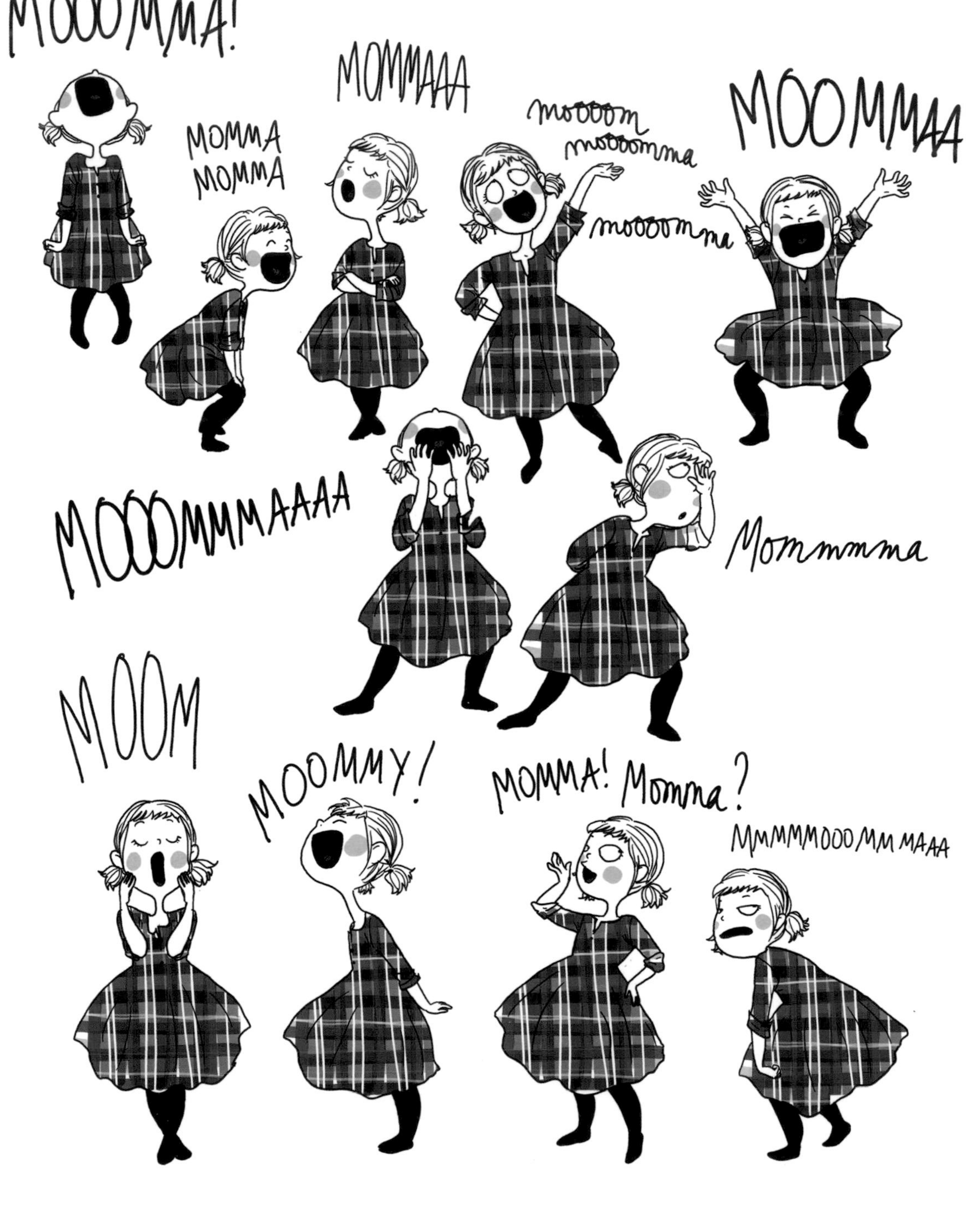
MOOOMMA!
MOMMA MOMMA
MOMMAAA
moooom mooooomma
MOOMMAA
mooooomma
MOOOMMMAAAA
Mommmma
MOOM
MOOMMY!
MOMMA! Momma?
MMMMMOOOMMMAAA

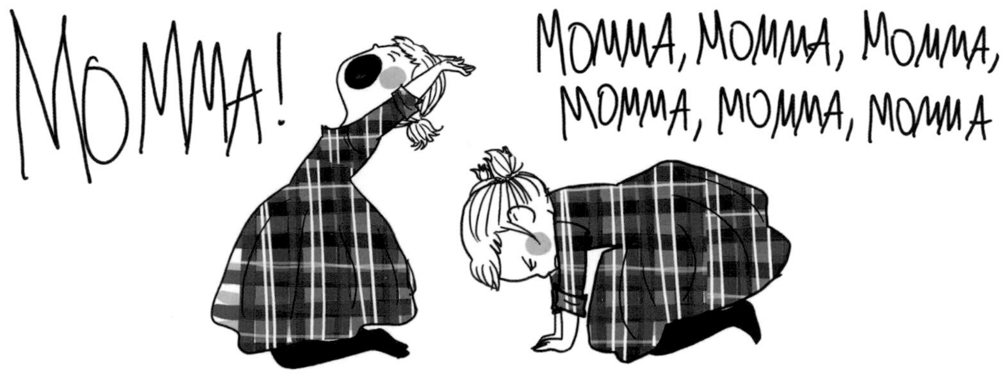
MOMMA!
MOMMA, MOMMA, MOMMA, MOMMA, MOMMA, MOMMA

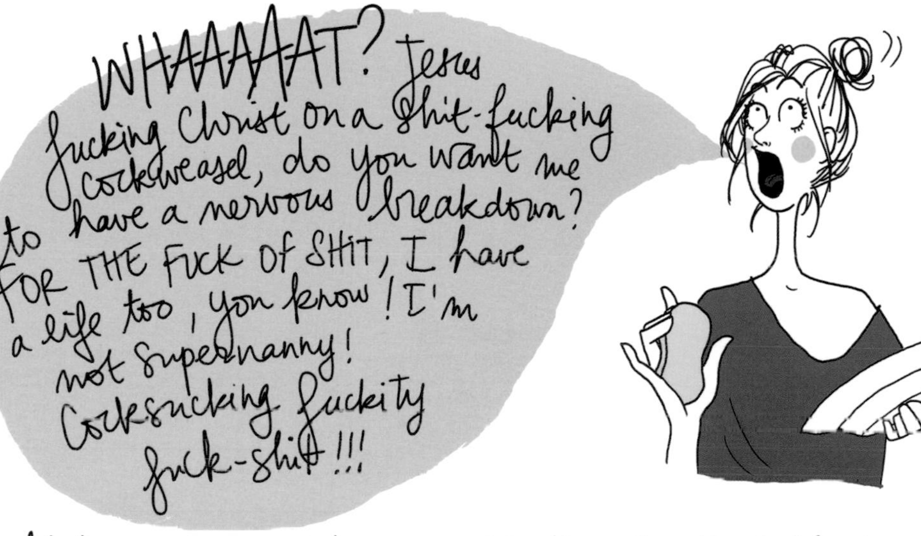
WHAAAAAT? Jesus fucking Christ on a shit-fucking cockweasel, do you want me to have a nervous breakdown? FOR THE FUCK OF SHIT, I have a life too, you know! I'm not supernanny! Cocksucking fuckity fuck-shit!!!

I would looooove to be able to respond like that. But that's life. My mother, Dr. Spock, Child Protection Services and the police department would come down on me like a ton of bricks if I responded like that. So:

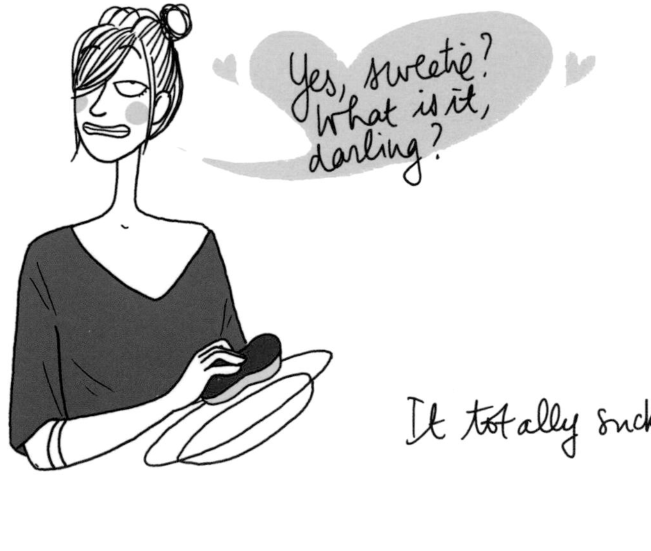
Yes, sweetie? What is it, darling?

It totally sucks.

Weekend

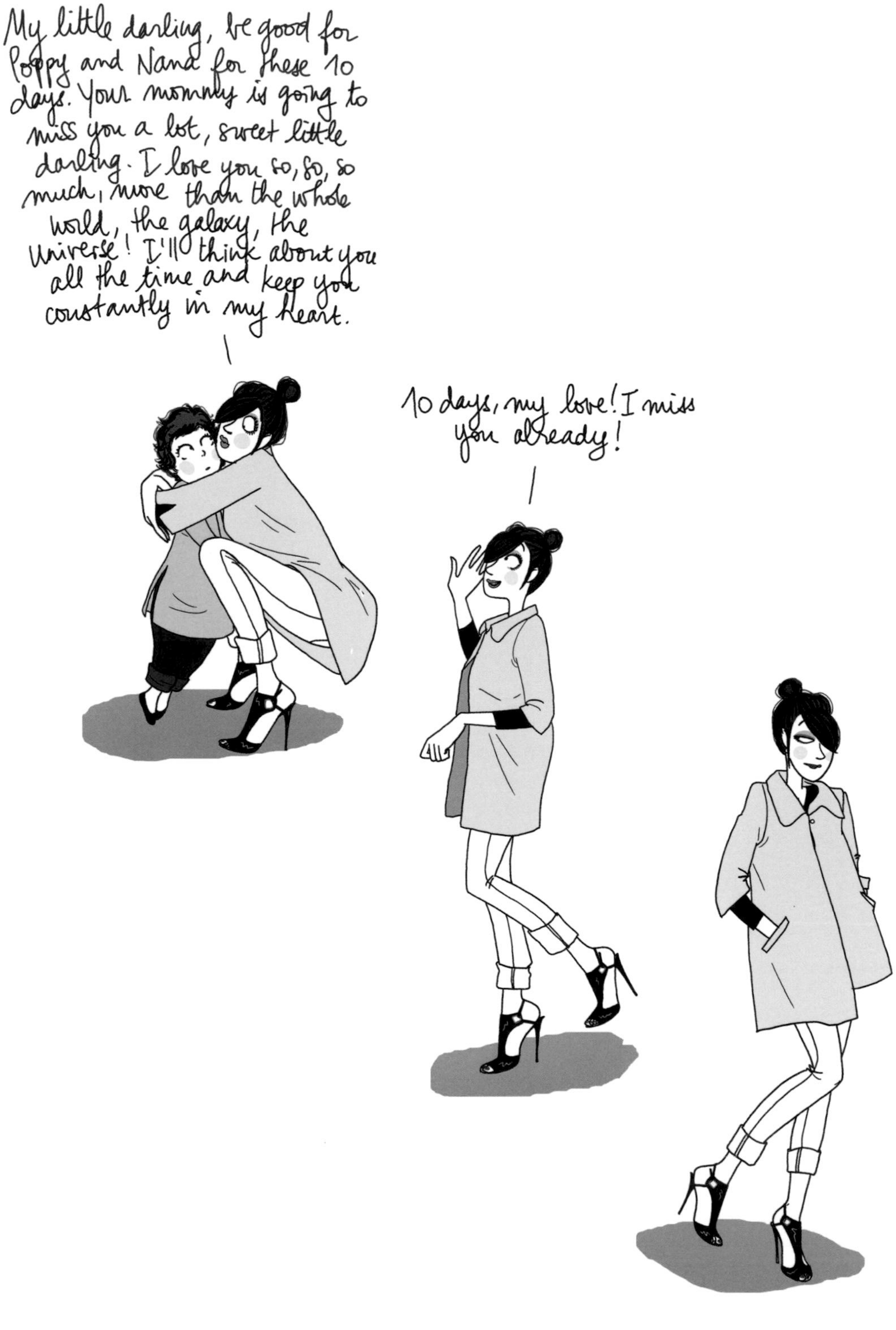
My little darling, be good for Poppy and Nana for these 10 days. Your mommy is going to miss you a lot, sweet little darling. I love you so, so, so much, more than the whole world, the galaxy, the universe! I'll think about you all the time and keep you constantly in my heart.
10 days, my love! I miss you already!

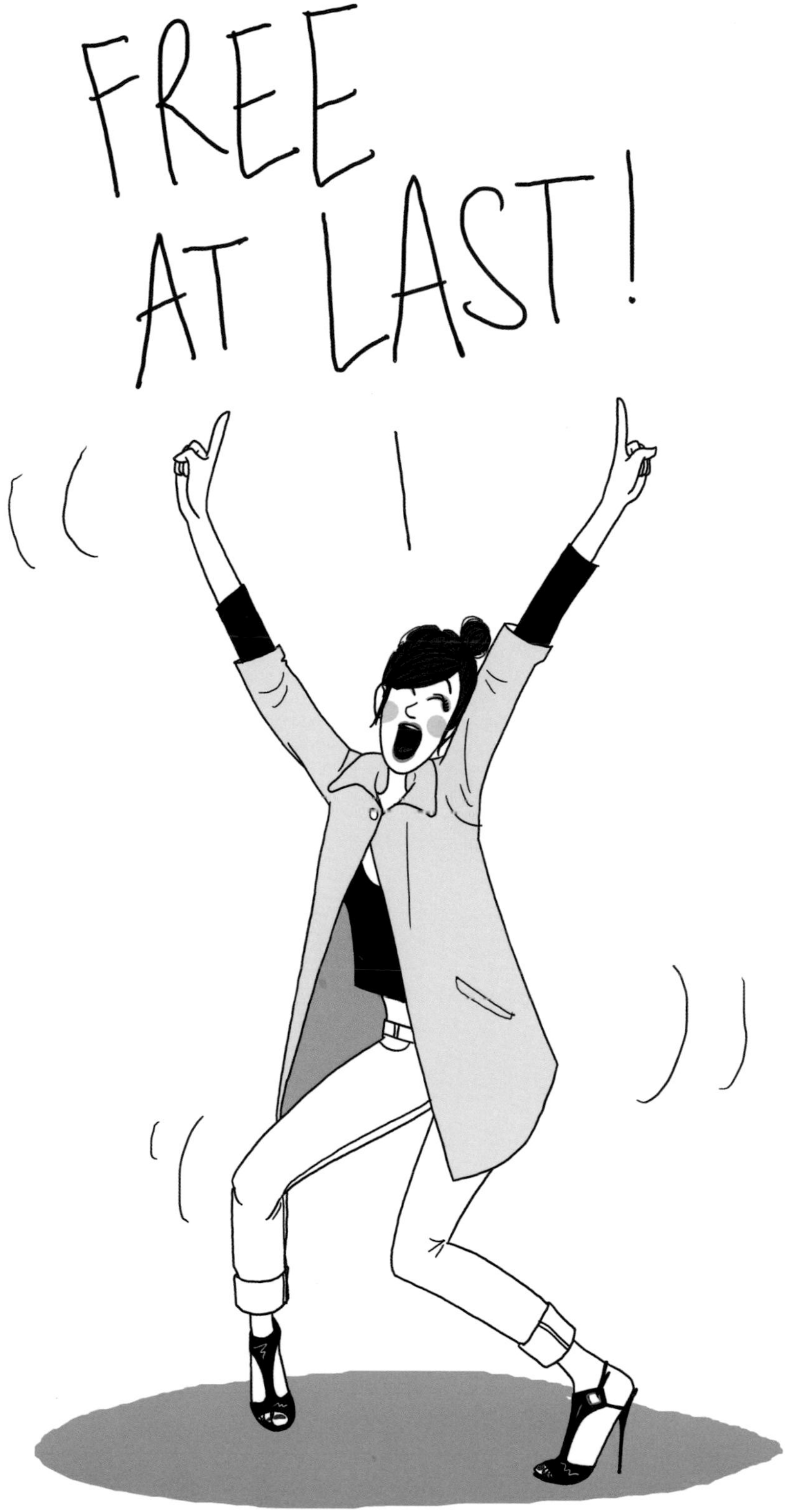
FREE AT LAST!

Wooooo, lucky devil!

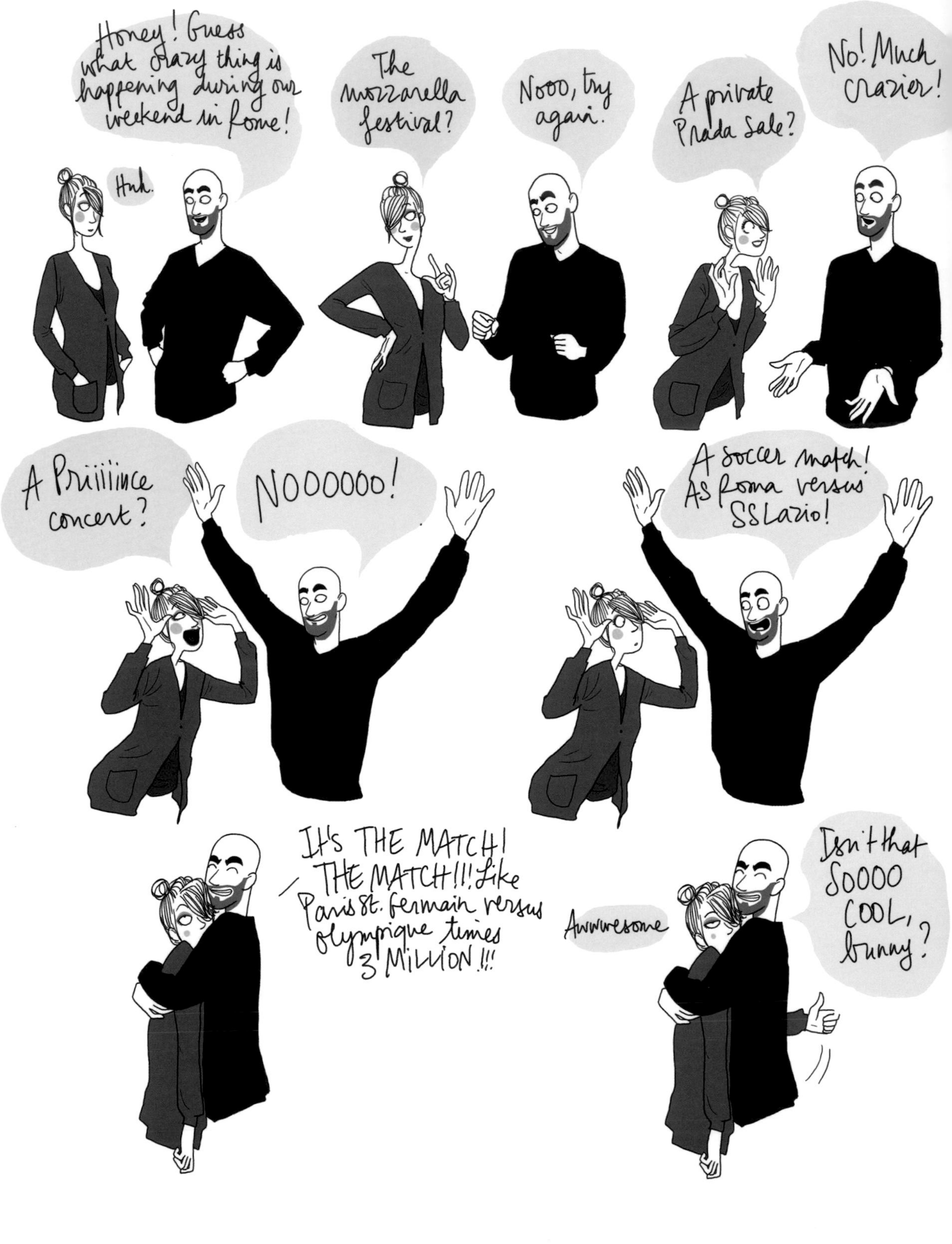

Honey! Guess what crazy thing is happening during our weekend in Rome!
Huh.
The mozzarella festival?
Nooo, try again.
A private Prada Sale?
No! Much crazier!
A Priiiiince concert?
NOOOOOO!
A soccer match! AS Roma versus SS Lazio!
IT'S THE MATCH! THE MATCH!!! Like Paris St. Germain versus Olympique times 3 MILLION!!!
Isn't that SOOOO COOL, bunny?
Awwwesome

Rome weekend, part 1: mental preparation

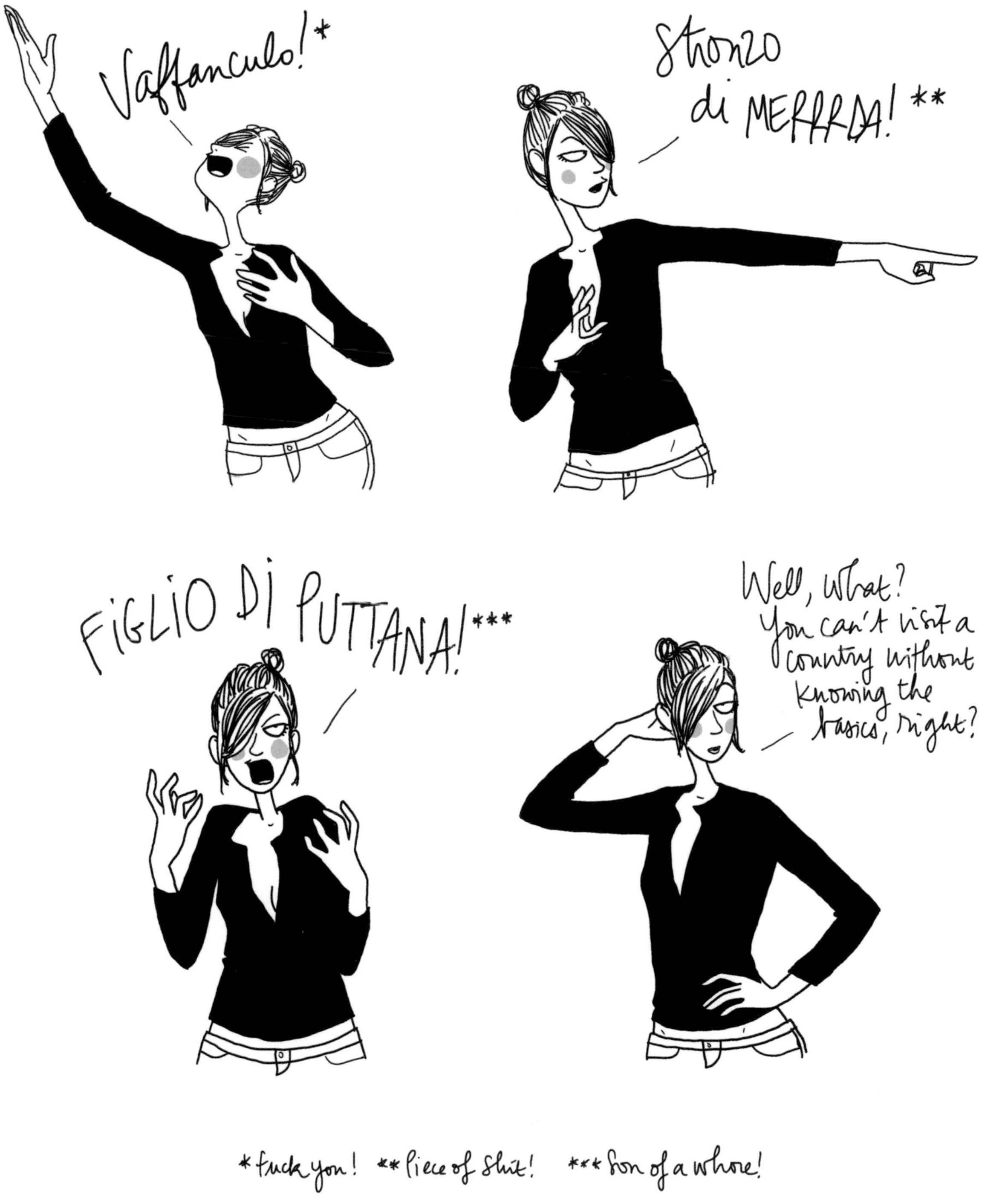
Vaffanculo!*
Stronzo di MERRRDA!**
FIGLIO DI PUTTANA!***
Well, what? You can't visit a country without knowing the basics, right?
*fuck you! **piece of shit! ***son of a whore!

Rome weekend, part 2: mini-SAT on the plane

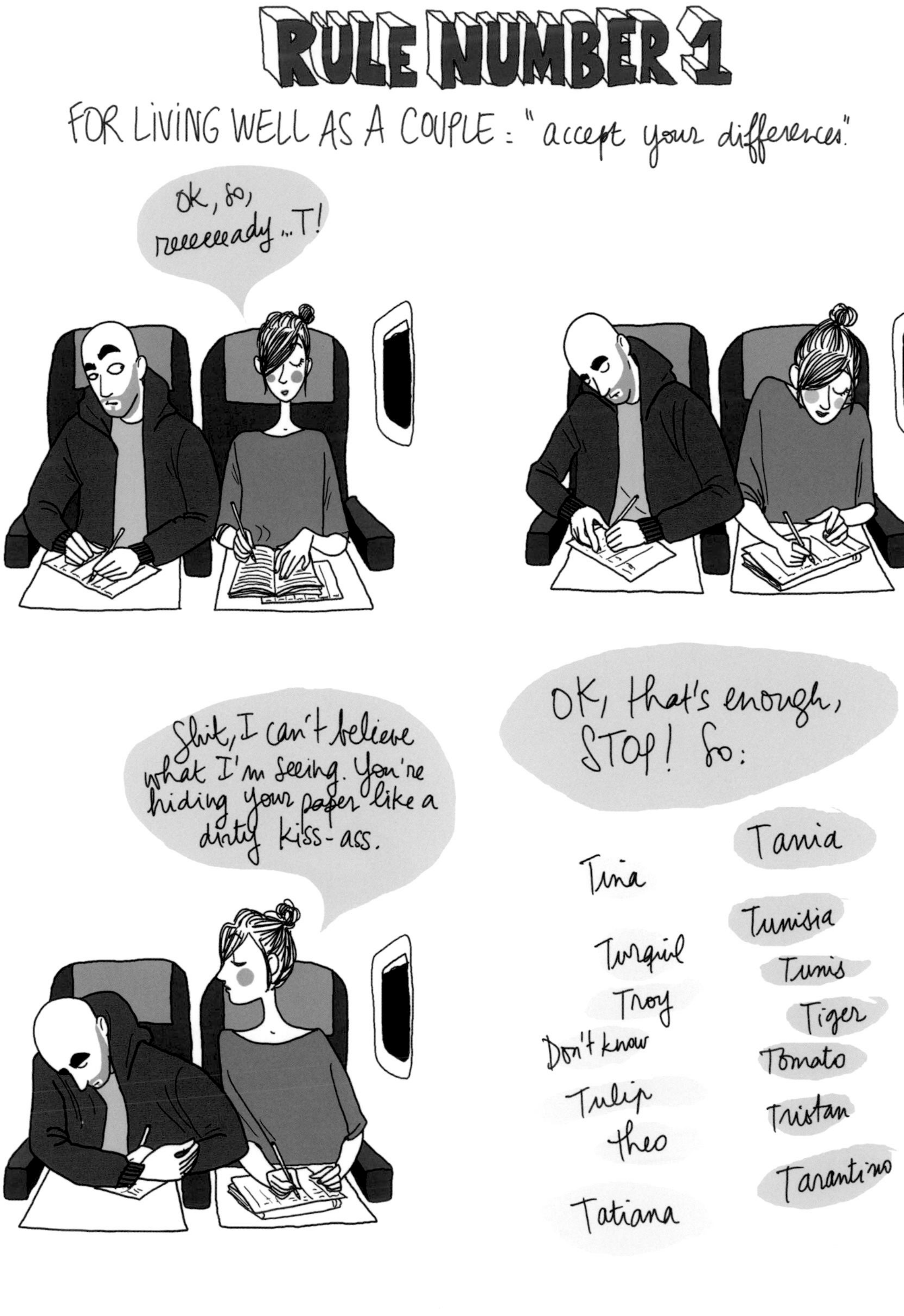
RULE NUMBER 1
FOR LIVING WELL AS A COUPLE: "accept your differences"
OK, so, reeeeeady...T!
Shit, I can't believe what I'm seeing. You're hiding your paper like a dirty kiss-ass.
OK, that's enough, STOP! So:
Tina
Torquil
Troy
Don't know
Tulip
theo
Tatiana
Tania
Tunisia
Tunis
Tiger
Tomato
Tristan
Tarantino

TATIANA!
Are you shitting me? There's no celebrity named Tatiana!
Uh-huh honey, there's Tatiana on Temptation Island!
Well there you go.

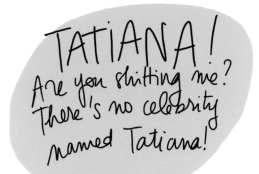

Rome weekend, part 3: Roman women

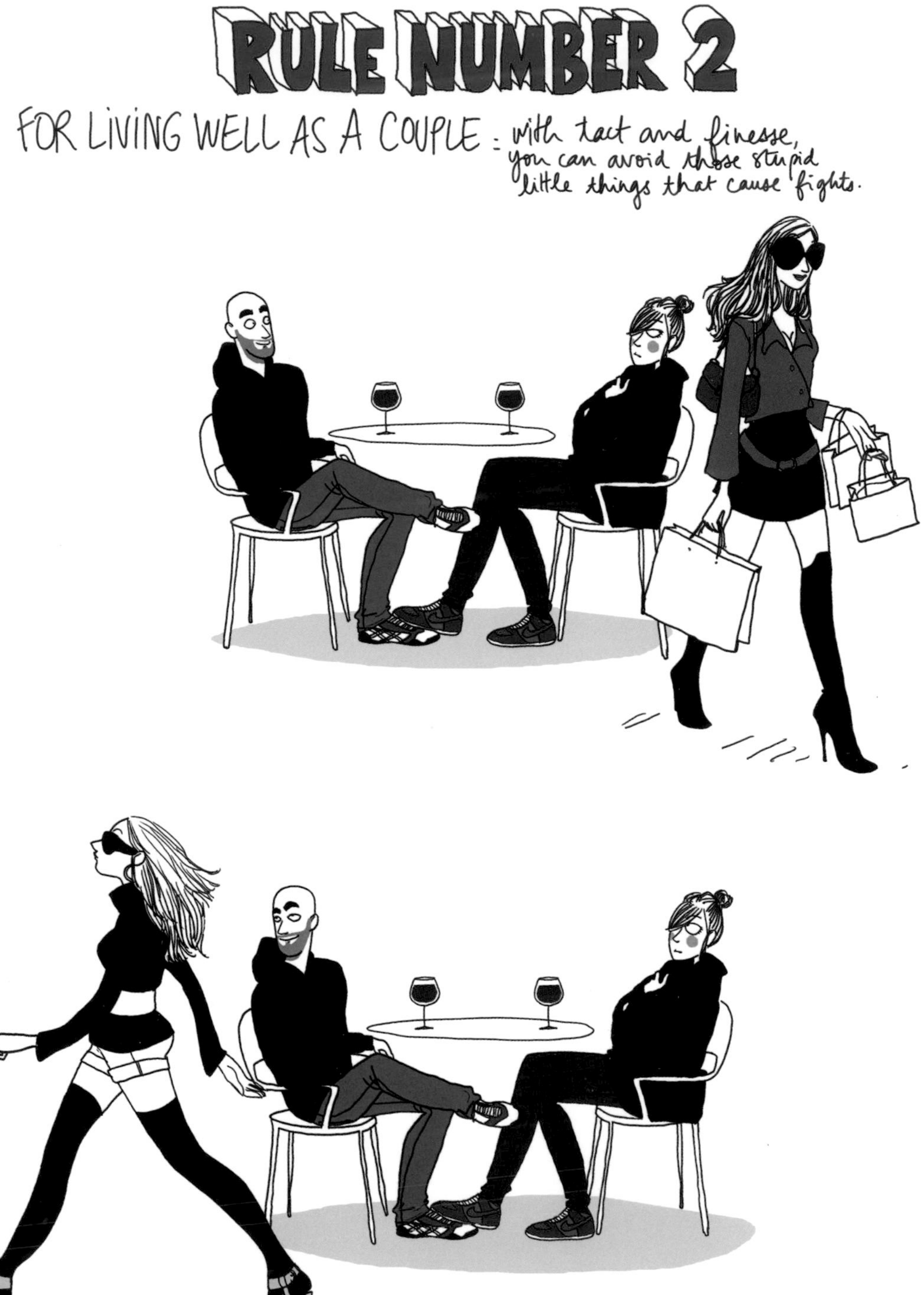
RULE NUMBER 2
FOR LIVING WELL AS A COUPLE: with tact and finesse, you can avoid those stupid little things that cause fights.

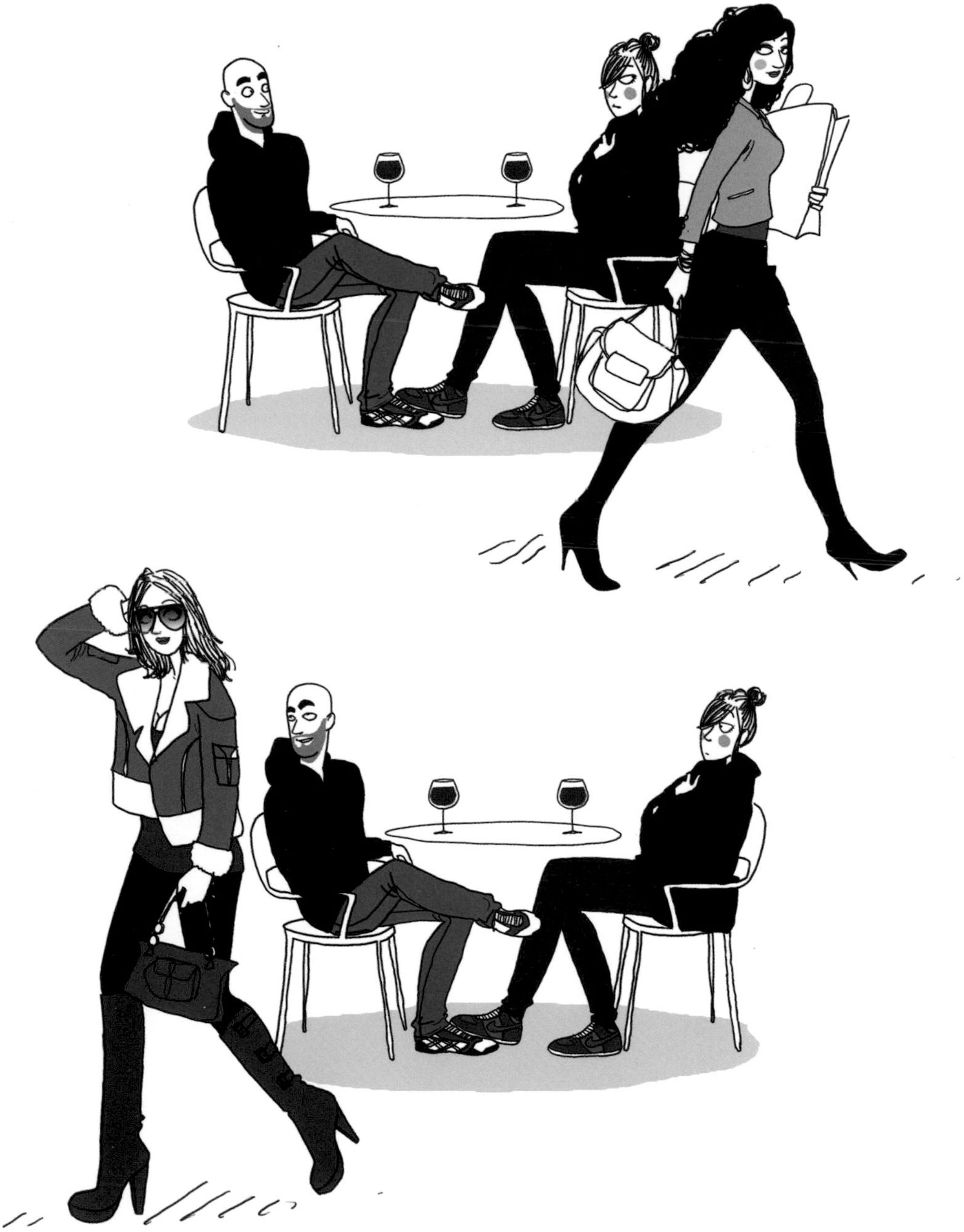

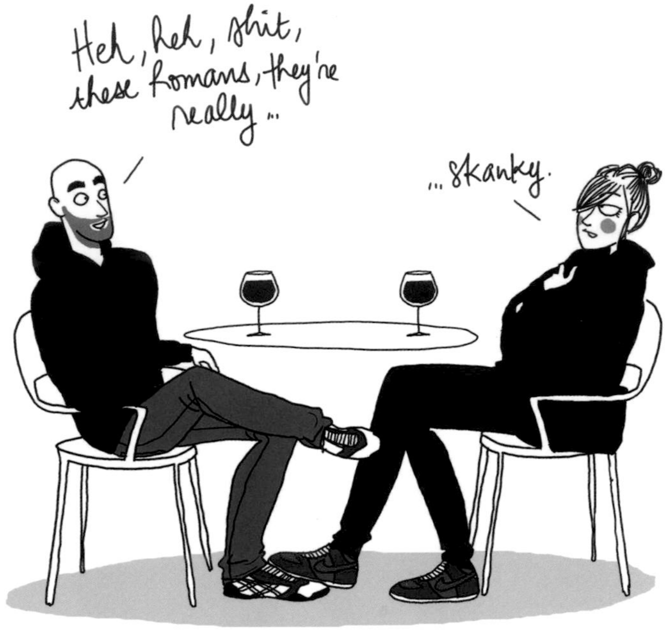
Heh, heh, shit, these Romans, they're really...
...skanky.

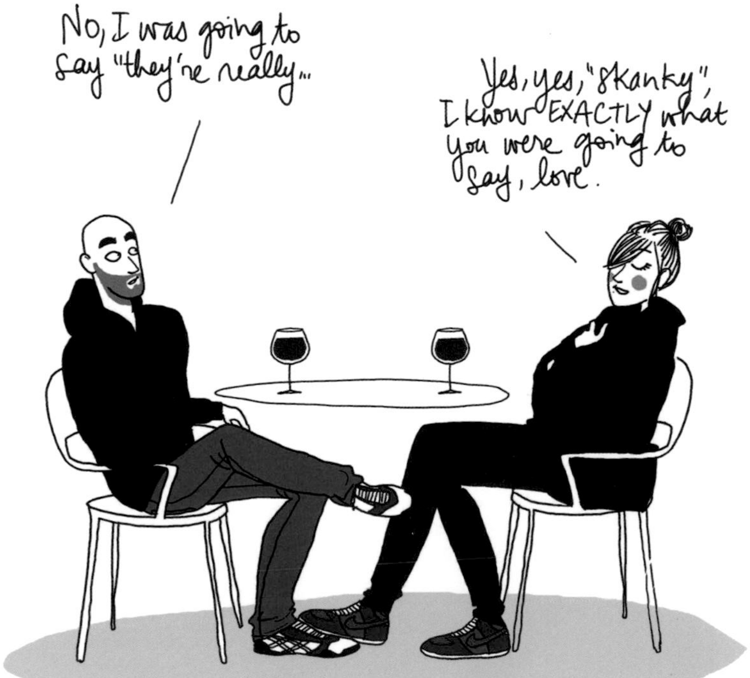
No, I was going to say "they're really...
Yes, yes, "skanky", I know EXACTLY what you were going to say, love.

On our Rome weekend...

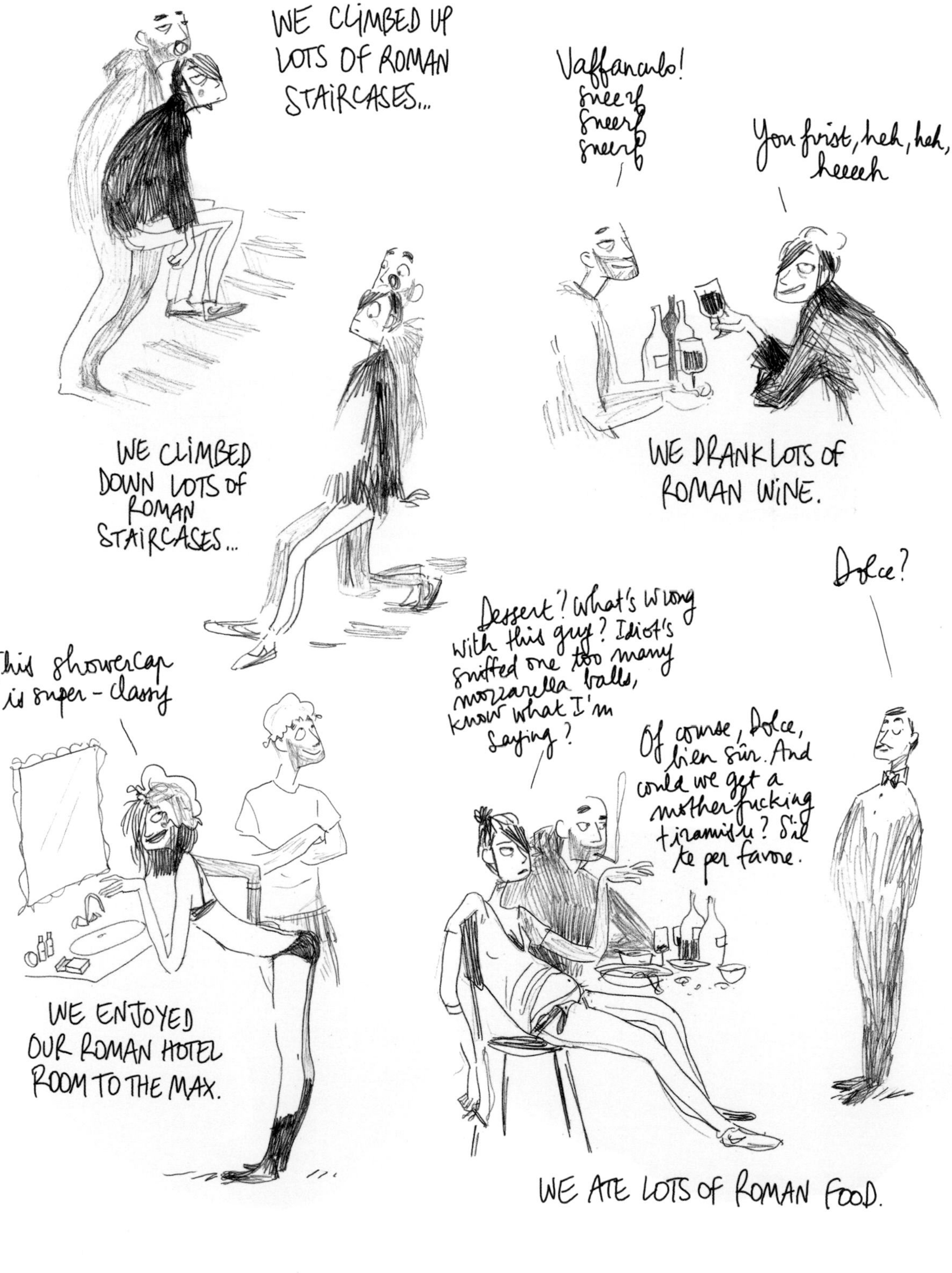

WE CLIMBED UP LOTS OF ROMAN STAIRCASES...
WE CLIMBED DOWN LOTS OF ROMAN STAIRCASES...
Vaffanculo! sneerf sneerf sneerf
You first, heh, heh, heeeeh
WE DRANK LOTS OF ROMAN WINE.
This showercap is super-classy
WE ENJOYED OUR ROMAN HOTEL ROOM TO THE MAX.
Dolce?
Dessert? What's wrong with this guy? Idiot's sniffed one too many mozzarella balls, know what I'm saying?
Of course, Dolce, bien sûr. And could we get a motherfucking tiramisu? Sil te per favore.
WE ATE LOTS OF ROMAN FOOD.

WE DISCOVERED LOTS OF TINY, TYPICALLY ROMAN SHOPS...

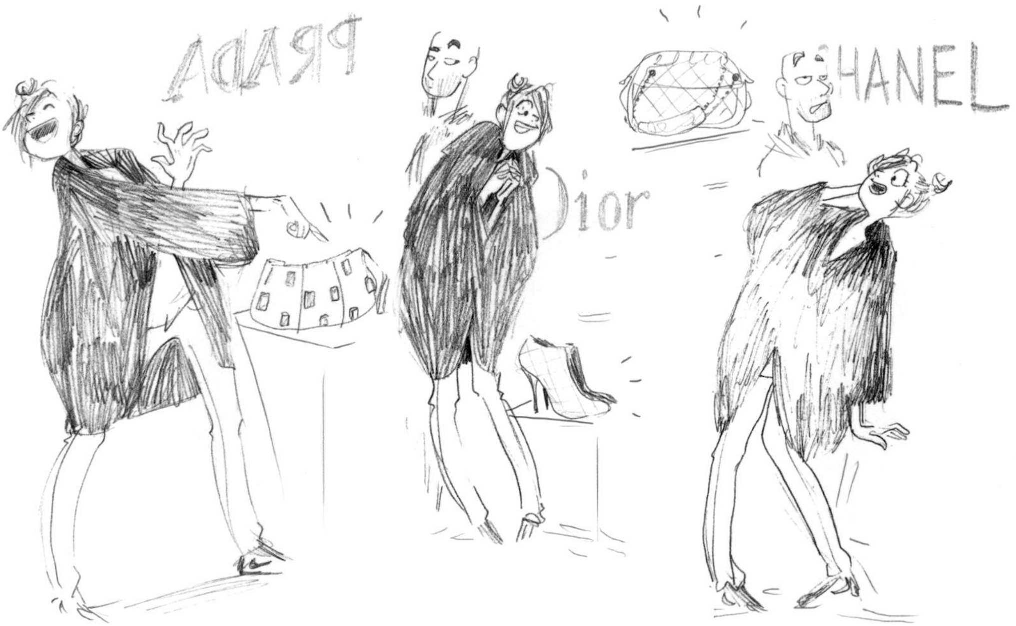
PRADA
Dior
HANEL

WE HAD OUR MINDS BLOWN BY ROMAN ARCHITECTURE

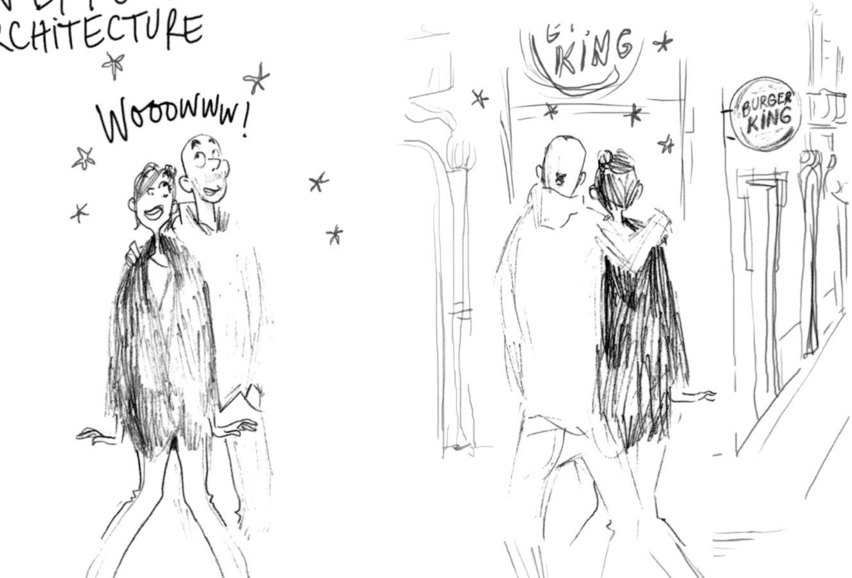
WOOOWWW!
KING
BURGER KING

The creative spirit of a non-artist is a funny thing

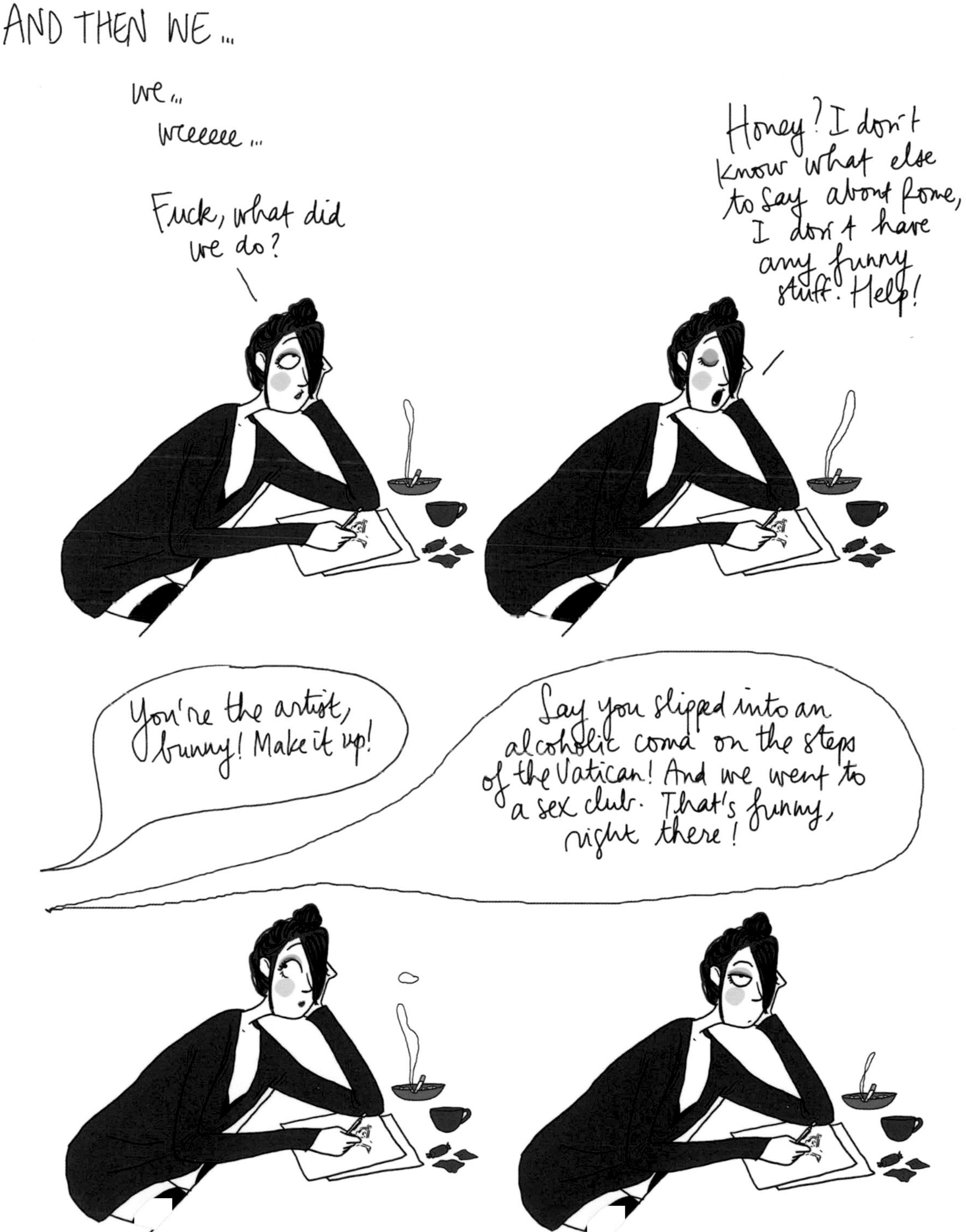
AND THEN WE...
we...
weeeee...
Fuck, what did we do?
Honey? I don't know what else to say about Rome, I don't have any funny stuff. Help!
You're the artist, bunny! Make it up!
Say you slipped into an alcoholic coma on the steps of the Vatican! And we went to a sex club. That's funny, right there!

Epilogue

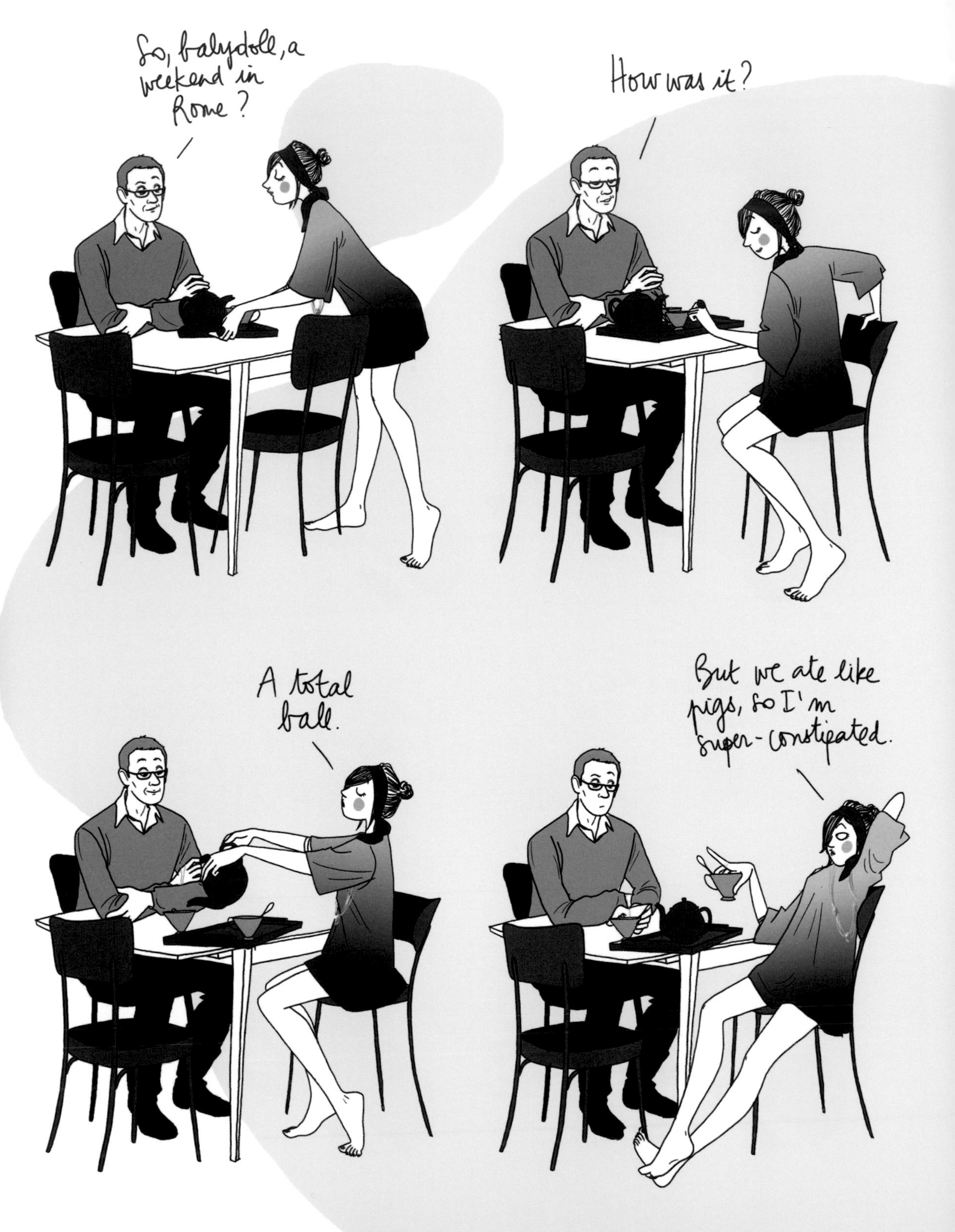
So, babydoll, a weekend in Rome?
How was it?
A total ball.
But we ate like pigs, so I'm super-constipated.

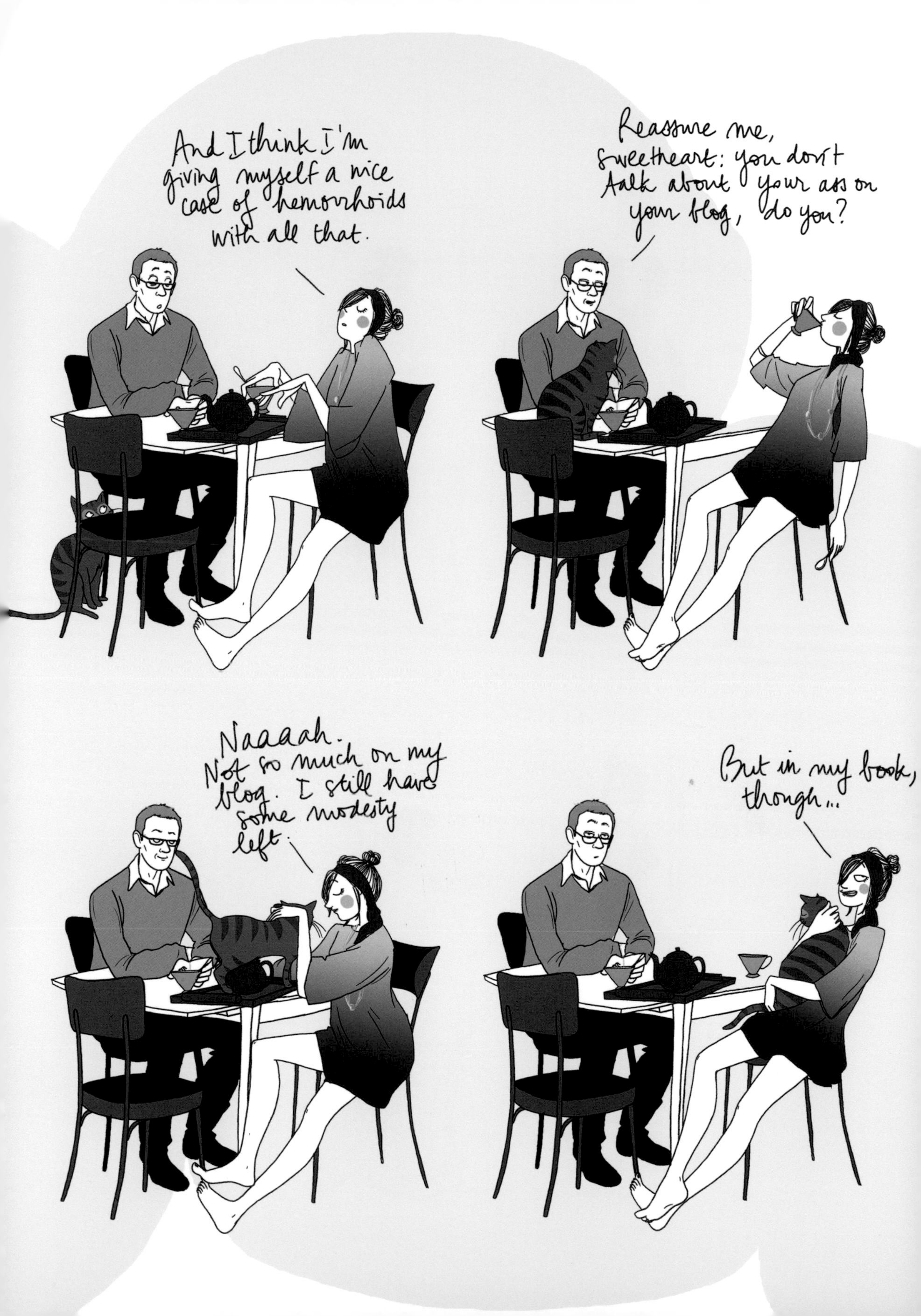
And I think I'm giving myself a nice case of hemorrhoids with all that.
Reassure me, sweetheart: you don't talk about your ass on your blog, do you?
Naaaah. Not so much on my blog. I still have some modesty left.
But in my book, though...

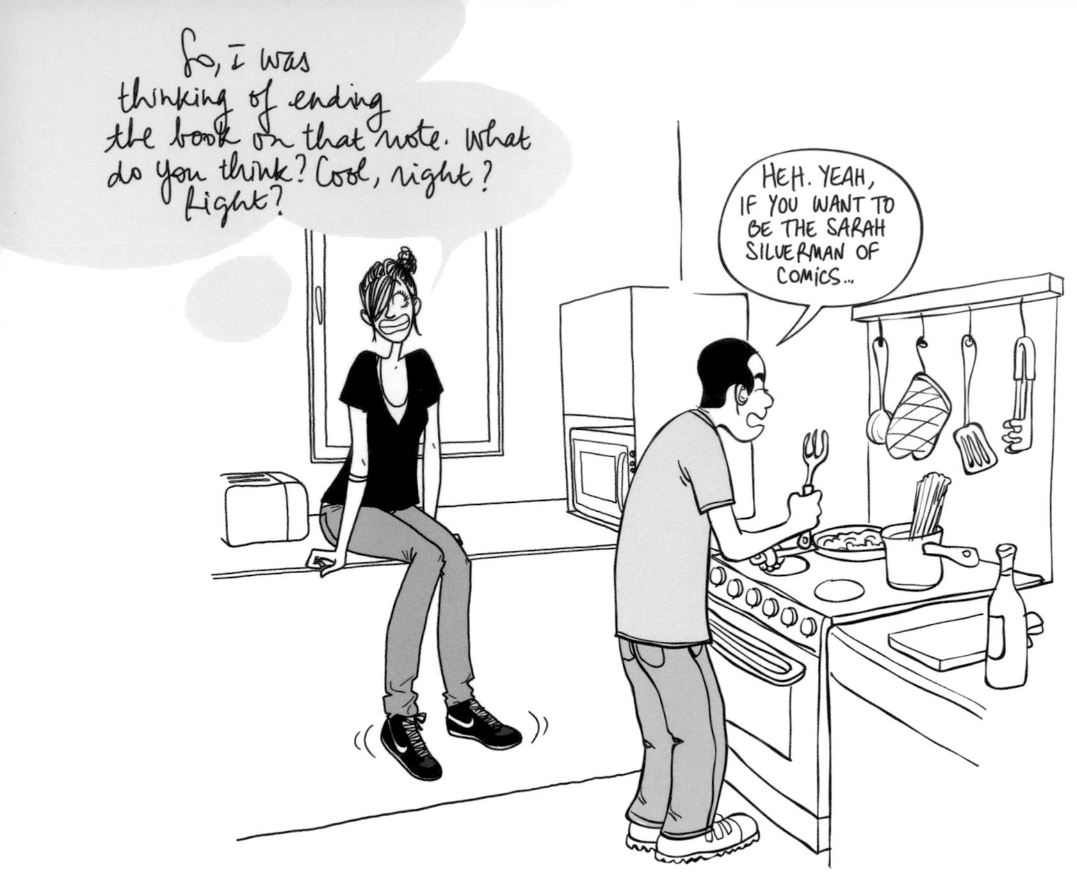
So, I was thinking of ending the book on that note. What do you think? Cool, right? Right?
HEH. YEAH, IF YOU WANT TO BE THE SARAH SILVERMAN OF COMICS...

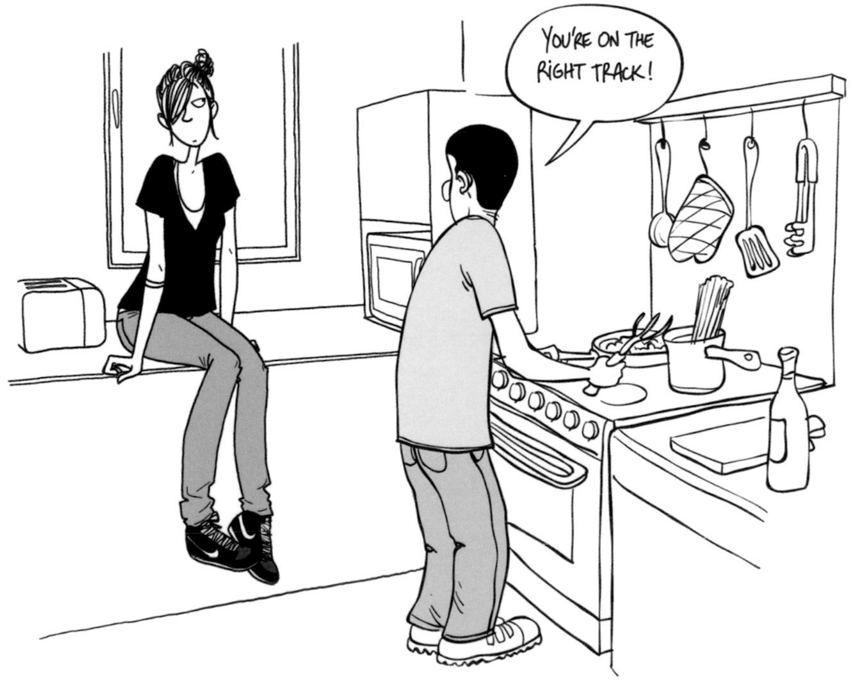
YOU'RE ON THE RIGHT TRACK!

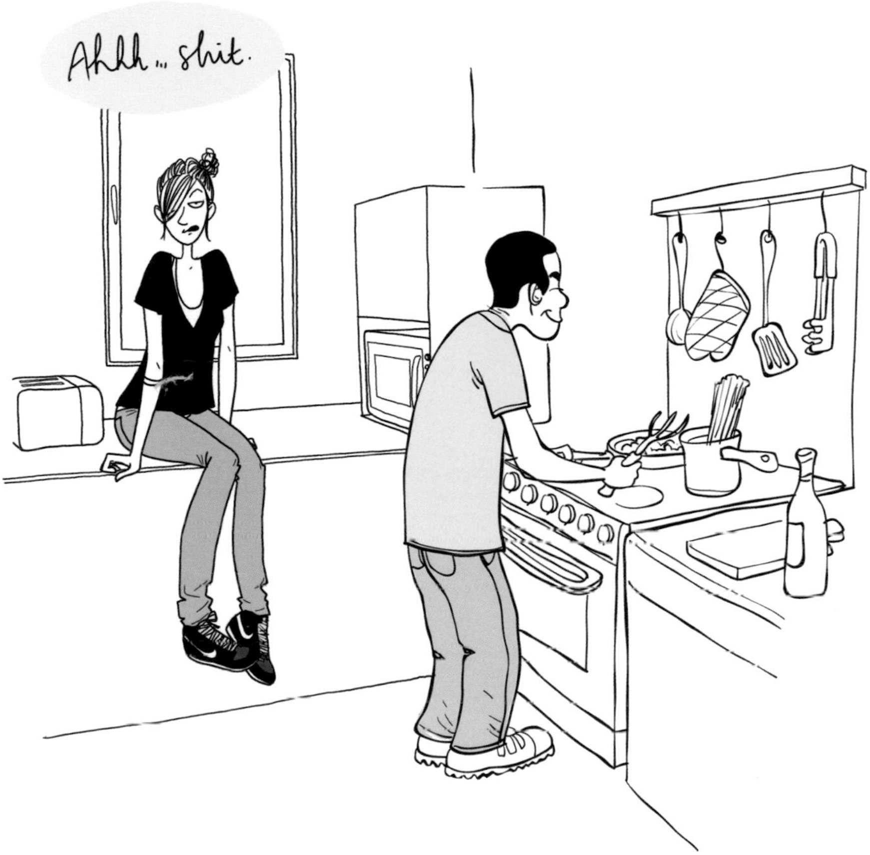
Ahhh... shit.

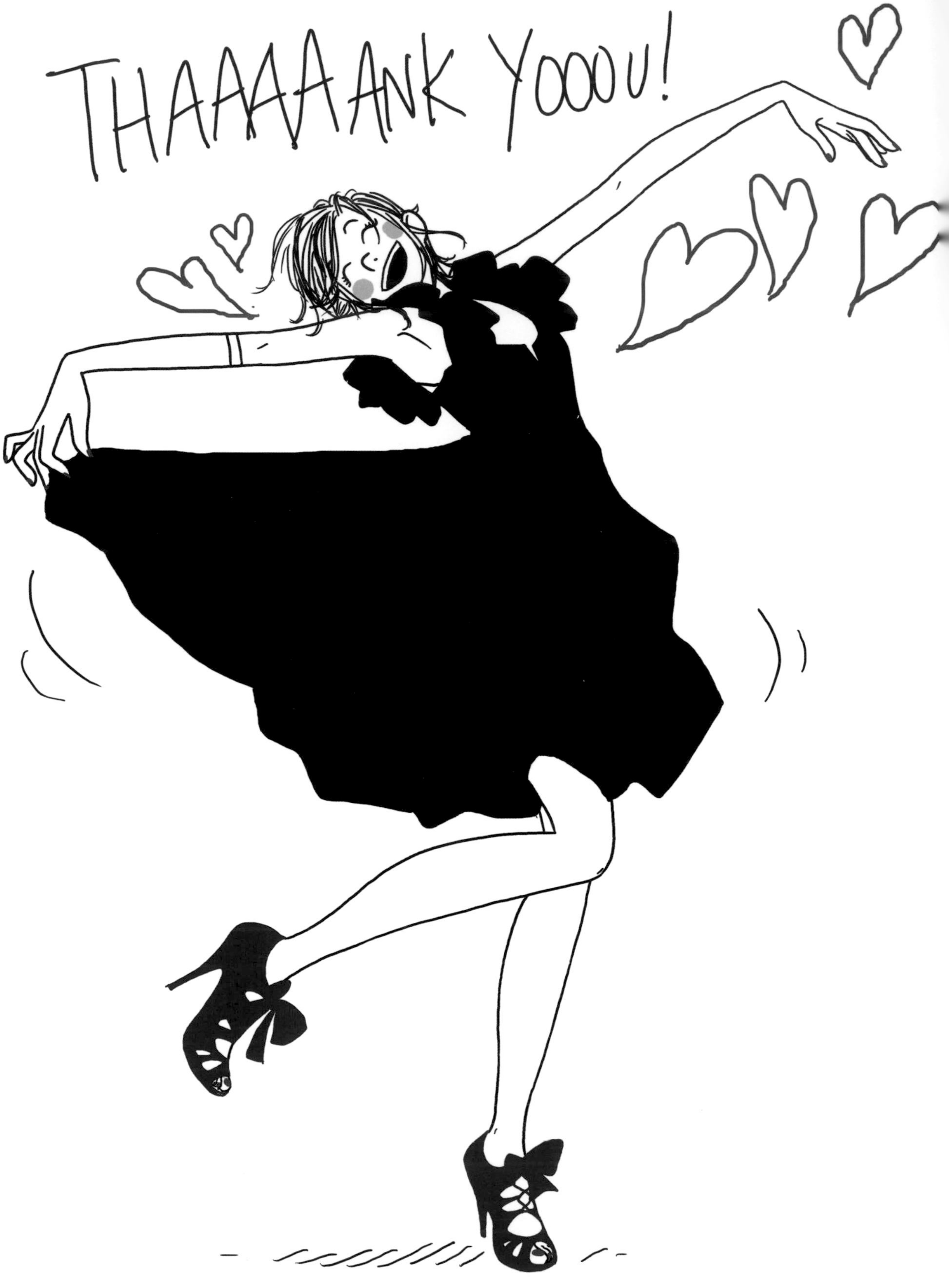
THAAAAANK YOOOOU!

To my dearest mother and my beloved father, and my lovely sister for everything, absolutely everything, unconditionally everything. ♥ To my honey and my kiddo, the nerve center of everything I love, for the patience, the laughs, our entire life together. ♥ To my precious, tiny little family, my Normandy, my Rue d'Agon, my Verte Mare and she who looked after me and watched over me, out on my limb. ♥ To my Krotte, for his continued support since the beginning, I was a crappy best friend while preparing this book and you were there, thanks. ♥ To Cath and Mélu, the head honchos at Muteen, in memory of the good old days and because you gave me my first chance; everything happened because of you, I won't forget it! ♥ To Virginie, who took me under her wing six years ago, who believed in me, helped me move forward, who's been by my side with her team of little fairies since the beginning. ♥ To my real-life besties, whom I bailed on for a few months to finish this project, but with whom I plan to fully enjoy all the good times to come now that IT IS DONE! Thank you for letting me do my hermit thing and for standing quietly in the shadows and for being in the book! ♥ To Gerald, my sort of fairy godmother, for having faith in me since I was wielding Crayolas and especially for always telling me so. ♥ To each netizen, particularly those who know perfectly well I'm talking about them here, thank you, thank you for your presence, for making this possible, for the love, the support, the stupid jokes, the music, for the huge delirium of the year that just went by. ♥ To Roca and Meri, who appeared with the blog and have now become a part of my life, girls, thank you for proving to me such real things can come from the virtual world. ♥ To my wooooooorst bestie, Pacco, my evil twin, for your illustration participation, and for all the crazy stuff there, the connection, the progress, the energy, in short, my darlin', you know. ♥ To Lisa, for her patience, her curiosity, her confidence and her precious savoir-faire.

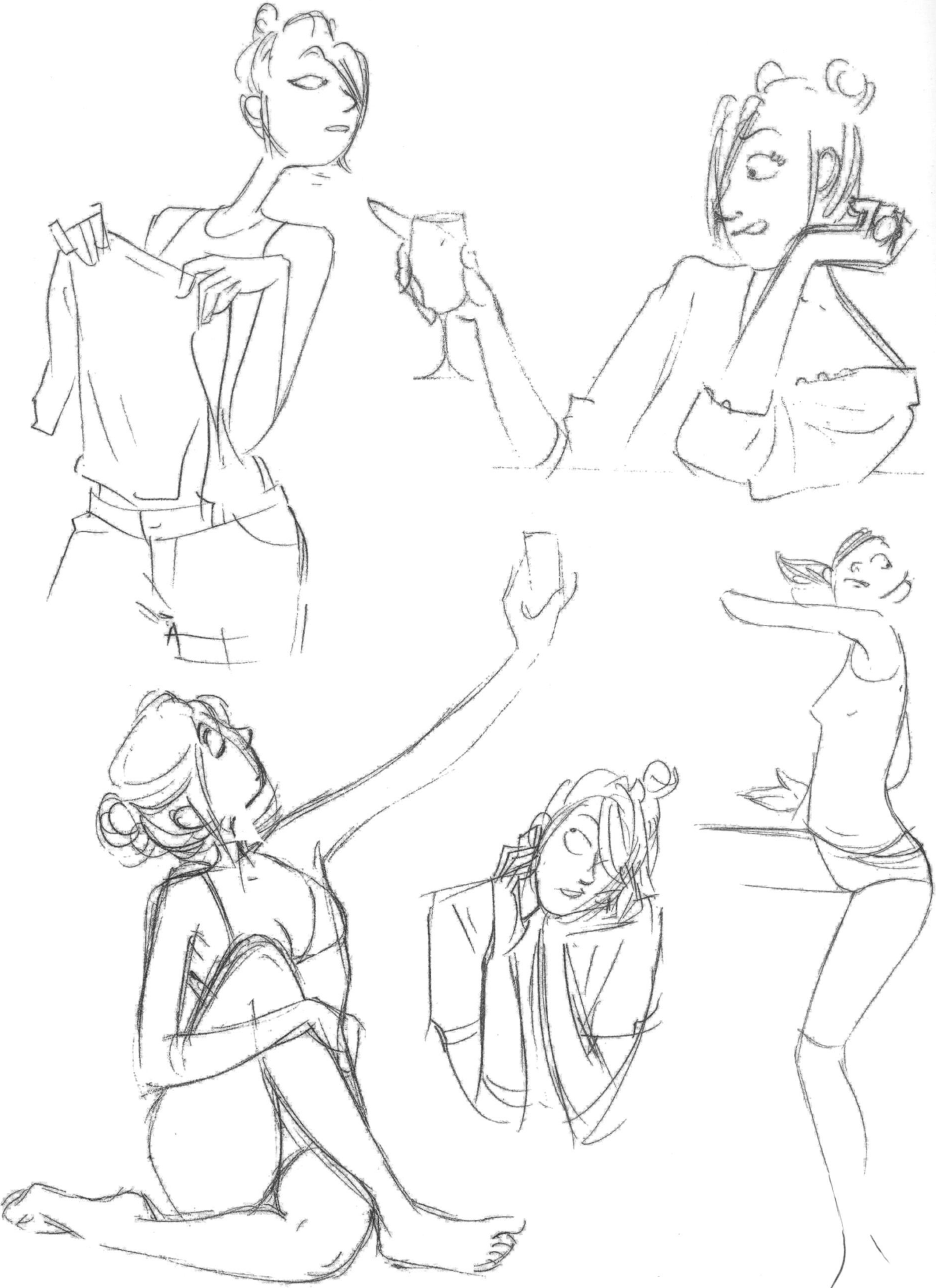